Immigration in Europe: Issues, Policies and Case Studies

Immigration in Europe: Issues, Policies and Case Studies

Edited by

David Turton
University of Oxford

Julia González
University of Deusto

Technical Editor

Almudena Garrido
University of Deusto

2003
University of Deusto
Bilbao

Publication printed on ecological paper

Illustration of front page: Xabi Otero

I.S.B.N.: 84-7485-905-0
Legal Deposit: BI - 2.716-03

Printed in Spain/Impreso en España

Design by: IPAR, S. Coop. - Bilbao

Printed by: Artes Gráficas Rontegui, S.A.L.

Contents

Preface

This book has been published within the framework of HumanitarianNet: Thematic Network on Humanitarian Development Studies, with the support of the European Commission DG for Education and Culture. HumanitarianNet consists of over 100 universities, research centres, and governmental and non-governmental organisations. The activities of the network are developed using a holistic, interdisciplinary approach with a European dimension.

This volume focuses on the challenges facing the different stakeholders involved in the immigration debate in Europe, including governments, NGOs and migrants themselves. Participants include policymakers, representatives of NGOs from different European countries, and academic experts, not only from the Migration group of HumanitarianNet, but also from other fields within the Thematic Network: Human Rights, Poverty and Development, Humanitarian Assistance, and Peace and Conflict Studies.

This is the fourth book to have been produced by the Migration group on the theme of Migration, Cultural Identities, and Territory in Europe. The others were *Cultural Identities and Ethnic Minorities in Europe* (ed. D. Turton and J. Gonzalez, 1999); *Ethnic Diversity in Europe: Challenges to the Nation State* (ed. D. Turton and J. Gonzalez, 2000); and *Diversity in the City* (ed. M. Martiniello and B. Piquard, 2002).

We would like to thank Eduardo Ruiz Vieytez and Ann-Marie Gallagher and the staff of both the Institute of Human Rights and the Department of International Relations at the University of Deusto, for hosting the conference and providing the necessary resources for the success of the event. We also wish to express our gratitude to Margaret Okole of the Refugee Studies Centre, University of Oxford, for her meticulous and skilful copy editing.

THE EDITORS

Introduction

David Turton and Julia González

The papers collected in this book were presented at a conference convened by the Thematic Network on Humanitarian Development Studies ("HumanitarianNet") and held at the University of Deusto, 30 and 31 January, 2003. A core set of papers (Martiniello, Similä, Ma Mung, Bosswick, Pace, Doomernik, Ruiz and Husband) focused on eight different member states of the European Union. Authors of these case studies were asked to provide an overview of the recent history of immigration in the country concerned, including a summary of laws and policies. They were also asked to discuss some of the most important challenges facing these countries in the area of immigration, in the context of European integration. There were, in addition, seven other papers dealing with immigration policies in the EU as a whole (Gallagher, de Vinuesa, Niessen and Boutruche) and with specific issues relevant to the migration debate in Europe (Brüß, Pekari and Vicente).[1] By way of providing the reader with a kind of "overture" to the book as a whole, we discuss here some of the linking and overlapping themes that run through the chapters.

New patterns of migration and the blurring of migrant categories

It is clear that the immigration and asylum policies of the member states of the EU have been affected, not only by attempts to create a common European policy in these areas, but also by recent changes in

[1] One paper presented at the conference, by William Berthomière, was a detailed study of the consequences of immigration from the former Soviet Union for the "territorial strategy" of the Israeli state. We decided not to include this excellent paper in the book, in order to maintain an exclusive focus on migration to the EU.

global migration flows. To understand immigration in Europe, therefore, we have to take into account certain general features of international migration which have emerged during the last twenty years or so. The most important of these was a rapid increase in migration from the less developed to the more developed world, causing some European countries, which had traditionally seen themselves as countries of emigration, to become countries of immigration (even if their political leaders have been slow to recognise this in public). In Spain, for example, although the number of resident foreigners remains small compared with countries of northern Europe, it was ten times greater in 1998 than in 1962, while the proportion of resident foreigners originating from developed countries has fallen from eighty to thirty% over the past fifty years (Ruiz). Former "guest worker" countries, such as the Netherlands and Germany, continued to receive a steady flow of immigrants, even after these schemes had been halted in the early 1970s, first through "family reunion" migration and then by asylum applications (Bosswick and Doomernik). In the Netherlands, "chain migration" has resulted in "ethnic communities" around ten times as large as the original guest worker population (Doomernik). There has been a dramatic rise in the number of "spontaneous arrivals" —illegal immigrants and asylum seekers— most of whom make use of the flourishing industry in people smuggling and trafficking which has developed since the 1970s in response to growing restrictions on legal immigration. There has also been an increase in —or at least an increased recognition of— the participation of women in migratory movements, not simply as the dependants of male migrants but as independent actors (Vicente).

Perhaps the most salient result of these new patterns of international migration has been a blurring of the traditional categories that served to structure the immigration and asylum policies of states. The chain migrations just referred to, whereby the movement of people from, for example, Turkey to Germany and other European countries, continued into the 1970s and 1980s, through the "side doors" of family reunion and the asylum system, are a good illustration of this (Bosswick). This blurring is also seen in the use by asylum seekers of migrant networks and smugglers and the use by economic migrants of the "asylum route". This has led European governments to impose ever stricter controls on asylum —with the avowed aim of making determination procedures more "efficient" (Boutruche), and thereby preserving the "integrity" of the asylum system. Even historical countries of immigration, such as Canada, Australia and the US have felt the same need. Thus, Canada's Minister of Citizenship and Immigration, Elinor Caplan, in introducing a new Immigration and Refugee Protection Bill in May 2000, stated that,

> ...closing the back door to those who would abuse the system will allow us to open the front door wider —both to genuine refugees, and to the immigrants Canada will need to grow and prosper in the future (quoted in VAN KESSEL, 2001, p. 13).

This sounds reasonable enough, until one recognises that, by focusing attention on their "back doors", as a condition for opening their "front doors", the rich industrialised countries are making asylum policy a function of immigration policy. Their obligation under international law to provide protection for refugees is being subsumed under their overriding domestic agenda, which is to control the movement of people and, above all, to pursue the "fight" against illegal immigration. Hence, "refugee protection in the North has almost entirely been taken over by the strengthening of the immigration control regime" (COLLINSON, 1999, p. 16). Asylum, in other words, has come to be treated, to all intents and purposes, as a loophole to be closed, rather than as a right to be protected.

The danger this poses for refugee protection is a recurrent theme of the contributors. Gallagher writes of the need for governments to "separate out" the issues of immigration and asylum in order to meet their obligations under international refugee law. Vinuesa, while recognising that most refugees arriving in Europe today do not conform to the traditional profile of a "Convention refugee", makes the same point: defending the rights of refugees is a matter of international law, not of the discretionary immigration policies of states. Boutruche points out that the restrictive measures introduced by European governments to deter the arrival of undocumented migrants (such as carrier sanctions and visa requirements) not only fail to take into account the particular situation of asylum seekers but have provided fertile ground for the growth of a huge international business in people smuggling and trafficking. His call for a "more balanced" and "complementary" EU asylum and immigration regime appears to rest on the hope that an expansion of legal immigration would help to reduce the pressure on the asylum route. This in turn would open up the space needed for states to meet their obligations under international law to refugees, a specific group of immigrants in need of international protection.

As Boutruche admits, it is by no means certain that the expansion of opportunities for legal immigration would have a downward impact on asylum applications. If it is indeed the case that most asylum seekers are economic migrants using the asylum route to circumvent immigration controls, then such an effect could logically be expected. But, as GIBNEY and HANSEN point out (2002, p.20), the expansion of high skilled migration that has taken place in the UK and Germany in recent years, and the regularisation of low skilled economic migrants in Spain and Italy in the 1990s, does not appear to have had an observable and significant impact on asylum applications. There are, however, other arguments for the expansion of immigration opportunities, which we discuss in the next section.

Arguments for a more liberal immigration regime

First, there is the simple need to meet shortages of both skilled and unskilled labour. The case studies make it clear that there is a growing awareness amongst EU member states of the need for increased labour immigration to help deal with such shortages This new awareness is conveniently marked by a Communication from the European Commission to the Council and the European Parliament on a Common Immigration Policy (2000), in which it is noted that "as a result of growing shortages of labour at both skilled and unskilled levels, a number of member States have already begun to recruit third country nationals from outside the Union" (quoted by Doomernik). It urges Member States to re-think their immigration policies in the light of their expected needs for labour immigration. The thinking behind this Communication is that labour immigration policies should address the supply side (by means, for example, of a quota system) as well as the demand side (by using immigration to target specific sectors of the labour market). For some countries, however, this would be, as Doomernik puts it for the Netherlands, "a bridge too far". In Spain also, there is a basic consensus that immigrants should only be admitted where there are no Spanish workers to fill the jobs (Ruiz).

The greatest stirrings of potential change in this area have perhaps been seen in Germany, where an independent Commission on immigration reported in 2001 that the expansion of immigration had become an economic necessity. It even went so far as to recommend a points system similar to the Canadian model (Bosswick). Although a new immigration act, incorporating this and other recommendations of the Commission, was blocked in the second chamber, Bosswick describes these proposals as heralding an "historic change in Germany's policies towards immigrants and foreign residents". In France there has been talk over the last few years, at least amongst the "political classes", of the need to expand the immigration of unskilled as well as skilled labour (Ma Mung), while in Belgium the government is holding back on a more liberal approach to immigration, presumably because of worries about public opinion, even though the business world is in favour of expanded immigration to help meet shortages of high skilled labour (Martiniello).

Second, there is a related but more fundamental and long term argument to be made in favour of expanding immigration flows, namely that this is necessary to meet Europe's "demographic deficit". Niessen would like to shift the debate about immigration in the EU from a preoccupation with the need to exclude third country nationals to the need for increased immigration in the context of a declining population. The average number of children per woman of childbearing age in the EU in 2000 was 1.53, as against 2.1 needed to replace the population. Because of increased life expectancy, the proportion of those aged 65 and over will reach 22 % in 2025, having risen from 16 % in 1998. The result is that the population of working age will have fallen by about 40 million in 2050 and the ratio of workers to pensioners will have declined from four to one, to two to one. Notwithstanding regional variations, this demographic arithmetic has stark implications for the future of pensions and health care systems in European welfare states. While it seems obvious that the expansion of immigration could play a part (along with policies to increase fertility and encourage greater participation in the labour force) in helping to turn this situation round in the short term, the long term effects of increased immigration on the labour market cannot be easily predicted because, as Niessen points out, immigrants are also subject to the ageing process!

Both of the above arguments might be called Euro-centric, in that they are based upon the economic self-interest of European welfare states. A third argument is based on the potential contribution of an increased flow of labour migrants from less developed to more developed countries (and an opposite flow of remittances) to raising the living standards and life chances of the world's poor. Since this argument is not presented in any detail by the contributors to this book, we give some space to it here because we believe it is potentially the most important and, therefore, one that deserves particular consideration. Nor is it is without a significant, if indirect, element of European self interest, if we assume that global inequality is the greatest long term threat to the security and well being of the inhabitants of the rich industrialised countries.

One of the most striking ways of representing the rich-poor divide in the world today is to note that farmers in the EU receive a subsidy of US$2 per day, for each of their cattle, while 1.3 billion of the world's poorest people live on an income of less than US$1 per day. In other words, cattle in the EU "enjoy" double the "income" of a third of the world's population. This way of representing the gap between rich and poor, based as it is on the EU's highly protective Common Agricultural Policy, is particularly apposite, given the so-called "Washington Consensus" of the 1980s and 1990s. This was the view that the best way to make globalisation pay for the poor is the ever wider adoption of policies of free trade and free investment, a view which has dominated the policies of the World Bank and the International Monetary Fund for the past twenty years.

With the benefit of hindsight, a new consensus appears to be growing among economists that it is not quite as simple as that (RODRIK, 2002). First, most developing countries grew faster *before* they abandoned trade protection policies. Second, while there has been a very small decrease in global poverty levels (0.2 % per year between 1988 and 1998), this is largely accounted for by the progress made by the world's most populous country, China. Having one of the most protected economies in the world, and having joined the World Trade Organisation only in 2001, China is hardly a glowing advert for the Washington Consensus. Third, if China did not get where it is today by following the dictates of the Washington Consensus, neither did the very countries which today preach its benefits. The EU's Common Agricultural Policy is one illustration of this. Another is the use made of protectionist policies by the US economy when it was catching up with and surpassing Britain's in the latter part of the nineteenth century (RODRIK, 2002, p. 4).

The other side of the coin of trade liberalisation, imposed by the rich countries through the multilateral financial institutions they control, is restrictive immigration policies, imposed unilaterally by individual welfare states.

> Thanks to the efforts of the United States and other rich countries, barriers to trade goods, financial services, and investment flows have now been brought down to historic lows. But the one market where poor nations have something in abundance to sell —the market for labor services— has remained untouched by this liberalizing trend. Rules on cross-border flows are determined almost always unilaterally (rather than multilaterally as in other areas of economic exchange) and remain highly restrictive. Even a small relaxation of these rules would produce huge gains for the world economy, and for poor nations in particular. (RODRIK, loc. cit.)

This is because the gap between what people can earn from the same —even menial— jobs in rich countries and poor countries is much wider than the gap between the prices of goods traded between those countries. According to Rodrik, a "back-of-the-envelope calculation" suggests that an expansion of labour migration from poor to rich countries, amounting to 3 % of the rich countries' labour force, "would easily yield $200 billion of income annually for the citizens of developing nations, which is vastly more than the existing WTO trade agenda is expected to produce" (loc.cit.)[2] Similar, if less dramatic, conclusions are reached by WINTERS *et al.* (2002) using, not the back of an envelope but a computer simulation. They conclude that

> ...by increasing developed economies' quotas on inward movements of both skilled and unskilled labour by just 3% of their labour forces, world welfare would rise by $US156 billion...This figure is half as large again as the gains expected from the liberalisation of all remaining goods trade restrictions ($US 104 billion). In general, developing countries gain most ...with higher gains from the increase in quotas on unskilled labour than on skilled labour. (p. 3)

If these arguments are correct, then the main reason why the gap between rich and poor countries continues to grow, with all the dangers this holds for the long term peace and security of the rich as well as the poor, is the restrictive immigration policies of the rich industrialised nations. By maintaining these policies, while forcing through trade and investment liberalisation (except where it is harmful to their own producers!), they ensure that their own citizens hold on to the lion's share of the benefits of globalisation.

There are at least two criticisms that can be made of the argument that the liberalisation of international migration would have a dramatic and positive impact on global inequality. The first is that Rodrik and others are assuming a more straightforward relationship between migrants' remittances and development in their countries of origin than is justified by the evidence. There has been much research on this topic, with no clear-cut conclusions.

---

[2] The current level of remittances already amounts to twice that of international development assistance. "Estimated at about US$75 billion a year in the early 1990s... and at US$100 billion in 2000 (Martin, 2001), migrants' remittances represent a large proportion of world financial flows and amount to substantially more than global overseas development assistance... By the mid 1990s. [international development assistance]... had stagnated at the level of US$50 billion net of debt repayments... To underline their importance for the developing world, 60 percent of remittances were thought to go to developing countries in the year 2000 (Martin, 2001).' (SØRENSEN *et al.*, 2002, p. 20).

> The relationship between migration and development in poor countries has been a topic of debate for a long time. There are two main views. The negative view holds that international migration results in an increase in the dependency of the country of origin on remittances and, furthermore, it distorts the development process since the remittances only benefit the "lucky" few, creating wealth disparities and therefore political and economic unrest. The other view regards remittances as one of the key factors in poverty alleviation in labour-sending countries and a good source of economic development (LEON-LEDESMA/PIRACHA, 2001, p. 1).

Thus, according to Stephen Castles, "..migration can present effective individual strategies for survival and improvement in life chances, but it cannot provide general solutions to global disparities... There is little evidence that migration under current arrangements, does anything to support development in the areas of origin" (2000a, pp. 91-92). On the other hand, a recent "Policy Study" carried out by the Centre for Development Research, Copenhagen, on the "migration-development nexus" (SØRENSEN *et al.*, 2002) states that "there is increasing evidence that remittances from abroad are crucial to the survival of communities in developing countries.." (p. 19). In their own study of the effect of economic flows derived from migration on Central and East European economies, León-Ledesma and Piracha found that remittances had a positive effect on productivity and employment, through their effect on investment. But this raises another important qualification —namely that the benefits of remittances to economic development are unevenly distributed across poor countries and it does not appear to be the poorest which benefit most.[3]

The second possible flaw in the arguments of Rodrik and Winters *et al.* lies in their assumption that the increased flows of migrant labour they envisage could be restricted to temporary migrants, who would be replaced by others after three or four years. This time limit is necessary in order to ensure that opportunities for increased labour migration are enjoyed by a sufficiently wide range and large number of migrants, without creating popular antagonism to the policy in host countries. Rodrik thinks this could be achieved "by building specific incentives into the scheme" —such as withholding a portion of the migrant's earnings until he or she returned home, or reducing the sending countries' quotas in proportion to the numbers who failed to

---

[3] Sub-Saharan Africa's share of global remittances declined from 8% to 4% between 1980 and 1999, while the "winners" have been Eastern Europe, Central Asia, South and Central America and the Caribbean (GAMMELTOFT, 2002, p. ii).

return (loc.cit.). Considering the history of immigration in Europe since the 1970s,[4] one could be forgiven for seeing this as another indication that the predictions of economists are more convincing, the less they are encumbered by the complexities of the real world, and the behaviour of real people.

The best we can conclude, perhaps, is that increased labour migration, especially by unskilled workers, could make a more significant contribution to reducing global inequality than the liberalisation of trade and investment. But the usual caveat applies: it should not be seen as a panacea or, in Castles' words, a "general solution". Still less should it be seen as a substitute for carefully targeted international development assistance, bearing in mind the regional differences in the contribution made by remittances to the economies of developing countries.

Identity, belonging and citizenship

The issue of the integration of cultural minorities in European societies naturally figures prominently in the chapters which follow. It is an issue which raises fundamental questions about membership, identity and citizenship and, ultimately, about the future of the nation-state model of political organisation itself. These questions must be faced by all countries with significant immigrant minorities, but they are perhaps most keenly felt in those which, until recently, either were not, or did not see themselves as, countries of immigration.

Germany comes into the latter category. Bosswick's chapter traces the slow and painful process by which, over the past fifty years, German politicians came to terms with the fact that Germany was a "*de facto* country of immigration".[5] A key aspect of this process has been the erosion of the ethnic concept of the German nation, through the introduction of changes in German citizenship and naturalisation law. During the early 1990s, the number of children born in Germany of foreign parents was 80 % more than the number of foreigners who became citizens through naturalisation. Since 1 January 2000, however, children of foreign parents born in Germany have automatically become German citizens, provided one parent holds residence rights, while

4 In particular, the failed efforts of such countries as France and Germany to induce significant numbers of immigrants to return to their home countries after the clamp-down on legal immigration in the early 1970s (Bosswick, Ma Mung).

5 During this period, there was a net gain of 9 million people through immigration, with an annual net immigration average of 200,000 foreign citizens (Bosswick).

those born since 1990 have been able to apply for naturalisation. Other foreigners are now entitled to citizenship after eight years of legal residence, on condition that they do not have a criminal record, that they are not dependent on social welfare and that they have a certain level of proficiency in the German language.

The imposition of these conditions suggests that the successful (from the immigrants' point of view) integration of immigrant minorities in German society is still hampered by a stereotypical characterisation of immigrant communities as having more than their fare share of criminals and welfare scroungers. This impression is supported by Brüß's chapter, in which he compares the attitudes of German adolescents to adolescents from settled Turkish immigrant familes who had been in Germany for decades, and "Resettler" adolescents (that is "Aussiedler" or "ethnic Germans"), who came from the ex-USSR and Eastern Europe since the mid 1980s. His results show that there is more "social distance" between German and Turkish adolescents than between German and Resettler adolescents and that Turkish adolescents therefore run the risk of social marginalisation.

Bosswick draws attention, at the end of his chapter, to the important point that the integration of immigrants is not a one-way process —it always implies a process of adjustment and adaptation by members of the host society, a process which has led in Germany to a rethinking of the notion of the German nation as a homogeneous, ethnic entity. This, no doubt, is why the process has been slow and painful, and why it has proceeded in fits and starts In other European countries, where immigration from the South is a relatively new phenomenon compared to Germany, such as Spain, Finland and Italy, this process is only beginning and promises to be equally painful and equally far-reaching.

In Spain, there has been a "qualitative change" in the nature of immigration since the 1980s, with a large increase in immigrants from Latin America and Africa (Ruiz). But while this relatively rapid and recent increase in cultural plurality has begun to affect Spanish "collective psychology", policies to protect the rights of cultural minorities are "practically nonexistent", the overriding concern of the authorities being to control immigration. This reflects public concerns and anxieties about immigration, which is now considered "one of the main problems of the country". And yet, by European standards, Spain has a low population of resident foreigners —1.5 million (a quarter of whom are European citizens) out of a total population of 40 million.

Finland, unlike other "Nordic welfare states" has been, like Spain, a country of emigration until the last ten years, during which there has been a relatively large influx of refugees and asylum seekers (Similä). It has a fairly homogeneous population of about five million, of which only arournd 18,000 belong to national minorities (Sami, Roma, Jews and Tatars). With the need for labour immigration likely to grow, Finland is faced, more or less for the first time in its history, with the familiar problem of how to reconcile the universalistic values of the liberal democratic state with the need to accommodate cultural diversity.

In Italy, another country which has moved in a very short time from being, predominantly, a country of emigration to a country of immigration, and in which access to citizenship is based upon the principle of *jus sanguinis* ("law of the blood"), the problem presents itself as how to maintain Italian identity (Pace). There is, according to Pace, a growing awareness among the Italian public of the need to arrive at a new basis for "social solidarity", which in time will presumably involve moving away from the present ethnic model of the Italian nation (itself a fairly recent "invention") to a new understanding of what it means to be Italian.

Two countries covered in this book, France and the United Kingdom, have long and significant histories as countries of immigration, although each has followed a different approach when it comes to the integration of minorities. The French "Republican model" of immigration has involved the integration of individuals rather than groups (Ma Mung). This is perhaps best described as assimilation rather than integration since, as Ma Mung puts it, according to this model, "The foreigner is tolerated only on condition that he/she disappears". The British approach to the management of ethnic and cultural diversity has contained elements of assimilationism, but has combined this with a strong emphasis on "cultural pluralism", which has been the hallmark of the "classical" countries of immigration —Canada, the USA and Australia (CASTLES, 2000b, 134-140).

The Republican model remained paramount in France after the cessation of labour immigration in the 1970s but began to change in the 1990s as a result of the interplay of both progressive and repressive policies towards immigrants. On the one hand, there was a new focus on the problem of discrimination. The recognition that individuals are discriminated against because of their ethnic group, clearly entails policies designed to help the integration of groups rather than individuals and therefore represents a move away from an assimilationist approach to the management of ethnic diversity. On the other hand, the toughening of immigration policy through the so-called "Pasqua Laws"[6] had the effect,

---

[6] Named after the Minister of the Interior of the right-wing Balladur government which came to power in 1993.

among other things, of taking away the automatic entitlement of foreigners to become French. According to Ma Mung, European integration and new forms of international migration, which have made the principle of "mono-belonging" to a single nation-state increasingly outmoded, are profoundly affecting the founding principles of the French nation-state. They "invite us", he writes, "to rethink our relations with the foreigner, otherness and exteriority: in other words, with the world."

The interplay of progressive and repressive policies, which can be detected in Ma Mung's account of changes in the traditional French approach to the integration of foreigners, is the central issue in Husband's chapter on the UK. He contrasts the "creep of progressive legislation" designed to combat discrimination and promote cultural pluralism, which has been accompanied by little in the way of public fanfare, with increasingly restrictive policies towards asylum seekers and illegal immigrants, which have been pursued with "a robust and explicit political rhetoric". The two policies are clearly in opposition to each other, since the "fight" against illegal immigrants (code for "asylum seekers"), accompanied as it is by a lurid media campaign, is hardly calculated to increase tolerance and respect for immigrant minorities amongst the host population. It is difficult not to agree with Husband that the public assault on "bogus" asylum seekers has more to do with calculations of short term electoral advantage than it has either with the protection of "genuine" refugees or with the promotion of multicultural values.

And yet it is not quite as simple as this. What all these examples illustrate is a contradiction, within the nation-state model of political organisation, between citizenship, as the universal source of individual rights, and nationality as the primary and fundamental source of an individual's social identity. The contradiction between citizenship and nationality arises from two interrelated assumptions which lie at the heart of the nation-state model but which have become increasingly problematic in the face of growing levels of international migration and the development of transnational networks. First, there is the assumption that the population living in the territory of a state is a homogeneous national community, with common values, sentiments and attachments. This was always a myth, but it has become increasingly difficult to sustain in today's conditions of globalisation, where membership of indigenous and ethnic minorities has become an increasingly salient basis of sub-national identity. Second, there is what JOPPKE calls the "principle of sedentariness" (1998, p. 6), the assumption that an individual's national identity, unlike any other basis of social differentiation, is all embracing and exclusive.

> ...states are an archaic anomaly within the organization of modern society, which is based on the principle of non-territorial, functional differentiation. This functional order integrates individuals only in certain specific respects (e.g. as workers, consumers or churchgoers), but never in their totality, thus requiring them to be multiply oriented and allied, and in this sense perpetually flexible and mobile. States are an exception to this. They include the individual as a whole and involuntarily by ascription at birth, further expecting her to be attached to just one state among a plurality of similarly conceived states, and not to change this attachment over a lifetime.....Unlike Schumpeter's classes, states cannot afford to be like buses, always full but always filled by different people (see Schumpeter, 1953, p. 171). (JOPPKE, 1998, p. 6).

Clearly, what is needed is a trade-off, or balance, between the mobility and flexibility which "the organisation of modern society" requires of the individual, and the "sedentariness" which is necessary for political life to be organised by the nation-state model. The same need for balance is expressed by Hirschman in terms of an opposition between "exit" and "loyalty" (1970, pp. 69-71, cited in JORDAN/DÜVELL, 2003, p. 23). By "exit" he refers to the need for individuals, in a market system, to shop around between different products and firms to find the one offering the greatest advantage for themselves. Political institutions, on the other hand, require "loyalty", if members are to be persuaded that it is worth their while taking part in collective decision making.

> Hirschman argued that all kinds of organizations —firms and NGOs as well as states— should try to balance exit...and loyalty... Whatever membership systems evolve or are created in this century will face this challenge, and the fate of democracy as a principle of collective rule will depend on the achievement of this balance. (JORDAN/DÜVELL, 2003, p. 23).

There has, presumably, always been the need for states to achieve such a "balance". Pursuing this metaphor, we might say that what is new today is that the level and intensity of international migration over the past few decades, linked to other globalising trends, has pushed the "balancing point" to the limit of the scale. Finding a new balancing point, therefore, will involve radical changes in the notions of membership, citizenship and identity to which we have become accustomed during the triumphant rise of the nation-state to its present position as the dominant political organising principle of the modern world. One example of a small but significant step towards the achievement of such a balance is provided by Pekari, in her chapter on the extension of the right to vote in local elections in Vienna to "third country nationals" —long term residents who are neither Austrian nor EU citizens. This proposal (which had not entered into force at the time Pekari was writing) breaks the link between citizenship and voting rights (albeit at the most local level), by recognising that resident non-citizens have the right to participate in political decision-making processes that affect citizens and non-citizens alike.

The role of academics and civil society

Academics who write about immigration and asylum are, like the contributors to this book, more often than not highly critical of the policies pursued by the governments of liberal democratic states, particularly over the past few decades. One basis for criticism is ethical and philosophical and concerns the failure of governments to protect the rights of immigrants and to honour their obligations towards refugees and asylum seekers under international law. Another common criticism is pragmatic, and concerns the frequently noted tendency of immigration policy to be ambivalent and inconsistent in its aims and to have unforeseen consequences, sometimes the direct opposite of what the policy-makers intended.

The most obvious example of this to be found in the chapters which follow are the restrictions imposed by European countries on labour immigration in the 1970s and 80s, and on the entrance of asylum seekers, particularly in the 1990s. One "unintended side effect" of the halt on recruitment of foreign workers to Germany in 1973, and the accompanying unsuccessful attempts to promote significant voluntary return, was that many foreigners stayed on precisely because they would not have the option of returning to Germany if they went home (Bosswick). All in all, and taken together with measures intended to reduce asylum applications, recent efforts by European states to gain greater control over immigration have, as noted earlier, contributed to a huge and ever more resourceful international "industry" in people smuggling and trafficking. As Boutruche remarks, "probably the most striking paradox of the EU immigration policy" was that "by giving the highest priority to the combat against illegal migration, it fostered the problem it was initially supposed to tackle".

These criticisms of European immigration policy, both ethical and pragmatic, raise questions about the effectiveness of research and advocacy as a means of influencing the process of political decision making. Gallagher, based on US experience, emphasises the impact academics and advocates can have on policy, if they work closely together and are sufficiently well organised. She clearly believes, no doubt rightly, that European academics and advocates have a long way to go in this direction by comparison with their American counterparts. Pace sees local level activity by "the movements of civil society", working at the level of schools and work-places, as virtually the only hope of stemming the outlandish fears of the Italian public about foreigners taking away their jobs, schools and identity.

Ruiz, on the other hand, is less sanguine about the contribution of NGOs to improving immigration policy in Spain. The number of these organisations working in the area of migration has "grown spectacularly" in recent years but, at the same time, their independence, and therefore their capacity to have a "transformative" effect on society, has been compromised by their economic dependence on public funds. They have become, in effect, subcontractors to "the powers that be", supplying services that are legitimised by government policy.

These remarks hold a warning also for academics working in the immigration and refugee field, for they also are often dependent on government funding and they certainly strive to make their research "relevant" to problems as perceived and defined by policy makers. We should like to end this Introduction by suggesting that, paradoxically, academic research is likely to have a more beneficial impact on policy, the more distanced it is from the immediate concerns and preoccupations of policy makers and from the concepts and categories by which those concerns and preoccupations are structured.[7]

How to bridge the so-called "research-practice divide" is a familiar topic of debate in any problem-oriented field of enquiry. At first sight, the answer seems obvious. If we want our research to influence policy, then we had better define its aims and objectives in terms of categories and concepts which are employed by policy makers. This was the approach adopted by refugee studies, when it emerged as a field of academic enquiry in the 1980s. Its concern to be "relevant" and, it must be admitted, its need for funding, led it to adopt policy related categories and concerns in defining its subject matter and setting its research agenda. The trouble with this approach is that the categories and concepts employed by policy makers may not be helpful —indeed, they are likely to be downright unhelpful— when it comes to the pursuit of scientific understanding. This, after all, is not their main

---

[7] The following paragraphs are based upon an argument also presented in TURTON (in press, 2003).

purpose.[8] And yet, we must assume that the more rigorous the science, both theoretically and methodologically, the more likely it is to have a beneficial impact on policy.

Perhaps the most common way of characterising the "gap" between research and practice is to distinguish between two kinds of people, academics and practitioners, each engaged in a different kind of professional activity. and each with a different objective: academics, it is sometimes said, want to understand the world, while practitioners want to change it. This apparently clear distinction soon becomes blurred, however, when one seeks to give it empirical content. For, on the one hand, it turns out to be no easy matter to sort individuals unambiguously into the two categories (academics often want to change the world too!) and, on the other, understanding the world is obviously a prerequisite for deliberately, systematically and beneficially changing it.

A more productive way of approaching the issue might be to distinguish, not between two kinds of people or professional activities, each focused on a different objective, but between two kinds of knowledge, scientific (or academic) and practical, which the same person can happily combine and make use of, depending on context and situation. Since all knowledge is socially produced, an obvious basis on which to distinguish between different kinds of knowledge is to focus on differences in their modes of production and reproduction. Thus, we can say that practical knowledge is produced "by doing" —that is, through the very performance of a task or activity which is not aimed primarily at producing knowledge— while scientific knowledge is produced by an activity which has precisely that objective. We can say, further, that it is a characteristic of practical knowledge to be unreflective and unself-conscious (though not necessarily false) because it is produced by "doing" and that it is a characteristic of scientific knowledge to be reflective and self-conscious (though not necessarily true) because it is produced by the deliberate application of scientific method.

From this point of view, the best way to make academic knowledge "relevant" to policy and practice is to use it to scrutinise and problematise what practical knowledge takes for granted, not to sustain or legitimise it. It follows that we should at least consider the possibility that, the "unintended" and "unforeseen" consequences of immigration policy may be partly the result of research in this area being too closely tied to

[8] Quite what *is* their main purpose is another matter. In any case, we assume that it is the first priority of any institution, political or otherwise, to pursue its own vested interests and to ensure its own survival.

the immediate, short term problems of the policy world (CASTLES, 2003, p. 26). Good research will always call into question the adequacy and usefulness of taken for granted generalisations, assumptions and categories —one might say that this is what research is for. It is by such questioning, therefore, that research can play its most effective part in the general improvement of human welfare. In the words of Louis Pasteur, a scientist whose practical contribution to the improvement of human welfare it is difficult to exaggerate: "Il n'existe pas de sciences appliquées mais seulement des applications de la science" (1872, p. 42).

References

CASTLES, S. (2000a) "Migration and Minorities in Europe: Perspectives for the 1990s: Eleven Hypotheses". In: S. Castles, *Ethnicity and Globalization: From Migrant Worker to Transnational Citizen.* Sage Publications, London.

CASTLES, S. (2000 b) "Multicultural Citizenship: The Australian Experience". In: S.Castles, *Ethnicity and Globalization:From Migrant worker to Transnational Citizen,* Sage Publications, London.

CASTLES, S. (2003) "Towards a Sociology of Forced Migration and Social Transformation". In: *Sociology* 37 (1), pp. 13-34.

COLLINSON, S. (1999) *Globalisation and the Dynamics of International Migration: Implications for the Refugee Regime.* Working Paper No. 1, New Issues in Refugee Research, UNHCR, Geneva.

GAMMELTOFT, P. (2002) *Remittances and other Financial Flows to Developing Countries.* Expert Working Paper, Centre for Development Research, Copenhagen.

GIBNEY, M.; HANSEN, R. (2002) "Asylum policy in the West: Past trends, future Possibilities". Paper prepared for the WIDER International Conference on Poverty, International Migration and Asylum, Helsinki, 27-28 September.

HIRSCHMAN, A.O. (1970) *Exit, Voice and Loyalty: Responses to Decline in Firms, Organisations and States.* .Harvard University Press, Harvard, MA.

JOPPKE, C. (1998) "Immigration Challenges to the Nation-State". In: *Challenges to the Nation-State: Immigration in Western Europe and the United States,* ed. C. Joppke. Oxford University Press, Oxford.

JORDAN, B.; DÜVELL, F. (2003) *Migration: The Boundaries of Equality and Justice.* Polity Press, Cambridge.

LEÓN-LEDESMA, M.; PIRACHA, M. (2001) "International Migration and the Role of Remittances in Eastern Europe". Department of Economics, University of Kent at Canterbury. www.ukc.ac.uk/economics/papers/papers-pdf/2001/0113.pdf (read, 1/10/03).

MARTIN, S. (2001) *Remittance Flows and Impact.* Paper prepared for the Regional Conference on Remittances as a Development Tool, organized by the Multilateral Investment Fund and the Inter-American Development Bank.

PASTEUR, L. (1872) *Comptes rendus des travaux du Congrès viticole et séricicole de Lyon,* 9-14 September

RODRIK, D. 2002 "Globalization for whom? Time to change the rules —and focus on poor workers". *Harvard Magazine*, 104:6, July-August 2002. www.harvard-magazine.com/on-line/070280.html (read 23/9/03).

SCHUMPETER, J. (1953) "Die sozialen Klassen im ethnisch homogenen Milieu". In: *Aufsätze zur Soziologie,* ed. J. Schumpeter, Mohr, Tübingen [first published in 1927].

SØRENSEN, N.N.; VAN HEAR, N.; ENGBERG-PEDERSEN, P. (2002) *The Migration - Development Nexus: Evidence and Policy Options. State of the Art Overview.* Working Paper 02.6, Centre for Development Research, Copenhagen.

TURTON, D. (in press, 2003) *Refugees, forced resettlers and "other forced migrants": towards a unitary study of forced migration*. Working Paper, New Issues in Refugee Research, UNHCR, Geneva.

VAN KESSEL, G. (2001) "Global Migration and Asylum". In: *Forced Migration Review,* 10, pp. 10-13.

WINTERS, L.A.; WALMSLEY, T.L.; WANG, Z.K.; GRYNBERG, R. (2002) *Liberalising the Temporary Movement of Natural Persons.* Economics Discussion Paper No. 87, University of Sussex, UK.

Framing the issues and meeting the challenges: the role of practitioners and academics

Anna Marie Gallagher

Introduction

We are a people on the move. In a world population of over 6 billion (US BUREAU OF CENSUS, 2003), there are approximately 37 million refugees, asylum seekers and internally displaced persons worldwide (USCR, 2002, p. 3, 4). In a population of over 375 million people within the European Union (EU), less than a million persons are refugees and asylum seekers (ibid.). Over 13 million immigrants from outside the EU are currently living in EU member states. The number of undocumented persons or de facto residents has been estimated to be as high as 5 million persons in Europe.

Today immigration and asylum are among the most important issues facing EU member states. Finding ways to develop and formulate just and fair policies regarding refugees and asylum seekers on the one hand and those seeking to immigrate or those already present in the EU on the other hand poses some of the greatest challenges facing the EU and its member states in the twenty first century.

Frequently, government policy makers mistakenly combine issues relating to these two very separate groups —migrants on the one hand and asylum seekers and refugees on the other— when discussing, debating and finally formulating migration and refugee policy in their countries. Real or imagined fear of potential mass influxes of refugees causes governments to pursue restrictive policies towards immigrants generally as well as refugees and asylum seekers specifically.

In order for countries to satisfy their moral and legal obligations under international refugee law, EU member states must respect the rights of refugees and asylum seekers. This respect should not be modified or qualified by real or imagined concerns regarding irregular immigration and border security issues. In separating out the issues, member states should carefully examine their own economic and social needs in devising and developing a sound immigration policy to benefit the host communities, immigrants themselves and the communities that they leave behind.

The issue of asylum and immigration in Europe is one of the four broad themes on which the current Greek Presidency of the EU will focus its energies. In the Draft Programme of the Council for 2003, the Greek and Italian Presidencies state that progress on developing a common EU policy on the separate but related issues of asylum and immigration are a political priority for both. As advocates and academics, we should urge the current presidency to examine and discuss these issues separately in order to protect and promote respect for the rights of all migrants, refugees and asylum seekers.

Specific challenges facing Europe

Introduction

The migration context in Europe has changed dramatically over the last few decades. Many countries have converted from countries of emigration to countries of immigration. Some are old hands in the debate, such as France, Germany and England. Others are relative newcomers, such as Ireland, Italy and Spain. All member states within the EU are faced with many migration-related challenges and conflicting priorities.

Some of the specific challenges facing member states include irregular migration, integration, burden of sharing responsibility for asylum seekers and refugees, and last, but certainly not least, addressing the root causes of migration. The ultimate challenge will be to create and promote policies with the participation of and for the benefit of all affected parties, including national governments, regional bodies, migrants, refugees and the host communities which receive them.

Root causes of migration

One of the most pressing and important challenges facing the EU is to identify and address the root causes of migration. This will involve long term planning and commitment by the member states. Many states do recognise the importance of this issue; unfortunately, however, it is not included as an integral and equal part in immigration policy and planning by governments.

Most migrants, refugees and asylum seekers, leave their countries because they have to, not because they want to. Many migrants are compelled to flee their countries because of extreme poverty, political conflict or natural disaster. After reaching their final destinations and finding work, the great majority become a primary source of support for those left behind. For most migrants, the issue of immigration is an issue of survival for themselves and their loved ones.

In order to seriously and sincerely address the root causes of migration, the EU must look at its level of overseas development aid (ODA). In Europe, the ODA contribution has been as low as 0.14 % of GDP. The recommended United Nations target is 0.7 % of GDP. In 2001, if every country worldwide had met this target, an extra $112 billion could have been available for support of work in developing countries (JRS, 2002, p. 2). Overseas aid is key to helping poorer economies develop and create the conditions necessary for people to stay and support their families in their own communities.

In devising immigration policies, member states must include the issue of overseas aid as an integral part of any plan. Member states should work closely with the governments of sending countries to identify regions with the highest numbers of out migration and develop projects in those regions to support and sustain the livelihoods of potential migrants and their family members.

Irregular migration

Member states in the EU are confronted with and fear continued irregular immigration. Uncontrolled irregular migration harms both the migrants themselves —some lose their lives in transit, while all face difficult conditions after arrival— and the receiving communities, which may have inadequate resources to accommodate the needs of large numbers of undocumented persons.

How should Europe address the issue of the increasing number of undocumented persons living within its borders? Their presence is a reality. Most flee situations of political instability or poverty in their home countries. Many enter illegally. They work in Europe, raise their children here, contribute to the economy and often play a major role in the support and development of the villages and communities they were forced to leave behind. They contribute to the labour market and cultural richness in Europe and to the development of the rest of the world. However, they are the most vulnerable of populations. Most irregular migrants receive low pay, have little or no access to health care, and face limited educational opportunities.[1] What can and should Europe do to protect the rights of these de facto residents? How should Europe recognise their contributions?

In spite of attempts by governments to control and clamp down on irregular immigration and despite the increasingly dangerous conditions faced by many undocumented migrants in their journey north, the numbers continue to rise. Some estimate the number of undocumented persons in Europe to be 5 million. Others believe the number may be even higher. The distinction between regular and irregular migration is likely to remain a feature of immigration reality in Europe for years to come. EU member states should exhibit the same respect for the human rights of undocumented migrants within their borders as they do for the human rights of persons living in unstable and dangerous regimes abroad. Although improving basic conditions for undocumented persons may be seen by member states as incompatible with their desire to curb illegal migration, this so called "pull factor" should not be exaggerated.

Therefore, a major challenge for the EU is the creation of a well-conceived and developed immigration policy —aside from issues of border control and enforcement— which includes as one of its goals the reduction of irregular migration. Any such plan should recognise the contributions of long-term de facto residents, including granting legal status to long-term residents with significant ties to their host communities. Many studies have shown that EU member states need both skilled and unskilled workers. Therefore, an effective and fair plan cannot be developed without realistically examining the labour needs of each country and whether the native population can meet those needs.

At the meeting of the European Council in Seville in June 2002, a large amount of time was devoted to the debate on the development of a future common policy on immigration and asylum. Discussions primarily focused on issues relating to border surveillance, repatriation to countries of origin and the cooperation of police in fighting illegal

---

[1] For general information about undocumented persons in Europe, visit the website of the Platform for International Cooperation on the Rights of Undocumented Migrants at http://www.picum.org. Also, see, *Outside the Protection of the Law: The Situation of Irregular Migrants in Europe,* by Dr. Matthew GIBNEY. This report summarises the research sponsored by the Jesuit Refugee Service regarding the situation of undocumented persons in Germany, the United Kingdom and Spain. More information about this research and copies of the reports are available on the JRS website at http://www.jesref.org under the Research section of the Resources division.

immigration. The challenge for the EU and its member states will be to move further in the policy debate and address issues relating to common policy on labour needs and immigration and the protection of the human rights of both undocumented migrants and asylum seekers.

Burden sharing

Another challenge for a growing EU is the issue of burden sharing. Legally and morally, what contributions should each member state make towards receiving and accommodating refugee populations? What contributions should member states make to poorer countries throughout the world to support them in accepting and protecting refugees?

Although not specifically required by conventions or international law norms, a limited number of countries admit refugees on a permanent basis through refugee resettlement programmes. Canada, the United States and Australia have admitted refugees under their immigration programmes for decades. In addition to processing asylum claims of persons within and at their borders, Canada, the United States and Australia yearly identify refugees in third countries for admission and participation in refugee resettlement programmes. In 2001, the United States admitted over 68,000 refugees; Canada admitted over 12,000; and, Australia admitted over 6,000 (see UNHCR, 2002, p. 60). Unfortunately, these numbers represent an 8 % reduction in the number of refugee resettlement cases accepted the previous year.

Europe, on the other hand, is primarily confronted with asylum seekers, many who end up staying. Only a handful of EU member states regularly admit a yearly number of permanent refugees through resettlement programmes. However, the European Commission has created a European Refugee Fund which distributes money and assists member states in processing and hosting refugees already in Europe. Hopefully, member states will access and use some of these funds to support the creation of permanent refugee resettlement programmes.

Although developed countries contribute most of the funding for programmes that assist refugees, the least-developed and poorest countries host the overwhelming majority of the world's refugees (USCR, 2002, p. 10, 11). Poor countries are thus faced with a double burden: how to provide for their own nationals during times of great economic and social crisis and, at the same time, attempt to protect and serve large numbers of refugees crossing into their territories. If a united effort by both sending and receiving countries is not made to adjust the burdens borne by poor countries, the number of migrants fleeing political and economic strife will continue to soar.

Integration

Another major challenge facing both migrants and their host communities is the issue of integration. Migrants to Europe come from all over the world. Often, the places that receive them are overwhelmingly large cities which quickly become a rich mix of cultures, identities and histories. These cities are the foundations of integration where the cultural diversity of the new immigrants and the challenges of living together as a community are brought together in neighbourhoods that are truly multiethnic urban villages.

In order to understand the ways in which immigrants and their children build lives in new communities, we must conceive of integration as something more than simple notions of a unidirectional assimilation. Integration is now understood as sustained mutual interaction between immigrants and the societies that receive them, an interaction that may last for generations. Recent North American and European research shows that immigrants quickly adopt many of the traditional norms and values of the receiving society but also maintain strong and positive values for their own cultures and languages. Unfortunately, socio-economic integration and mobility may be proceeding at a slower pace.

The degree of social integration and socio-economic mobility of immigrants is generally assessed by looking at a variety of variables, including the following:

—**Linguistic Integration**: Language used in public interactions, competency in the new language, language used at home, language used among family members.

—**Labour Market Integration**: Education level, labour force participation of men and women, unemployment rate, socio-professional mobility, individual or household income.

—**Civic/Political Integration:** Participation in political parties, unions, neighbourhood associations, religious institutions and/or community groups.

—**Educational Integration:** School performance, school drop-out rates, choice of school, post-secondary education attainment, parent-teacher communication.

—**Residential Integration:** Degree of residential concentration/ segregation, residential mobility, homeownership rates, dwelling size/crowding, discrimination in rental markets.

Immigrants and their children face daily challenges in their new worlds. Meeting those challenges in part will demand effective social and economic policies on the part of host communities to help address problems faced by immigrants in places where they settle. Integration policies and programmes will succeed only if they are based on the particular socio-economic, cultural and political circumstances of the communities that receive them.

Host communities themselves will be faced with new challenges, including whether they have the capacity, the will and the resources to address the needs of newcomers fairly and adequately. If not, how can they access such resources? If they are not capable of integrating newcomers, what accounts for this inability? How can member states promote education campaigns to curb the rise of racism and xenophobia in response to increasing immigration? These are only some of the many questions that need to be asked, discussed and answered in devising sound integration policy and programmes to benefit both immigrants and the members of the host communities.

Academics, non-governmental organisations and practitioners working together: an American perspective

Non-governmental organisations (NGOs), academics and practitioners in the United States have come together over the last fifteen years to create a dynamic, collaborative relationship to advocate for the rights of immigrants, refugees and asylum seekers in the United States. That collaboration has resulted in the provision of direct legal, social and educational services to immigrants and asylum seekers, direct lobbying on their behalf before local, regional and national decision makers and federal court litigation to challenge unfair and discriminatory laws and policies. A large, diverse and powerful NGO community across the United States is devoted to promoting respect for the rights of migrants, refugees and asylum seekers. The immigration bar association —the American Immigration Lawyers Association— has over 8,000 members who are lawyers practising in the field of immigration law, primarily in the United States (see their website at http://www.aila.org). Academics dedicated to migration and refugee issues have organised sophisticated networks and associations through which they share ideas, information and research.[2]

---

[2] In the field of immigration, nationality and constitutional law, many legal academics and scholars belong to focus groups within the American Association of Law Schools (AALS). For information on AALS and those groups, visits its website at http://www.aals.org Additionally, immigration and nationality law professors in the United States have organised a list serve, known as the immprof list, with close to 200 participants.

A well-developed network of NGOs across the United States work together locally, regionally and nationally to promote the development of sound immigration policies which protect the rights of all immigrants, regardless of legal status.[3] Many NGOs have headquarters in Washington, D.C. where staff are primarily responsible for lobbying the governmental agencies, the White House itself and the United States Congress for promotion of better policies, laws and regulations relating to immigration in the United States. NGOs often serve as a source of information on the lives and needs of immigrants, legally, socially and economically, for the government, academic researchers and the press.

NGOs work together in coalition to devise effective, unified lobbying strategies based on their direct experiences with and knowledge of immigrant communities. Local NGO representatives in cities across the United States regularly meet with local Immigration and Naturalization Service (INS) personnel to discuss ongoing problems and challenges facing the communities they represent. NGOs also liaise with local government officials, including police, municipal authorities and school board officials, on all matters affecting immigrants, including housing, education and safety issues.

National NGOs work together to promote better laws and policies for immigrants and their family members before the United States Congress. They meet regularly with members of Congress and their staff to discuss immigration policy issues and to educate them on the complexities of implementation and interpretation of the many immigration laws and regulations in force. Many times, members of Congress will ask NGO representatives to draft portions of proposed legislation in immigration related bills. NGO representatives serve as a source of information to the United States Congress on all areas of immigration law and policy.

NGO representatives in Washington, D.C. also regularly meet with high officials in the INS and other governmental agencies with jurisdiction over immigration matters to discuss topics relating to immigrants in the United States, including backlogs in adjudication of immigration applications, detention of immigrants, and refugee and asylum issues. Over the last ten years, the relationship between the NGO community and the INS and other governmental agencies has become more open and fluid.

The NGO community and governmental officials have worked together on a variety of initiatives which have resulted in greater

---

[3] For more information regarding these organisations, visit the website of the American Immigration Law Foundation at http://www.ailf.org and click on Links.

protection of immigrants' rights in the United States. The NGO community worked closely with the INS in the early 1990s on a major reform and overhaul of the asylum system. This collaboration resulted in the creation of much improved policies, laws and regulations to protect the rights of refugees and asylum seekers in the United States. In fact, many NGO representatives involved in the asylum reform process later were hired by the INS as asylum officers within its Asylum Offices across the country.

The NGO community and the INS worked together to draft and publish Detention Standards governing the treatment of INS detainees in prisons and detention centres across the country pending the outcome of their deportation cases. At the request of the INS, several NGOs developed "Know Your Rights" programmes which provide information to INS detainees regarding their rights to remain in the United States, including providing pro bono representation to detainees. In a joint collaboration between the Board of Immigration Appeals —the immigration appellate authority which decides appeals from local immigration court decisions— and the NGO community, a Pro Bono Project was created to provide free representation to INS detainees around the country in appeals of their cases. These are a few examples of the many collaborative efforts which have resulted from strong and unified lobbying by NGOs across the United States.

Unfortunately, since John Ashcroft has been named Attorney General, the relationship between the NGO community and the INS (which is under the jurisdiction of the United States Department of Justice) has become somewhat strained. Attorney General Ashcroft has taken the lead in promoting secretive immigration policies, has drafted regulations authorising secret deportation hearings, has stripped the administrative appellate body in charge of immigration related appeals —the Board of Immigration Appeals— of much of its authority and has generally promoted the restriction of immigrant rights after September 11, 2001.[4] In response to these attacks on immigrants' rights, NGOs have filed litigation seeking open hearings and challenging new restrictions on the rights of immigrants. They have also developed media campaigns to publicise and report on what is happening to

---

[4] For more information on actions by US government agencies relating to immigration since September 11, 2001, visit the American Immigration Law Foundation website at http://www.ailf.org. Click on the Legal Action Center to access Post September 11 Legal Resources which lists Executive Branch Actions since September 11, 2001. This list includes all the initiatives taken by Attorney General John Ashcroft restricting immigrant rights in the United States.

immigrants and their family members as a result of special registration procedures, secret proceedings and detention of long time residents.

NGO representatives and academics from universities throughout the United States have also developed a close working relationship over the last fifteen years. In the area of immigration law and policy, immigration and constitutional law professors have provided direct assistance to NGOs and private attorneys in drafting complaints and legal briefs in support of the many lawsuits filed in the federal courts challenging unfair and discriminatory immigration laws. Law professors, NGO representatives and private practitioners have challenged the INS practice of indefinite detention of immigrants with deportation orders who cannot be deported for diplomatic reasons. They have worked together to challenge unfair asylum procedures which eventually resulted in a major reform of the asylum system in the early 1990s.

Law professors across the United States have established over 30 refugee and immigration law clinics within university law faculties. These clinics serve two purposes: to provide quality, free legal representation to immigrants and asylum seekers, and to train law students to effectively and assertively advocate on behalf of these vulnerable groups. Many law students continue to provide pro bono representation to asylum seekers and immigrants for many years after their clinical experience in law school.

Law professors have also promoted the creation and development of NGOs which provide direct legal services to immigrants and asylum seekers in their communities. They have helped immigrants and family members create and establish their own NGOs to lobby on behalf of themselves and their family members adversely affected by unfair immigration laws and practices.[5]

Academics also serve as an important source of information to the press and public. As academics, they are seen as credible and thoughtful analysts of issues relating to immigration policies and practices in the United States and, therefore, serve as a powerful voice on behalf of migrants, refugees and asylum seekers.

Academics play an important and integral role in litigation of immigration matters before the federal courts. There have been many instances where the NGOs and the INS have been unable to reach agreements in resolving problems. NGOs, therefore, have been forced

---

[5] Citizens and Immigrants for Equal Justice is an NGO created with support from faculty at the New York University Law School. It fights for the rights of long term residents whom the INS seeks to deport as a result of the commission of crimes, most of which are minor. For more on CIEJ, see http://www.ciej.org

to bring matters before the courts for resolution. In those instances, the NGOs have worked closely with private lawyers and law professors in drafting complaints, filing lawsuits and preparing and submitting legal briefs to the courts in support of their positions. Because of their credibility within the legal community, academics play an important and influential part in immigration related litigation.

Finally, and perhaps most importantly, academics in the United States often shape the terms and influence the outcome of the immigration debate. For example, law professors in the United States regularly write articles and books analysing and criticising discriminatory and ineffective immigration law and policies and often offer proposed alternatives to such. Supreme Court Justices and federal court judges look to these articles in reviewing and deciding important immigration cases before them. It is also quite common for immigration and constitutional law professors to serve in high positions within the Department of Justice and the Immigration and Naturalization Service for different periods of time during their professional careers.[6]

Conclusion

In light of the many pressing issues and challenges facing Europe, and the role that academics and NGOs can play, it is vital that we work together to promote the investigation, publication and dissemination of credible and reliable information about migrants and refugees available for use by migrants, their advocates and the decision makers throughout Europe. The thoughtful and analytical qualities possessed by academics combined with the energy, experience and knowledge of NGO advocates and practitioners working with and for migrant communities provide the best setting to meet and address the many migration-related challenges facing Europe in the twenty-first century.

References

JRS (2002): *JRS-Europe annual report 2001-2002*, available on the JRS-Europe website at http://www.jrseurope.org.

---

6 David Martín, a law professor at the University of Virginia School of Law and Alex Aleinikoff, a law professsor at the Georgetown University Law Center have both served at different times during the 1990s as General Counsel of the Immigration and Naturalization Service.

US Bureau of Census (2003): International Programs Center, U.S. Bureau of Census at http://blue.census.gov/ipc, providing world population statistics as of January 29, 2003.

USCR (2002): *World Refugee Survey 2002* available from the USCR website at http://www.refugees.org

UNHCR (2002): *Statistical Yearbook 2001*, UNHCR, Geneva.

Building a rights based asylum system for Europe: a UNHCR perspective

Belén García de Vinuesa

The Amsterdam Treaty, with the EU Member States' agreement to relinquish their sovereign right to pursue national policies in the fields of asylum and immigration, represents the most significant step towards the building of a common EU asylum system. The Member States thereby «agreed to agree» on the principles of *who* is to receive protection, *what* it entails, *where* and *how* it is to be implemented. Four out of the five years of the Amsterdam timeframe have gone by, and three instruments have been adopted: the Council Decision creating a European Refugee Fund; the Directive on Temporary Protection; and the Directive setting minimum standards for the reception of asylum seekers. Political agreement has been reached on one further instrument: the Regulation replacing the Dublin Convention for determining the State responsible for examining an application for asylum. However, most of those questions I have just mentioned on the common asylum system remain unanswered.

If we take a close look at the context in which a common EU asylum system is emerging, we cannot ignore that it is not the best of times for the birth of a regional asylum system to be taken as a model by many, if not all, regions in the world. The portrait that many have of a refugee —often close to a caricature— no longer corresponds to the earlier image of a political opponent to a communist regime received in a Western State. Nor does it even correspond to the victims running away from ethnic cleansing shown by the terrible images on the CNN. The refugee who currently knocks at our doors is a peasant milked by a guerrilla army who cannot pay any longer because he or she is ruined, or a woman who fears genital mutilation and in some cases is forced into prostitution upon arrival in our country. It is indeed a new profile of refugees, and some say that such persons are not real refugees, although they acknowledge that they might be in need of protection.

Many refugees nowadays arrive together with many of their country people who have suffered the consequences of economic inequality and the aftermath of a conflict and see themselves forced to choose between a hopeless struggle to survive at home, or an uprooted existence where they might nonetheless regain the hope of leading a dignified life. They reach what has been called a "fortress" Europe and seek the best way to enter its territory, be it through the available legal means, including the asylum procedures, or with the aid of smugglers and traffickers who take them across borders concealed in lorries, at high financial cost and great personal risk.

In an attempt to manage these migration flows, European States create new tools and mechanisms that might, or might not be effective for such purpose, but often put asylum systems at risk, if not the mere possibility of having access to the territory of a State where an asylum application can be lodged. Even when an asylum seeker manages to enter the territory of one of the Member States and lodge an application, he or she risks being sent back to any 'safe third country' outside the Union through which he or she passed en route to Europe. Although the definition of a safe third country implies that such country is a party to the 1951 Convention on the Status of Refugees and has status determination procedures in compliance with this, often there is no guarantee that the asylum seeker will find effective protection in it.

European States are increasingly preoccupied with the integrity of their asylum systems and the prevention of their abuse. They study the low recognition rates and make calculations of the money spent in deciding who is and who is not an asylum seeker, as well as the costs of repatriating unsuccessful asylum seekers where this is achieved. They compare these figures to UNHCR's overall budget and the money spent to assist refugees worldwide and wonder whether it would not be more cost-effective to spend their money in assisting what they consider to be the «real refugees» in regions of origin.

Migration and asylum issues become major themes of election campaigns, which have nothing to do with international solidarity and international human rights commitments, and turn them into "problems" which are to be solved by any means as a first step to solving any other problem at the national level. These trends, reflected and fuelled by the mass media, result in increasing xenophobic and paranoid attitudes among European citizens, who, under a revolving door effect, demand stricter migration and asylum policies from their Governments.

All these elements, together with the fact that unanimous voting is required to adopt any of the measures foreseen by the Treaty of

Amsterdam, make the building of a common European asylum system, as said earlier, a difficult task, which requires a solid legal framework and a firm and clear common understanding of the premises upon which it is built.

From the perspective of UNHCR, the motive for developing a common asylum system is the need to provide a predictable and structured framework for ensuring effective international protection of persons whose life or liberty is at risk in their country of origin. When a person must, out of necessity, exercise his or her human right to seek asylum, that person's treatment and fate at the hands of a State are a matter of international law and obligations, not a matter of the State's discretionary immigration policy. The scope and content of a common European asylum system must be determined, therefore, against the backdrop of established principles and standards of international refugee and human rights law.

The construction of a coherent, rights-based asylum system rests on certain assumptions. The UNHCR Bureau for Europe sets out seven premises in this area (UNHCR, unpublished).

First, the scope of the 1951 Convention is a matter of international law. Therefore, its interpretation is not, or should not be, subject to variations on the basis of the history, legal culture or political necessity of each State Party to the Convention. As observed, for instance, by the UK House of Lords (2000), "in principle there can only be one true interpretation of a treaty" and "there is not a band of permissible meanings of Article 1A(2) [of the 1951 Convention]." As such, the 1951 Convention must be given an "autonomous and international meaning" derivable from the sources mentioned in Articles 31 and 32 of the Vienna Convention on the Law of Treaties.[1]

Second, the true meaning of the refugee concept must be determined independently from the financial or other costs attaching to the granting of asylum, the management issues pertaining to asylum procedures, or any other limitations on a State's capacity to meet international obligations as regards the treatment of refugees. The level of legal obligations that a State Party has to assume once it grants refugee status cannot be a justifiable ground to circumscribe the internationally-agreed refugee definition in a narrow conception which limits the

---

[1] According to the House of Lords, one such source that should be relied on for the enquiry into the "true autonomous meaning" of the refugee concept is the UNHCR *Handbook*, because of its "high persuasive authority" and the fact that it constitutes "good evidence of what has come to be international practice within Article 31(3)(*b*) of the Vienna Convention."

numbers of those who qualify for refugee status. A person who satisfies the established definitional criteria of the Convention is, and remains, a refugee regardless of whether the State is able or willing to meet its international obligations to provide for the rights and entitlements set out in the Convention. It may be useful to recall in this context the declaratory nature of refugee status. As set out in paragraph 28 of the UNHCR *Handbook*, a person does not *become* a refugee because of recognition of his or her refugee status, but is recognised as such because he or she *is* a refugee.

Third, the oft-repeated argument about the changing character of the refugee problem today as grounds for narrowing down the applicability of the 1951 Convention requires a more careful, objective appraisal. What has actually been different in recent years when compared to 1951? Refugee problems have become more widespread and countries of origin more diverse, encompassing virtually all corners of the globe. Other recent changes concern the multiplicity and increasing complexity of the causes of flight. There have also been significant changes in the patterns of refugee movements, with a disproportionate shift of the burden towards the poor nations and regions least able to receive and care for refugees.

In the post-Cold War era, internal conflicts fuelled by national, ethnic and religious differences and resulting intolerance have increasingly become the main cause of refugee flight. This era has witnessed more and more frequently the use of war and violence as instruments of persecution, the means chosen by the persecutor to repress or "cleanse" specific groups merely on account of their ethnicity, religion or other affiliations. In many of today's wars, the plight of the civilian population is not simply a matter of being caught in the cross-fire or suffering the unintended consequences of armed conflict, but being specifically targeted by the combatants and subjected to extortion, sexual violence, forced labour and displacement.

If these are the basic changes that have marked the global refugee situation in recent years, they do not in any way put into question the relevance and validity of the 1951 Convention and its 1967 Protocol. Today's refugees, whether their vulnerability and victimisation occur in the context of war or in peacetime, are just as deserving of international protection as those who preceded them. There can be no denying that the 1951 Convention and its 1967 Protocol, even while they need to be supplemented with other protection tools or regimes, continue to be both effective and relevant in ensuring a coherent rights-based approach to the protection of most of today's refugees. All that is needed is to apply them in the spirit in which they were drafted and adopted, i.e. in a less rigid and more principled, protection-minded way.[2]

Fourth, restrictive asylum policies of one State or region do not deter refugees from fleeing persecution in their country. They may only divert refugee movements elsewhere, often to those States in the region of origin that are least able to guarantee effective protection. Clearly, responsibilities for refugee protection and the resulting costs should not be a matter of a State's geographical position, but rather a coherent, planned strategy for a collective humanitarian response to the victims of human rights violations, persecution or armed conflict.

Fifth, neither the definition of refugee in Article 1 of the 1951 Convention nor the observance of the principle of *non-refoulement* in Article 33 is entirely an inter-State treaty obligation. The obligation is as much towards the refugee, whose fundamental human rights are the subject of the Convention. Even when there is a specific formal agreement among a group of States to apportion responsibility for receiving and considering applications for refugee status, any number of these States would bear the responsibility for direct or indirect breach of the *non-refoulement* obligation if this were to occur.[3]

Sixth, employing a narrow construction of the refugee concept will not help reduce the numbers of non-refugee migrants claiming asylum. At best, it limits the number of refugees who are recognised as such. In a rather circular logic, States have sometimes found it convenient to inflate the rate of rejections of refugee claims so as to justify stringent measures against the "abusers" of the asylum system.

In no way does rejection of a refugee claim imply that the applicant abused the asylum system. Some unsuccessful refugee claimants are people who actually meet the requisite criteria for refugee status, but whose claims are rejected only because of a restrictive application of the refugee definition or stringent evidentiary requirements. Yet others are

---

[2] See, for example, UK Court of Appeal, Regina *v.* Secretary of State for the Home Department Ex parte Adan and Aitsegeur [1999] 3 W.L.R, 1274, at p. 1296: "It is clear that the signatory States intended that the Convention should afford continuing protection for refugees in the changing circumstances of the present and future world. The Convention has to be regarded as a living instrument."

[3] See, for example, the European Court of Human Rights, T.I. *v.* the United Kingdom judgement of 7 March 2000, at p. 16: "Where States establish international organisations, or *mutatis mutandis* international agreements, to pursue co-operation in certain fields of activities, there may be implications for the protection of fundamental rights. It would be incompatible with the purpose and object of the Convention if Contracting States were thereby absolved from their responsibility under the Convention in relation to the field of activity covered by such attribution."

people who genuinely view themselves as refugees, but, understandably, without having expert knowledge about legal definitions and thresholds that must be met. Furthermore, not every so-called "economic migrant" is by definition an abuser or a cheater. Many economic migrants who have recourse to asylum systems may lack sufficient understanding that the solution to their problems lies within international development and economic co-operation, not within the institution of asylum.

Finally, Governments and communities have, as a matter of course, legitimate interests to ensure that their hospitality and generosity are not exploited. Problems of real and serious misuse of States' asylum systems can and should find their effective redress within the established national procedures for the determination of refugee status, but certainly not through political discourse edging on xenophobia or by downgrading generally accepted protection standards. Likewise, refugee applicants have duties to the country of asylum to conform to its laws and regulations, and to fully co-operate with and facilitate the tasks of the authorities charged with status determination.

It should, however, be recognised that in the adversarial refugee status determination systems which presently exist in most European States, it is often difficult for refugee claimants to know what attitude to take towards the status determiners who simultaneously act as both judges and prosecutors. Given the prosecutorial posture dominating the refugee status determination process — with the authorities challenging every asylum claim brought before them — claimants often feel impelled likewise to employ whatever means possible to "defend themselves" rather than simply recounting truthfully the facts and events surrounding their claims. Refugee status determination should not be an adversarial contest. Justice would be better served if the refugee applicant and the decision-maker properly shared the duty to ascertain all the relevant facts rather than oppose each other. This requires, above all, the restoration of mutual trust and confidence in the refugee status determination processes.

It is important to bear in mind that the instruments to be adopted under the asylum agenda represent but a first phase towards a common asylum system. Important changes are still necessary to achieve this goal. In UNHCR's view, important gains in efficiency can be made in such a common asylum system, while still maintaining high standards of fairness. Such gains should override the costs of necessary legislative changes on a national level. The development of such a common system requires, however, willingness on the part of Member States to question and revise current national systems and practices. Reservations, "standstill" clauses and other flexible provisions in EC instruments setting minimum standards on asylum eventually defeat the purpose of harmonisation, while agreement at the lowest common denominator can only be harmful to bona fide asylum-seekers and refugees. However, this development also requires that all of us, who are committed to the defence of the rights of asylum seekers and refugees in Europe, do not give up a continued dialogue with our Governments and other actors, in order to uphold the human rights of these persons, which, as said before, is a matter of international law and obligations, and not of the State's discretionary immigration policy.

References

UK House of Lords (2000): *Regina v. Secretary of State for the Home Department, Ex parte Adan and Aitseguer*, Judgement of 19 December 2000.

UNHCR (unpublished): "Towards a common European asylum system: a view from UNHCR". Draft article to be published in the European Series.

The consequences of demographic change: is there a role for immigration?

Jan Niessen and Yongmi Schibel

The Migration Policy Group (MPG) is an independent organisation committed to policy development on mobility, migration, diversity, equality and anti-discrimination by facilitating the exchange between stakeholders from all sectors of society, with the aim of contributing to innovative and effective responses to the challenges posed by migration and diversity.

This paper aims to make the case for including immigration in debates on Europe's social and economic goals and objectives. A subsequent paper will examine how to link international migration with foreign and development policies.

Introduction

Can immigration become one of the multiple responses to the challenges Europe and the expanding European Union are facing? Can immigrants play a meaningful role in shaping Europe's future? These questions seem to be out of place considering the almost exclusive attention migration restriction and prevention are currently receiving in public and policy debates. Concerns expressed in these debates are about the real and feared consequences of uncontrolled migration and the perceived or real unsuccessful integration of immigrants. In response governments design and refine policies that tighten the admission of immigrants.

Nevertheless, the questions deserve to be answered. Certain trends in the labour market with undesired implications for Europe's economy and welfare system warrant an examination of the role of immigration as a complementary labour market strategy. In a situation of steady population decline and worsening demographic imbalances immigrants could contribute to reversing these developments.

This paper argues that immigration should be considered as an option in the policy debates on strategic economic and social goals and fundamental values that underpin Europe's social market economy. Immigrants should be valued for their contribution to achieve these goals and this will enhance their integration into society. Immigration is about sustainable development, economic interests and social values.

In other words, this paper is an attempt to change the terms of the current debate on international migration: from a debate that focuses almost exclusively on admission issues to one where these issues are only discussed in the context of an assessment of immigration needs against the backdrop of a declining and ageing population. This makes the migration debate distinct from the refugee debate, which is about protection needs and human rights commitments. It also makes it distinct from the debate on all forms of forced migration to be addressed by Europe's foreign and development policies.

First we examine briefly the significance of demographic factors for economic development. We then look at future demographic trends and spell out the implications for labour markets, pension and health care systems. This is followed by an overview of policies to address emerging challenges and by some final remarks. We focus on the expanding European Union and refer regularly to work undertaken within the Council of Europe.

Why demography matters

The European Union has embarked upon an ambitious programme of becoming 'the most competitive and dynamic knowledge-based economy in the world capable of sustained economic growth with more and better jobs and greater social cohesion' (Presidency conclusions, Lisbon European Council, 23 and 24 March 2000). Such goals crucially depend on people: people who will generate growth, create and fill jobs, and contribute to social security systems; and people who will live in and shape the societies that benefit from economic development. How many people live in Europe, and how many will there be in twenty or fifty years? What is their age profile, and how is it changing? The achievement of Europe's long-term goals is intimately bound up with the size and age of its population. Demography and demographic change, then, matter for social and economic progress in Europe.

Some trends

Demographic projections show that Europe's population is diminishing in size as well as becoming older. While on average around 2.1 children per woman of childbearing age are required to replace the population, the EU average is 1.53. In addition to the decline in fertility, life expectancy is increasing. The proportion of those aged 65 and over is projected to rise from about 16 % of the total population in 1998 to 22 % by 2025. Within this, the relative number of people of 80 and older is rising faster still (EUROPEAN COMMISSION, n.d.). This means that a growing number of people above retirement age will need to be supported by those in employment. On present trends, for the current 15 member states, the population of working age will fall by approximately 40 million people from 2000 until 2050 and the old age dependency ratio will double from 24 % to 49 % (COM, 2002).

Regional differences are significant for all the measures examined. For instance, whereas a number of regions including the south of France and Greece will not face population decline for decades, population is already declining in some regions of Spain, Italy, Germany and the Nordic countries, and in most of the candidate countries. With regard to the old-age dependency ratio —the number aged 65 and over relative to those of working age (15 to 64)— the most marked increases are expected to take place in Italy, Sweden, Finland and Germany and the smallest in Ireland, Portugal and Luxembourg. For the current 15 members, the old age dependency ratio was 24 % in 2000. An increase to 27 % is projected by 2010 (EUROPEAN COMMISSION, 2001, p. 63).

In looking at demographic change, total population size is an important measure. However, the size of the labour force and the balance between economically active and inactive persons are the most policy relevant dimensions because of their impact on the labour market, on pensions and on health care systems. At the same time as there is demographic decline in Europe, there is also an employment creation process. A low labour supply aggravates labour market mismatches and shortages, particularly if combined with an unfavourable skill profile. The negative economic effects resulting from these imbalances affect the state's revenue base and can endanger spending on pensions and health care. More directly, the fewer people work, the narrower is the base of contributions on which pensions and health care systems rest. The higher the number of older persons, the heavier is the burden that these systems have to bear.

Which of these factors should be addressed by policy? The increase in the number of older persons is a result of the fall in mortality rates.

Life expectancy has increased over the last 50 years by about 10 years in total. This is a positive development, which is projected to continue. The attention of policy makers should therefore be on maintaining or enlarging labour supply (the sum of employed and unemployed persons), in order to keep the "economic dependency ratio" as low as possible. Labour supply can expand in two ways: through having more people in the labour force ages, or through increases in labour force participation rates MACDONALD/KIPPEN, 2000, p. 4). Increases in fertility and immigration are two ways of adding to the number of people in the labour force ages, while higher participation rates lift the percentage of those in the labour force ages who are, in fact, part of the labour force. Projections and scenarios for demographic change in Europe thus depend on developments in fertility rates, labour market participation and immigration.

Fertility

Fertility is the most influential determinant of demographic change in the long term. Changes in fertility not only affect the number of children but also of succeeding generations. For this reason relatively small changes in fertility can have very significant consequences on future population size and age structure (LUTZ/ SCHERBOV, 1999, p. 2).

Along with most other developed countries, European societies experience the sustained slippage of birth rates below replacement fertility (2.1). The total fertility rate for the EU was 1.53 in 2000 (EUROPEAN COMMISSION, 2001, p. 63). The situation differs between countries. In the Mediterranean countries (Spain, Italy, Greece and Portugal), fertility dropped relatively late, but fast and to very low levels. Spain (1.19) and Italy now have the lowest fertility rates in the European Union. Ireland (1.89), France and the Nordic countries have relatively high rates, although they are still below replacement level. Developments in Belgium and the Netherlands are characterised by fluctuating fertility rates, whereas Austria has had low and stagnating birth rates for almost 20 years. Accession countries have seen a particularly dramatic decline in fertility (EUROPEAN COMMISSION, 2002, p. 5; BAGAVOS/MARTIN, 2000, p. 47f). However, with the exception of the accession countries, projections for fertility rates are for stagnation at low levels rather than further decline. In 2000, the only EU countries that still experienced a decline in birth rates were the United Kingdom and Germany.

Participation in the labour market

While participation in the labour market is not strictly a demographic measure, it is an effective tool for determining the impact of demographic change on a society. It gives information about the employment component of the working age population rather than about its size only. This is relevant because large parts of the working age population may be in education, retired, or may not be actively seeking work because of personal responsibilities. They may not form part of the labour force because of illness or incapacity, or not seek work because of discouragement about the availability of work (PUNCH/PEARCE, 2000, p. 47).

The labour force participation rate (i.e. the share of the population that is actively involved in the labour market) varies substantively for men and women, as well as for people in different age groups. On the one hand, of the men of prime working age, 25 to 54, almost 93 % are economically active. On the other hand, the participation of older men aged 55 to 64 is only 51.5 %, with figures around 35 % in Belgium and France. Low participation rates are also found among young men and women under 25 —the drop in their employment rates has effectively reduced the EU work force by almost 5 million since the mid-1980s. The participation rate of older women has risen but is still low at 30 %. The main source of labour force growth in the Union since the mid-1980s has been women aged 25 to 54, whose participation rate is now at 72.5 %. In recent years, however, the rate of increase in this group has shown signs of slowing down (ALGOE CONSULTANTS, 2002, p. 15; figures are for 2000).

It is difficult to project future changes in labour force participation rates. It is unlikely that Europeans aged less than 25 years will participate much more in the future, as educational requirements continue to rise. The participation of older persons is strongly influenced by the incentive systems in place and will be affected by political choices. The process of expansion in the participation rates of women has not come to an end, and several European countries may catch up with states such as Sweden, where women already have participation rates close to those of men. It is important to note that the general economic climate has a noticeable effect on participation rates, as low expectations for finding employment may induce people to drop out of the labour market.

Immigration

Since 1989, net migration has been the main component of annual population change in the Union. In 2000, the annual net migration rate was 2 per 1000 population, representing around 65 % of total population growth. Without positive net migration the populations of Germany, Greece, Italy and Sweden would be in decline. In addition, unrecorded immigration is significant in a number of member states, especially in southern Europe. A disproportionate number of immigrants into the EU have been men and women in their 20s. On average, people in this age group represented some 40 % of all immigrants in the second half of the 1990s, while those in their 30s accounted for another 20 %. Accordingly, immigrants of non-EU nationality added an average of 0.8 % a year to the resident population of 20 to 29 year olds in the Union over this period. However, this influx was partly offset by emigration. The specific age and sex structure of most immigrant groups means that apart from the direct demographic effect through the influx of persons, migration also has secondary effects, namely a higher number of births and a lower number of deaths compared with the host population. Many recent immigrant groups also have a higher fertility rate (HAUG, 2002, p. 2).

Migration is the most volatile of the components determining population size. While fertility and mortality rates change gradually, the number of people entering or leaving a country can vary significantly from one year to the next (LUTZ/SCHERBOV, 1999, p. 3). The past 10 years have witnessed great fluctuations in European migration levels, as well as significant regional variations. Future migration trends largely turn on policy decisions about migration needs in Europe. However, the supply side in the form of continuing migration pressure from outside the EU is also a much-discussed aspect. Researchers have added a demographic perspective to this theme by pointing out that the "stagnating entity" Europe is "surrounded by populations with run-away growth" (SCHMID, 2001). Projections suggest that while in the post-World War II era, the population of Spain was three times larger than Morocco's, in about 2050 Morocco's population might be 50 per cent larger than Spain's. A similar picture emerges when comparing France and Algeria or Germany and Turkey.

Consequences of demographic change in Europe

Demographic change is taking place, and it matters for the social and economic future of Europe. But how exactly will it affect European economies and societies? Where will it be felt first, and by whom? Labour markets are an obvious point of departure, with demand for workers at all skill levels projected to persist, and certain sectors already affected by a lack of labour supply. Having people in jobs also sustains Europe's pension and health care systems: those in employment need to support those out of employment, and the more unfavourable the proportion between the two groups, the higher the burdens will become. This section will examine the implications of population decline and ageing for these key components of the European social economy.

Implications for the labour market

Will the demographic changes described above have a negative impact on European labour markets? European economies are far from fully employed economies. The degree of labour under-utilisation is clearly greater than that indicated by unemployment rates. For instance, at the moment less than a quarter of people aged 60-64 are in employment. For these reasons, some researchers conclude that the size of the reserve labour force, which could be tapped into by raising participation rates, is enough to prevent any shortages on the labour market. They assert that "in this context, the fact that the new cohorts reaching working age are less numerous will not matter much" (PUNCH/PEARCE, 2000, p. 61). However, there remain questions as to how much participation rates can be raised before the social and cultural changes required become prohibitive, and whether such measures can, in fact, compensate for the effects of declining fertility. Like future labour supply, future labour demand is, to an extent, a matter of speculation. However, there are indications that advances in information technology will lead to greater demand for skilled labour. Labour-intensive services, from leisure to health and personal care, will be in demand by aged persons and by workers with affluent lifestyles. Low-skilled labour will also be required by the construction industry (MACDONALD/KIPPEN, 2000, p. 4). In addition to the demographically induced fall in labour supply, the historical trend indicates that the annual number of hours worked per individual is decreasing through time, as leisure becomes more important (PEDERSEN, 2002, p. 11).

Unsatisfied demand for labour at both the high and the low end of the skill spectrum can lead to shortages and skills deficiencies. The European Commission has acknowledged that these exist in the EU despite the high unemployment levels that remain, and that they may seriously limit Europe's capacity for further growth (EUROPEAN COMMISSION, 2001a, p. 45). More detail is given in the *Joint Employment Reports* adopted annually by Commission and Council in response to the *National Action Plans on Employment*, in which Member States describe the state of their labour market as well as their policy responses. The *2000 Joint Employment Report* mentions the tightening of the labour market supply of high tech professionals (p. 56). Specifically, the report identifies a tightening of the labour market supply in Sweden, Denmark, Ireland, the Netherlands, Northern Italy and Flanders. The *2001 Joint Employment Report* refers to Guideline 6 under the employability pillar, which asks Member States to identify and prevent emerging bottlenecks. It comments on the National Action Plans, in which Italy, Finland, Sweden, the United Kingdom and France state that their labour shortages are mainly limited to a few occupations/sectors and regions. At the other end of the spectrum, it notes that Finland, Ireland and the Netherlands find themselves in very tight labour markets, with shortages in both high and low skill occupations. It concludes that "most Member States anticipate the problems becoming more serious in the near and mid term future, based on combined economic and demographic forecasts" (EUROPEAN COMMISSION, 2001b, p. 24).

Apart from the size of the labour force, there is also a debate about its composition and about potentially negative effects of ageing. In particular, there is a discussion as to whether a smaller and older labour force would have a lower ability to innovate, which would affect the competitiveness of European economies.

Implications for pension and health care systems

Ageing has the effect of shortening the employed period with respect to the whole life. Concerns about the financial stability of pensions and wider social security systems are therefore often framed in terms of the old age dependency ratio or the proportion of persons in retirement ages relative to those of working age. It is important to note that this ratio does not accurately reflect the true ratio of beneficiaries to social contributors in the social security system. However, it gives an important indication of the demographic dynamics affecting the system, where fewer persons in employment will need to support more persons out of employment. In the European Union, it is projected that the ratio of workers to pensioners will decline from four to one to less than two to one by 2040.

In European welfare states, pensions account for, on average, 40-50 % of the total expenditure on social security (COUNCIL OF EUROPE, 2002). The proportion is especially high in Italy, while it is low in relatively "young" countries such as Ireland. It is a particular challenge to fund adequate pensions for those whose working career has not been sufficiently long or continuous to accumulate satisfactory pension requirements. This is frequently true for women, who predominate in older age groups and whose share of the population increases with advancing age. It is projected that public spending on pensions, health care and care for the elderly will increase between 4 % and 8 % of GDP by 2040 in most Member States (EUROPEAN COMMISSION, 2002a). For governments, pension spending could thus lead to higher deficits. For individuals, the demographic developments could mean "pay more, work longer, and get less" (BOLKESTEIN, 2001). As the financing of pensions is increasingly precarious, it is partly being shifted from the public to the private sector. Of the three pillars of pension systems —statutory social security schemes, occupational schemes and personal schemes— the third is growing the most rapidly. The importance of private pension schemes for the incomes of retired people may increase further as governments try to contain the burden of rising pension expenditure on public finances.

Health care systems likewise need to meet the challenge of ageing. Life expectancy in the European Union now stands at 81 years for women and 75 for men. When it comes to the provision of care for the elderly, the family network and the public sector (local and central government) are the two most important actors. However, there is a growing trend across Europe to use more publicly funded services. While in the Nordic countries the state is already the main supplier of services, in Southern countries the family is still the most important provider of care for the elderly. However, it is expected that these countries will expand their formal services (COUNCIL OF EUROPE, 1995). It is also important to note that age-related illnesses, which may be serious enough to make sufferers completely dependent on others, often require long-term care (outpatient care, in long-stay units or in psychiatric units). This may not be a matter for the conventional health system, but for the medical-social sector (EUROPEAN COMMISSION, 2001c). As is the case with other health services, such care will be labour-intensive.

Over the last decade, health expenditure in the majority of EU countries rose as a percentage of GDP, and in 1999 total EU expenditure on health represented 8 % of EU GDP. Clearly, older persons need more health care. However, in recent UN sponsored discussions around ageing the EU pointed out that population ageing is not a principal cause of the rising healthcare costs (UNECE, 2002). Indeed, research confirms that the rise in health expenses is higher than would have been predictable purely due to ageing. Thus some other factors must be contributing to inflate health expenses. One possible explanation is that health expenses are viewed as luxury goods and are allotted increasing shares of individual budgets as economic conditions improve. As many among the new cohorts of elderly people have experienced improved living conditions during their lifetime, they may have raised expectations and higher perceived needs. New and more sophisticated drugs are also developed and produced at greater cost. The question is how much health care should be publicly provided, and whether the (partial) privatisation of health expenses does not lead to rising inequality in health (DE SANTIS, 2001).

Pension and health care patterns interact with the labour market in a variety of ways. Firstly, the growing need for care for the elderly generates demand for both skilled and unskilled labour. Secondly, participation and social systems are interrelated. This is because choosing to participate in the labour market depends critically on the alternatives available to the individual. Choices about whether to enter the labour market or not will often hinge on financial incentives. The level of wages will interact with levels of social support and the tax system to determine whether there is a financial incentive to work (EUROPEAN COMMISSION, 2002b, p. 22). Finally, the revenue base of pension and social protection systems depends on a healthy labour market and economy, as the scope for taxation will grow with higher employment rates and high productivity.

Policy options

It can be argued that a decrease in the population in European countries would in fact have a favourable effect on the environment and quality of life. Individuals may benefit if competition for access to the labour market, education, and housing opportunities is less intense. On the macroeconomic level, a smaller work force may induce capital deepening and so have a positive impact on productivity and economic growth. On such a view, only adaptive measures should be taken to adjust social structures and services to the emerging ageing society.

However, the mounting of fiscal pressures and anxieties about the sustainability of pension and health care systems have combined with concerns about labour market shortages and lower economic growth to impel governments to respond to demographic change with a variety of policies. Some of these measures are general efforts to boost economic growth, in order to broaden the tax base and alleviate public finance problems. Many government policies in the social, economic, education, housing, migration and regional planning fields are affected by demographic trends and are now frequently taking on a demographic dimension. Three clusters of policies will be examined here, corresponding to the pivotal factors identified above: policies to increase fertility, policies to raise labour market participation rates, and migration policies.

Policies to increase fertility

Despite its importance, the consequences of low fertility are not explicitly discussed in all European countries. While discussion is lively in the UK and in Germany, public debate in Austria and Italy does not devote much space to the potential consequences of low fertility (STARK/KOHLER, 2000). Public pressure for government intervention on fertility is therefore low in most countries, and is controversial in others for historical reasons. At the European level, there is no competence in the field of "family policies", and no official definition of the family exists in the European treaties (EUROPEAN COMMISSION, 2002c, p. 3). However, in 2000 a European Commission-sponsored seminar on low fertility came to the conclusion that "fertility is unlikely to stay at very low levels for long because governments will be forced to do something about it due to the problems associated with massive ageing" (BAGAVOS/MARTIN, 2000, p. 45).

It has been suggested that fertility decisions, from an economic point of view, have changed from investment decisions to become 'consumption' decisions. As the economic role of children declines and less material benefits are expected from them later in life, the cost of bearing and rearing a child becomes the most important factor in parental decisions (PUNCH/PEARCE, 2000, p. 75). For governments aiming to bring down the economic costs of children, it is important to recognise that the actual monetary expenditure on a child (the direct cost) is less important than the earnings lost because of the need to spend time bearing and caring for the child (the indirect costs). Cash benefits and other measures with an impact on direct costs have not been very successful in encouraging childbearing. Policies to lower indirect costs, on the other hand, work by making it easier to combine work and family. The importance of this factor is borne out by the circumstances of very low fertility especially in Southern European countries. It can be argued that a powerful cause for very low fertility is the incoherence between gender equity in the areas of education and employment and the more traditional attitudes that dominate with regard to family (MACDONALD, 2000, p. 10; for factors in low fertility in Italy, see PALOMBA, 2001). Policies should therefore aim to increase gender equity in the family and avoid penalising women in the workplace.

Such policies would support workers with family responsibilities irrespective of gender and give more recognition to fathers as parents. They would include paid parental leave for both parents, flexible working time, and affordable childcare.

Reconciling work and family life has indeed become a priority in national family policies across Europe, reflected and encouraged by developments at the European level. In 1996, the Commission adopted a gender mainstreaming approach, which has since informed a wide variety of its policies especially in the field of Employment and Social Affairs. The European Employment Strategy's Equal Opportunities pillar has also been the site of much activity to encourage gender equity. The 2002 employment guidelines pay particular attention to reconciling work and family life and advise Member States to implement policies on career breaks, parental leave and part-time work. They emphasise that good quality care for children is crucial, as is an equal sharing of family responsibilities.

The fertility factor has a powerful effect on the size of the labour force, but it is not an easy target for policies. Any rise in birth rates needs twenty years to make an impact. Implementing policies to achieve such a rise would require major cultural and attitudinal changes, especially those relating to gender equity. There are also indications that good family policies cannot guarantee higher fertility. While in Norway the relative generosity of family policies, which reduce the costs of having children, seems to have contributed to higher fertility, this has not worked in Sweden to the same extent. It can therefore be argued that good family policies are a necessary but not a sufficient condition for higher fertility (RØNSEN, 2001). Decisions about childbearing are also crucially influenced by the general economic climate. High unemployment and precarious job opportunities frustrate the reproductive plans of couples and lead to lower fertility. Moreover, fertility tends to be lowest where female labour force participation is also low (SIRCELJ, 2002).

Policies to raise labour market participation rates

Policies aiming to raise labour market participation rates must take into account the diverse reasons that cause low participation in different groups. For example, lower than average and/or declining participation rates may be observed among young people due to longer time spent on education, the old because of early retirement or disability, women due to traditional gender norms or difficulties in reconciling work and family life, and migrant groups as a result of integration issues. More education for young people is generally regarded as a positive development, although governments do worry that for some, education is a default option because of a lack of opportunities on the labour market. The focus of policy activity, however, is on raising the participation rates of women and of older people. A recent study commissioned by the Directorate-General of Employment and Social Affairs points out that in all countries, the growth of participation of women is seen as the most important potential source of labour force growth. This is increasingly so in the southern Member States, where the involvement of women in the work force has historically been low. Increasing weight is also accorded to expanding the participation of older people, although the study's authors question the extent to which this is a priority among employers (ALGOE CONSULTANTS, 2002, p. 64).

Policies for raising the participation rates of older people can include support for flexible and gradual retirement formulas and promoting access to life long learning, which can improve employability. The quality of jobs is also important for retaining workers in employment. The European Commission advocates such policies, for instance in a report on "Increasing labour force participation and promoting active ageing" which it prepared for the Spring 2002 Council meeting in Barcelona. The report notes that the European Councils at Lisbon and Stockholm set ambitious targets for raising employment rates in the Union by 2010: to close to 70 % for the working-age population as a whole, to over 60 % for women and to 50 % for older workers. Reaching these targets would imply an increase in employment of about 20 million in total, of 11-12 million women and 5 million older workers. The report points out that at the moment, participation rates of men, particularly those in low skilled manual occupations, begin to decline rapidly from the age of 50 onwards. Those for women start to decline earlier, at around 45, but do so less rapidly. Much of the decline is due to the use of early retirement schemes during cyclical downturns. However, the report points out that these times should, on the contrary, be used to "prepare the labour force for the next upswing" and so workers' participation should be maintained. In fact, the 2002 European Council in Barcelona set the objective that in 2010, the age at which Europeans actually leave the labour market should be increased by five years. Today the European average is 58.

The extent of labour market participation of older people may also be limited by negative attitudes towards their employment. One of the dimensions addressed by the UN and EU alike is the inclusiveness of labour markets for older workers. The Madrid international plan of action on ageing, adopted in 2002 by the second world assembly on ageing, promotes the concept of a "society for all ages" and, in paragraph 31, specifically lists the objective of "Employment opportunities for all older persons who want to work". An implementation strategy for the UNECE region is to be adopted on 11-13 September 2002 in Berlin at a Ministerial Conference on Ageing.[1] At the EU level, the institutions aim to safeguard the inclusion of older persons through a rights-based approach linked to its anti-discrimination strategy. However, despite standard- and target-setting activities at the international level, a comprehensive approach towards active ageing policies is lacking in most Member States and measures taken remain limited in their scope and impact.

Raising the labour market participation of women has been the goal of a variety of policies addressing issues such as the wage gap and labour market segregation. Employment guidelines have consistently called for member state action in those areas and in the year 2000 also started examining the impact of gender issues in social protection and taxation on women's employment. These policies were clearly linked with demography and ageing in an Opinion of the Economic and Social Committee, which argued that "gender equality must be seen as a factor in productivity. It is quite clear that women must enter the labour market if the EU is to achieve the economic growth needed to sustain its social —and not least pension— systems. Equality is important to productivity in a Europe where older people will account for an increasingly greater proportion of the population. And if Europe is to be able to maintain its level of social protection, women must also be able to contribute to the economy through paid employment" (ECONOMIC AND SOCIAL COMMITTEE, 2000). In some countries, there has indeed been a notable rise in the number of women in work, which has been cited as a major achievement. However, the rise in participation has been significantly less in full-time equivalent (FTE) terms, i.e. in the amount of working time contributed to the labour force, than in terms of numbers. This is the result of the strong growth of part-time working, especially in the north of the Union. A recent study argues that the extent of part-time working is not necessarily a matter of choice but reflects the continuing lack of affordable childcare facilities, and that "in many cases, the increase in participation of women seems to have

---

[1] Regional Implementation Strategy for the Madrid International Action Plan on Ageing 2002, 4th consolidated draft, ECE/AC.23/2002/2/Rev.4, 19 June 2002. For the European Commission's contribution to the 2nd World Assembly on Ageing on April 8-12 2002, at which the Plan of Action was adopted, see Communication (COM (2002) 143), Promoting economic and social progress in an ageing world, 18.03.2002.

occurred despite the lack of supporting policies rather than because of them" (ALGOE CONSULTANTS, 2002, p. 19).

Raising the participation rates of non-EU nationals has been a stated goal under the Equal Opportunities pillar. Among the range of relevant perspectives, the link with gender equity has so far been the main focus. Indeed, employment rates for non-EU women are particularly low. In 2000, only around 53 % of women aged 25 to 54 of non-EU nationality living in the Union were economically active as against 73 % of nationals. This gap is common to all member states in the north of the Union, but is not evident in the south, in many parts of which participation rates of women are low. It also applies to people at all education attainment levels, but is especially wide for women with university degrees or the equivalent qualifications (ALGOE CONSULTANTS, 2002, p. 20; however, there are arguments that the number of economically active migrant women may be significantly underestimated by official statistics, considering the importance of the informal economy for many migrant communities). While a concern with the labour market participation of non-EU women is justified, a broader approach to this topic would increase governments' chances of making an impact in this area. The employment rates of non-EU nationals are broadly influenced by integration, anti-discrimination and immigration policies, which are currently undergoing changes in many member states as well as at EU level.

As is the case with policies to increase birth rates, the effectiveness of policies to raise labour market participation is not uncontroversial. It can be argued that the actual potential labour reserve in European countries is not as large as it may seem from the absolute number of inactive persons. For Europe as a whole, the major reasons for inactivity are personal or family responsibilities (almost 20 % of the total inactives), own illness or disability (9 %), education and training (27 %, almost 90 % in the 15-24 group) and retirement (16 %, about 90 % in the 55-64 group) (EUROPEAN COMMISSION, 2002b). While policies on the labour market, family and education will have an impact on these factors, the extent to which they will respond to government intervention may be limited. Availability may be constrained for reasons that are not open to change, or simply by the widespread and growing reluctance on the part of nationals to take low quality and low-paid jobs. In some countries such as Sweden, further large increases in participation are not feasible as labour force participation is already very high (around 85 % in the three Nordic countries). Lastly, while policies to raise labour market participation rates, if successful, can have a strong and immediate effect on the size of the labour force, this will necessarily be a "one-off" effect mobilising a limited reserve without provisions for its renewal. Implementing economic measures may mean buying time in the short or medium term, but it will not remove the necessity of addressing the issue of population renewal through fertility and migration (LESTAEGHE, 2000).

Policies to sustain health care and pension systems

Social policy systems across Europe differ widely from one another. Until now, national policies have been dominant, with standard setting and co-ordination activities being undertaken at the international level. The Council of Europe is active in developing and promoting standards for social security and in encouraging social security co-ordination among its member states, arguing that social rights are a legal basis for social cohesion. Its European Code for Social Security, which sets out a minimum level of social security protection, has so far been ratified by 18 member states, while its more extensive Protocol has been ratified by seven member states.[2] At EU level, the Commission sees its role as fostering the sharing of best practices and identifying challenges common to all member states. In a 2001 Communication, it suggested that the main challenge for health care systems in the European Union is that of attaining the three-fold objective of access to health care for all, a high level of quality in health care and ensuring the financial viability of health care systems (EUROPEAN COMMISSION, 2001c). Financial viability is the overriding concern, as it is with regard to pension systems. Public spending in these areas could lead to higher deficits and endanger the sound public finances required by the Stability and Growth pact. In this context, the Broad Economic Policy Guidelines for 2001 stress that member states need to develop comprehensive strategies for addressing the economic and budgetary challenges posed by ageing populations. Strategy measures might include reform of pension and health care systems, and care for the elderly.

The Commission has issued two Communications on "safe and sustainable pensions" and suggested the introduction of an "open method of co-ordination" in this area (EUROPEAN COMMISSION,

---

[2] Council of Europe, *Implications of labour migration for social security systems in European countries - activities of the Council of Europe*, report of the 8th Conference of European Ministers responsible for Social Security, Bratislava, 22 and 23 May 2002. The seven member States that have signed the 'Protocol' are Belgium, Germany, Luxembourg, the Netherlands, Norway, Portugal and Sweden. Note that a revised 'European Code of Social Security' was adopted in 1990, but has not yet entered into force.

2000, 2001d). These plans were adopted by the Council of Ministers in December 2001. Pensions remain a national responsibility, but member states agree on common objectives and annual policy review along the lines of the Employment Strategy. The first national reports on pensions were due in September 2002, and the first Joint Report on pensions is expected for the European Council meeting in Spring 2003. An initial review of pension systems and reform activities by member states records some progress, although it notes that in some cases (Germany, Austria, Portugal) additional measures may be required in the future to secure financial sustainability. Belgium, Spain, France and Italy are singled out as member states where reforms need to proceed as a matter of urgency. The report observes that reserve funds have been created in a number of member states (Belgium, Spain, Ireland and France) but regrets their limited size (EUROPEAN COMMISSION, 2002d, p. 21).

A parallel effort that addresses both labour market participation and social protection is the Social Inclusion Process, which was agreed at the 2000 Lisbon summit. National action plans against poverty and social exclusion are submitted by member states every two years. The first set of reports from June 2001 remarks on the challenge of equal access to health care and also shows that pension systems are an important component of overall policies to combat poverty and social exclusion. In its Draft Joint Report on Social Inclusion, which builds on the National Action Plans, the Commission again underlines the dual role of social policy as a productive factor and as a key instrument to reduce inequalities and promote social cohesion. It notes that certain countries (Luxembourg, Netherlands, Denmark, Sweden and Ireland) have emphasised the need to increase the labour participation of specific groups, such as older people, immigrants or people with disabilities "also with a view to tackling current labour shortages" (EUROPEAN COMMISSION, 2001e, p. 26).[3] With regard to health care, the report notes that "although the objective of affordability is shared by all Member States, the degree of coverage and the quality of care provided under the different systems may differ widely across countries" (p. 39). A common concern is how to face a growing number of situations of dependency, given the limitations of public care services and the declining support role of families. On this question, different policy instruments have been envisaged across the EU, ranging from the development of long-term care facilities to the implementation of

[3] European Commission, Draft Joint Report on Social Inclusion, COM (2001) 565 final, Brussels, 10 October 2001, p. 26 pp.

long-term care insurance schemes. However, the general impression is one of dispersed and limited policy initiatives.

As with other policies to address demographic change, the general economic climate is a critical determinant of success in this area. While the modernisation of pension and health care systems themselves is an important objective, coherent employment, social and economic policies are needed to increase the revenue base on which such systems rest. Moreover, a drop in public debt can lower interest payments and help governments to offset some of the projected increase in spending on pensions and health care. How do policies to sustain pension and health care systems interact with other policies mentioned in the context of demographic change? Higher employment rates reinforce the aim of financial viability as they improve the revenue base of pensions systems and as working to higher ages eases the pressure on these systems. On the other hand, increased employment rates of women mean that fewer of them will be available as informal health care providers. Such a development will require increased public provision of long-term health care for the elderly. With regard to fertility, it can be argued that policies that respond to fiscal pressure on social insurance systems, such as increasing taxes or social security contributions or reducing benefits provided by employers, do not encourage childbearing (MACDONALD, 2000, p.14). Similarly, less progressive taxation systems (which may stimulate investment and job creation, thereby raising participation rates) provide relatively higher benefits to higher income earners who tend not to be young people on the verge of family formation. There are examples for mutually reinforcing policies, such as the positive effects of increased childcare provision on both fertility and the participation rate of women. However, there are also indications that policies in the different areas affected by demographic change, such as fertility and social support systems, can have contradictory effects.

Immigration policies

Immigration for demographic reasons has long been debated by scientific experts and is now increasingly making the transition into policy debates. An example for the topic's rising profile is the European Population Conference 2003, which will be organised in Warsaw by the European Association for Population Studies in collaboration with Polish partners. The draft programme lists international migration, population ageing, and "population and policies" as topics to be discussed. In the framework of the Council of Europe, several studies completed under the aegis of the Population Committee have made the connection between labour market and migration policies. A current research project addresses reconciliation policies to combine work and family life, retirement policies, and international labour migration as different "aspects of the problem of an ageing population" (COUNCIL OF EUROPE, n.d.).

Within member state governments and EU institutions, migration is also increasingly being connected with demographic considerations and is entering into policies implemented to meet related challenges. The European Employment Strategy and the Broad Economic Policy Guidelines, the emerging policies on ageing and health, and activities to promote gender equity increasingly contain references to the immigration of third country nationals. In most cases, the relevant texts still take a cautious position, mentioning migration as an option but refraining from advocating it more strongly. For instance, the Commission's 2001 Communication on pensions states that "immigration can [..] make a significant contribution to stabilising total population and employment figures" but then maintains that no "realistic level of immigration" can halt the decline in the ratio of workers to pensioners. Similarly, the 2002 Social Situation report concludes that "immigration can contribute to filling certain specific gaps on the European labour market, but it can in no way stop or reverse the process of significant population ageing in Europe". The hesitancy of policy makers with regard to immigration as an answer to demographic challenges is connected to three main aspects: the composition of the immigrant flows involved, the social sustainability of large scale immigration, and the sustainability of immigration's effect on ageing.

With regard to composition, the debate is about the degree of selectivity that is possible and desirable when managing immigration, and about the criteria that should be employed when selecting immigrants. Many commentators advocate selecting immigrants who can provide the skills that are lacking in the domestic labour market. However, others warn that shortages in specific sectors are often short-term, while immigrants, at least from less affluent countries, tend to be permanent. Moreover, they point out that immigration should not be an 'easy' way of temporarily evading hard choices about the need to reform the European labour market, education, social protection and retirement policies. Some of the strongest voices for immigration come from those concerned with budgetary stability and the sustainability of public finances. To maximise the positive effects of immigration for pension and health care systems, the desired immigrants would be as young as possible. However, if the selection criteria were entirely dependent on demographic objectives, flows would have to be closely regulated and representatives of particular age groups would have to be selected. Such a policy of 'fine-tuning' would be impossible to implement (PUNCH/PEARCE, 2000, p. 107. This study further argues that "it cannot be expected that migratory flows will have a major impact on the structure of the population of Europe").

Apart from the composition of the immigrant intake, its size also remains a controversial issue. The UN 2000 report led to a polarised debate about numbers, which focused on the highest scenarios and neglected the amount of choice that societies have in designing policy responses to ageing. While now there is a greater acknowledgement of the need for immigration, numbers are still a sensitive issue. Some scholars assert that the proponents of migration for demographic reasons neglect to consider the "indirect economic costs and the social, cultural and political externalities of immigration" (COLEMAN, 2000). Such comments refer to the issue of social cohesion relating to migration, which is now high on the agenda of many European countries. While it is true that increased flows into countries with little historical experience of immigration would require social and cultural adjustments, it is important to keep in mind that alternative policies to meet demographic challenges may also demand far-reaching changes. Increasing the labour force participation rates for women and for older men would shift the social balance in countries such as Italy and Greece. "Fertility-friendly" changes in family culture and in the levels of social support for men and women with family responsibilities would require a degree of gender equity not currently feasible in many societies (MACDONALD/ KIPPEN, 2000, p. 18).

Scepticism about migration for demographic reasons questions the sustainability of the "migration effect" to counter population ageing. On this view, replacement migration is not a long-term solution to population ageing, because migrants also age. While increased immigration would certainly have an immediate impact on the working-age population, the long-term effects are less certain. Current immigrant populations in Europe have a relatively young age structure (the median age of new immigrants is on average about 30 years, compared with 36 years for the overall OECD population. Among the immigrant populations present in the EU, Turkish immigrants have the lowest old-age dependency ratio). A recent OECD commissioned study also notes that fertility rates among immigrant women are often relatively high, which "can help boost overall fertility and hence long-term population growth" (COPPEL/ DUMONT/VISCO, 2001, p. 21). However, these fertility levels may drop once the migrants are in the country, especially if they are temporary workers with little security of work and residence. Hence, the fertility factor remains key to the process of population ageing.

Some concluding remarks: migration as an option

The previous sections have tried to show that migration is and should be considered an important ingredient in a diversified approach to respond to demographic trends in Europe. Demographic trends suggest that keeping the "economic dependency ratio" —the relation of the economically active to the economically inactive— low will be crucial for creating a balanced labour market and for safeguarding the sustainability of pension and health care systems. A long-term view is indispensable here, both because population policy deals with long time periods such as generations and because uncertainty and lack of planning for the future lead to fear among European citizens. Thinking about demographic developments and about ways to respond to them implies making decisions about the shape of future European societies. Again, a broad and long-term view is vital in this context, and "it is not so much the individual policies that matter but the nature of the society as a whole" (MACDONALD, 2000, p. 21). Beyond the play of sanctions and incentives, the far-reaching changes required if the size of the labour force and the old age dependency ratio are to be kept at current levels will not be achieved without shifts in culture and attitudes. It is essential to raise support for these shifts and to promote a debate about their implications. This debate should ask how immigration could help to shape Europe's answer to demographic change, and which terms and conditions would best strengthen the positive role of immigration and the successful integration and equal treatment of immigrants.[4]

In the context of this debate one should have another look at the legislative proposals under consideration within the European Union. The Directorate-General for Justice and Home Affairs has presented several proposals for Directives setting out the parameters of a common immigration policy. The draft *Directive on the conditions of entry and residence of third-country nationals for the purpose of paid employment and self-employed activities* (COM (2001) 368) aims to provide a single national application procedure leading to one combined title for both residence and work permits. The draft *Directive on the conditions of entry and residence of third-country nationals for the purposes of studies, vocational training or voluntary service* (COM (2002) 548) was

---

[4] An important part of integration is anti-discrimination. Effective anti-discrimination law is essential in the promotion of equality and to avoid the social and economic costs of discrimination. For more information about MPG's work on anti-discrimination, please see MPG's website at www.migpolgroup.com.

presented on 7 October 2002 and covers non-employment related purposes of stay. These two texts aim to introduce a measure of harmonisation into the admission decisions of member states. Two further instruments have strong implications for the equal treatment and integration of third-country nationals. The *Directive on the right to family reunification* was initially presented in 1999, with amended versions proposed in 2000 and 2002 (COM (2002) 225). The *Directive on the status of third-country nationals who are long-term residents* (COM (2001) 127) proposes that after five years of legal residence in a member state long-stay third-country nationals will be entitled to a permanent residence permit that is valid for ten years and automatically renewable. The text also includes provisions for free movement, i.e. residence in another member state.

Since the 1999 European Council in Tampere, member states have repeatedly emphasised the centrality of the immigration agenda within Justice and Home Affairs, and consecutive presidencies have highlighted various parts of this agenda as priorities. Indeed, the importance of the proposed measures becomes even more evident when seen in the context of the demographic arguments made above. Once Europe has decided that immigrants are important, and why, its governments need to think about ways of attracting and admitting them, and they need to create a coherent system of rules that support integration. Integration, in turn, will be enhanced by valuing immigrants for their contribution to achieving Europe's socio-economic goals and alleviating the consequences of demographic change. It is crucial that the rights of immigrants, equal treatment and security of residence should form the cornerstone of immigration and integration policies throughout Europe. Discussion and adoption of the Commission's proposals, then, should be taken forward in parallel with the policy debates on demography and on the fundamental values that underpin Europe's social market economy.

This paper has consistently taken the European framework as its reference point, looking not only at the EU but also at its accession states and at the Council of Europe. It is difficult to see how purely national policies can be designed in a European Union that is both unifying and expanding. The establishment of a common market and the abolition of internal borders mean that common rules need to be devised regarding external borders as well. Beyond the internal market, Europe's states also seek to create a political community under Community law that protects fundamental rights and promotes a social policy agenda. These ambitious goals call for the joint development of a balanced immigration system, which looks beyond present concerns and is designed to meet the challenge of the long term.

The European Migration Policy Dialogue

One forum for discussion on these issues was created in May 2002 with the European Migration Policy Dialogue, a partnership to stimulate national and European debates on European migration policies. Dialogue is promoted between key stakeholders and between stakeholders and policymakers in the field. The European Migration Policy Dialogue seeks to increase the level of information and participation among non-governmental actors working on the national level in EU Member States as well as accession states. Its partners include NGOs, think tanks, foundations, and service delivering organisations providing advice and support to migrants while being active in policy development as well.

Partner organisations of the European Migration Policy Dialogue	
Austria	Viennese Fund for Integration (Wiener Integrationsfonds)
Belgium	King Baudouin Foundation (Fondation Roi Baudouin/Koning Boudewijnstichting)
Denmark	MS Movement for Solidarity (Mellemfolkeligt Samvirke)
Finland	Finnish League for Human Rights (Ihmisoikeusliitto)
France	CERI (Centre d'Etudes et de Recherches Internationales) Institut Panos
Germany	DGB Bildungswerk with Interkultureller Rat (Intercultural Council)
Greece	Hellenic League for Human Rights
Hungary	Research Group on International Migration and Refugees, Research Institute on Minority Issues, Hungarian Academy of Sciences
Ireland	NCCRI (National Consultative Committee on Racism and Interculturalism)
Italy	CIE (Centro di Iniziativa per l'Europa) CENSIS (Centro Studi Investimenti Sociali)
Luxembourg	ASTI (Association de Soutien aux Travailleurs Immigrés)
Netherlands	FORUM (Institut voor Multikulturele Ontwikkeling)
Poland	CSM (Center for International Relations) ISP (Institute for Public Affairs)
Portugal	Luso-American Foundation (Fundação Luso-Americana)
Spain	CIDOB Foundation (Fundació CIDOB) Ortega y Gasset Foundation (Fundación José Ortega y Gasset)
UK	UKREN (UK Race and Europe Network) IAS (Immigration Advisory Service)

References

ALGOÉ CONSULTANTS (2002): *The construction of an index of labour market adaptability for EU Member States*, report of a study funded by the European Commission and directed by Algoé Consultants in conjunction with Alphametrics Limited, Brussels.

BAGAVOS, C.; MARTIN, C. (2000): *Low fertility, families and public policies*, synthesis report of the European Observatory on Family Matters annual seminar, Seville, September 15-16, 2000, report published by the Austrian Institute for Family Studies

BOLKESTEIN, F. (2001): Internal Market and Taxation Commissioner, Defusing Europe's Pension Timebomb, speech of 6 February 2001. This speech can be found at: http://europa.eu.int/comm/internal_market/en/speeches/spch52.htm.

COLEMAN, D. (2000): *Why Europe does not need a 'European' migration policy*, evidence submitted to the inquiry on the European Commission Communication to the Council and the European Parliament 'On a Community Immigration Policy (COM (2000) 757 final) ', House of Lords Select Committee on the European Union Sub-Committee F (Social Affairs, Education and Home Affairs).

COM (2002): Commission Communication, Europe's Response to World Ageing, A Contribution of the European Commission to the 2nd World Assembly on Ageing (COM (2002) 143 final), 18 March 2002.

COPPEL, J.; DUMONT, J.-C.; VISCO, I. (2001): *Trends in Immigration and Economic Consequences*, OECD Economics Department Working Paper No. 284, ECO/WKP (2001) 10, OECD.

COUNCIL OF EUROPE (1995): European Population Studies Series, *Ageing and its consequences for the socio-medical system*.

COUNCIL OF EUROPE (2002): *Implications of labour migration for social security systems in European countries - activities of the Council of Europe*, summary of a conference held in Bratislava on 22 and 23 May 2002.

COUNCIL OF EUROPE (n.d.): Population Committee, outline of research project 'The economically active population in Europe: trends, perspectives and policies', www.coe.int.

DE SANTIS, G. (2001): *Population ageing in industrialised countries: challenges and issues*, IUSSP Policy and Research Paper No. 19, 2001.

ECONOMIC AND SOCIAL COMMITTEE (2000): Opinion SOC/036 on the Communication from the Commission Towards a Community framework strategy on gender equality (2001-2005) and on the proposal for a Council Decision on the Programme relating to the Community framework strategy on gender equality (2001-2005) (COM (2000) 335 final - 2000/0143 CNS), 30 November.

EUROPEAN COMMISSION (2000): The future evolution of social protection from a long-term point of view: safe and sustainable pensions, COM (2000) 622 final.

EUROPEAN COMMISSION (2001): "Union, solidarity, diversity for Europe, its people and its territory", second report on economic and social cohesion, adopted by the European Commission on 31 January.

EUROPEAN COMMISSION (2001a): *Employment in Europe 2001 - Recent Trends and Prospects*, July.

EUROPEAN COMMISSION (2001b): Draft *Joint Employment Report 2001*, COM (2001) 438 final, 12 September.

EUROPEAN COMMISSION (2001c): Communication, The future of health care and care for the elderly: guaranteeing accessibility, quality and financial viability, COM (2001) 723 final, 5 December.

EUROPEAN COMMISSION (2001d): Communication, Supporting national strategies for safe and sustainable pensions through an integrated approach, COM (2001) 362 final, 3 July.

EUROPEAN COMMISSION (2001e): Draft Joint Report on Social Inclusion, COM (2001) 565 final, Brussels, 10 October.

EUROPEAN COMMISSION (2002): Directorate-General for Employment and Social Affairs, *Family Benefits and Family Policies in Europe*, June.

EUROPEAN COMMISSION (2002a): Report on the Implementation of the 2001 Broad Economic Policy Guidelines, ECFIN/16/02, Brussels, 21 February.

EUROPEAN COMMISSION (2002b): report, Increasing labour force participation and promoting active ageing, COM (2002) 9 final, Brussels, 24 January.

EUROPEAN COMMISSION (2002c): Directorate-General for Employment and Social Affairs, *Family Benefits and Family Policies in Europe*, June.

EUROPEAN COMMISSION (2002d): Report on the Implementation of the 2001 Broad Economic Policy Guidelines, ECFIN/16/02, Brussels, 21 February.

EUROPEAN COMMISSION (n.d.): Employment and Social Affairs Directorate General, Introduction on Ageing Policy. This document can be found at: http://www.europa.eu.int/comm/employment_social/soc-prot/ageing/ intro_en.htm

HAUG, W. (2002): *The Demography of Immigrant Populations in Europe*, European Population Papers Series No.8, Council of Europe, April.

LESTAEGHE, R. (2000): *Europe's demographic issues: fertility, household formation and replacement migration*, Paper prepared for the UN expert group meeting on policy responses to population decline and ageing, New York, October 16-18.

LUTZ, W.; SCHERBOV, S. (1999): *First probabilistic population projections for the European Union*, Austrian Institute for Family Studies.

MACDONALD, P. (2000): *The "toolbox" of public policies to impact on fertility - a global view*, paper presented at the seminar "Low fertility, families and public policies".

MACDONALD, P.; KIPPEN, R. (2000): *The implications of below replacement fertility for labour supply and international migration, 2000-2050*, paper presented to the 2000 Annual Meeting of the Population Association of America, Los Angeles, California, March 23-25.

PEDERSEN, L. H. (2002): Ageing, Immigration, and Fiscal Sustainability, Danish Rational Economic Agents Model, March.

PALOMBA, R. (2001): *Postponement of family formation in Italy, within the Southern European context*, paper given at the IUSSP (International Union for the Scientific Study of Population) seminar on "International Perspectives on Low Fertility: Trends, theories and policies", Tokyo, March.

PUNCH, A.; PEARCE, D. L. (eds.) (2000): *Europe's population and labour market beyond 2000*, Council of Europe.
RØNSEN, M. (2001): *Fertility and family policy in Norway: is there a connection?,* paper given at the IUSSP seminar on "International Perspectives on Low Fertility: Trends, theories and policies", Tokyo, March.
SCHMID, J. (2001): *Political responses to immigration pressures in the European Union*, paper presented at the XXIV IUSSP General Population Conference, Salvador, Brazil, 18-24 August.
SIRCELJ, M. (2002): *The European Population Committee's Recent Demographic Studies and their Relevance for Social Cohesion*, Council of Europe European Population Paper Series No.2, Council of Europe.
STARK, L.; KOHLER, H.-P. (2000): *The Public Perception and Discussion of Falling Birth Rates: The Recent Debate over Low Fertility in the Popular Press*, MPIDR Working Paper, October 2000 (revised 8 June 2001).
UN (2000): *Replacement Migration: Is it a Solution to Declining and Ageing Populations?* New York: United Nations Population Division.
UNECE (2002): Regional Implementation Strategy for the Madrid International Action Plan on Ageing 2002, 4th consolidated draft, UNECE, 19 June.

Immigration and asylum in the harmonisation policies of the EU: the need for balance

Samuel Boutruche

"The *separate but closely related* issues of asylum and migration call for the development of a common EU policy" (author's emphasis). § 10 of the Conclusions of the Tampere European Council held on 15 and 16 October 1999, clearly illustrates the ambiguity of the nexus between these two issues.

Under the Amsterdam Treaty framework, asylum and migration are both embraced in the umbrella concept of the Area of Freedom, Security and Justice referred to in article 61 (Title IV of the EC treaty). This new objective of the EU developed in the Vienna Action Plan is designed as a set of fundamental rights to be offered first to EU nationals but also to third country nationals legally residing in the EU (BOELES, 2001, pp. 1-12). One of the key issues in implementing the AFSJ is therefore to determine the conditions of entry into this area for non-EU nationals. Since asylum and immigration both relate to the admission of third country nationals into the EU territory —yet for clearly different reasons— they are closely linked to the realisation of this objective. Article 63 of the Amsterdam treaty provides a single legal basis for the harmonisation process concerning asylum and refugee law on the one hand (§ 1 and § 2) and immigration on the other hand (§ 3 and § 4).

On one side, in a broad sense, asylum policy —understood as the elaboration of a common European asylum regime— includes the procedural and substantial aspects of asylum together with the other forms of protection offered to persons falling outside the scope of the 1951 Geneva Convention, the elaboration of a Temporary Protection scheme in case of mass influx and the setting up of a burden sharing mechanism (see Conclusions of the Presidency, Tampere). On the other side, immigration policy refers to the regulation of the conditions of entry and residence of legal migrants, and the prevention and fight against illegal immigration.

Asylum and immigration remain strictly different in nature and in scope: whereas asylum is seen as a human right (GOODWIN-GILL, 2001) —the right to seek asylum rather than the right to be granted asylum— for persons fleeing because of a reasonable fear of persecution, immigration refers to "voluntary" moves of populations triggered by socio-economic factors. The specific causes and conditions of the flight of asylum seekers allow them to apply for a certain protection which is legally defined under binding international or regional instruments. Indeed, the persons concerned are entitled to certain rights including the right to *non-refoulement* either on the ground of Article 33 of the Geneva Convention or on the ground of Article 3 of the European Convention on Human Rights. By contrast, the admission of economic migrants is entirely at the discretion of the sovereign receiving state.

Despite this legal distinction, drawing a clear dividing line between the "forced" and the "voluntary" population flows is rather theoretical. In reality, the displacement phenomenon is often prompted by a mixture of overlapping factors; identifying the prevailing cause is therefore difficult (CDR, 2002). The confusion is also due to the fact that asylum seekers are often deemed to resort to illegal migration networks to gain access to the EU territory. Finally, the imprecise use of the terminology by the media when dealing with refugee and immigration matters is also quite misleading (e.g. the covering of the Sangatte issue in the news in which the terms "refugees", "asylum seekers" and "immigrants" were used regardless of the distinctions between them).

For these reasons, determination of the need of protection becomes crucial, not only in asylum policy itself, by establishing a fair and efficient regime for processing asylum claims, but also in immigration policy by securing access to this regime. This is precisely what a number of restrictive measures in the field of immigration fail to achieve. UNHCR emphasises that denying the specificity of asylum seekers is the "major problem common to virtually all the immigration measures introduced by States(...)" (2002, p. 4).

The first aim of this paper is to analyse to what extent the restrictive trend observed in EU immigration policy interferes with the negotiations for the future European asylum regime. On the one hand, giving the highest priority to combat irregular entry of migrants (especially during the Seville Summit in June 2002) may contribute to create a major gap within the common immigration policy itself by neglecting the harmonisation of legal channels of migration towards the EU territory. On the other hand, this lack of attention to legal immigration together with the increase of deterrent restrictive measures also undermine the coherence and integrity of the asylum policy as a whole, by preventing the access of undocumented third country nationals to the EU territory regardless of their need for protection.

The second aim of this paper is to stress the necessity and the prospects for reconciling the legitimate interest of the member states in managing migratory flows and the specific rights of the people in need of protection. Beyond the negative impact of the immigration policy which is systematically highlighted, it can also be argued that a balanced regulation of migration can strengthen the future European asylum regime. This is particularly important in order to guarantee the coherence of the comprehensive "common EU policy" referred to in the Tampere Conclusions; indeed, far from being two contradictory policies to be carried out simultaneously, immigration and asylum could benefit from each other if designed in a complementary way without interference. The repeated call for a more balanced approach in various EU documents goes in that direction. In November 2000, the Commission presented a Communication on a Community immigration policy which aimed at clarifying "the way in which the other components of an overall immigration policy must be taken into consideration (...) and especially the humanitarian dimension —the asylum policy" (COM, 2000, p. 6). Even more relevant is the Communication on a common policy on illegal immigration where the Commission stressed that "the measures relating to the fight against illegal immigration have to balance the right to decide whether to accord or refuse admission to the territory to third country nationals and the obligation to protect those genuinely in need of international protection" (COM, 2001, p. 7).

The emerging common immigration policy and especially its component in the fight against illegal immigration put the asylum regime under a double strain: on the one hand, the restrictive measures to prevent illegal migration flows directly limit access to the asylum procedure for undocumented asylum seekers; on the other hand, specific deterrent measures have been taken under the asylum policy itself with the aim of fighting abuses. However, recent initiatives in the EU immigration policy may contribute to a more balanced approach and benefit to the asylum regime.

The consolidation of existing restrictive measures to fight illegal immigration

The focus in June 2002 at the Seville summit on combating illegal immigration must not be misleading: this has been a long lasting priority of the EU member states which contributed to orient the harmonisation process in the field of immigration. Beyond the worsening of the economic situation in the member states, another specific factor linked to the European integration process itself, is often put forward to justify the shift towards more restrictive migration controls: strengthening the controls at the external borders aims at compensating for the suppression of the internal barriers to freedom of movement of persons within the EU. The integrated notion of Area of Freedom, Security and Justice —singled out as one of the prime objectives of the EU (pursuant to Article 4 § 4 of the TEU)— clearly reflects this trend.

As a matter of fact, a number of recent developments of the EU harmonisation process with regard to immigration are mostly designed to strengthen the existing tools despite the repeated concern about their negative impact on the possibility of applying for asylum. The so called "fortress" Europe shows little signs of openness and consolidates in many ways the walls erected in the 1990s.

This paper does not aim at presenting an exhaustive list of all the current texts adopted or under negotiation concerning the fight against illegal migration and the increased control of EU external borders which may restrict access to the asylum procedure for people in need of protection. We shall only focus on several instruments to demonstrate that they fail to secure a clear distinction between economic migrants and asylum seekers and apply indifferently to both categories regardless of the humanitarian nature of the refugee problem. This is particularly worrying since these texts merely adapt the existing measures taken at the European and the national level (KJÆRUM, 2002, p. 516) instead of suggesting necessary improvements.

Throughout the 1990s, a set of restrictive tools to deter the arrival of undocumented third country nationals on the EU territory was adopted. In the absence of any chance to lodge an asylum application from the country of origin (NOLL/FAGERLUND, 2002), the exercise of this human right is therefore dependent on access to the EU territory. As a result, denying entry into the EU clearly amounts to denying access to the asylum procedure as such.

Moreover, in elaborating the policy to combat irregular migration, the member states placed a particular emphasis on the legal characteristic of the flows: no one could be admitted to the EU territory without specific identity and visa documents. These requirements, although legitimate to guarantee the efficiency of a planned management of migration flows, do not fit at all with the particular situation of asylum seekers. These latter are often fleeing a violent conflict without any possibility of applying for a visa. Moreover, they often destroy their own passports so as not to be identified in their home country. These particular circumstances are taken into account under Article 31 of the 1951 Convention which recognises that there are reasons justifying a refugee's unauthorised entry or presence in a receiving country. The texts elaborated at the EU level are therefore inconsistent with the member states' international commitments as they impede the undocumented asylum seekers from gaining access to the EU territory.

However, the instruments described hereafter continue to neglect the specificity of the asylum seekers.

The *carrier sanction mechanism* is probably the most troubling (LAMBERT, 1995, pp. 198-202). Article 26 of the Convention implementing the Schengen Agreement of 14 June 1985 signed on 19 June 1990 laid down the obligations and sanctions imposed upon the carriers transporting undocumented foreign third country nationals into the territory of the member states. First of all, the transfer to a private company of the sovereign competence of the state to control who is (not) entitled to enter the national territory is rather questionable. Moreover, these companies are by no means authorised, under international law, to assume asylum determination responsibilities, precisely because this process required particular legal training and practical skills to identify the protection need of the persons concerned. Despite these problems, the Council Directive of 28 June 2001 supplementing the provisions of Article 26 only strengthened the existing sanction mechanism and the obligations imposed to the carriers.[1]

A second example concerns the *visa policy* elaborated under Article 62 (§ 2 b) i.) of the Amsterdam treaty and formalised by the Council regulation of 15 March 2001.[2] This text lists the third countries whose nationals must be in possession of visas when crossing the external borders and those whose nationals are exempt from that requirement. Although this list is regularly reviewed, it includes a number of countries where there is documented evidence of grave human rights violations or widespread persecution in the context of ethnic or religious conflict (UNHCR, 2002, p. 6).

Finally, the recent *Commission Communication on the integrated management of the EU external borders* also comprises certain aspects

---

[1] Council Directive 2001/51/EC supplementing the provisions of Article 26 of the Convention implementing the Schengen Agreement of 14 June 1985, OJ L 187, 10 July 2001, p. 45.

[2] Council Regulation listing the third countries whose nationals must be in possession of visas when crossing the external borders and those whose nationals are exempt from that requirement, No 539/2001 of 15 March 2001, *Official Journal L 081, 21 March 2001*, pp. 1-7.

which may challenge the humanitarian dimension of the asylum institution if proper safeguards are not implemented. Among other initiatives such as a common unit of immigration practitioners or a European border guards corps, the future EU network of immigration liaison officers raises concerns. This network is designed as another preventive tool for controlling entry into the EU territory and supports the range of existing deterrent measures. Unlike the airline personnel, these officers belong to the member states' immigration offices but their capacity to deal with asylum cases remains unclear. These cases require particular skills and training to ensure that a person covered by the 1951 Geneva Convention or entitled to another form of protection will not be prevented from embarking for purely administrative reasons. Surprisingly enough, the same initiative (e.g. asylum liaison officers) has not yet been suggested in order to counterbalance the exclusive focus on border management and to take into account the "interrelated" dimension of asylum and immigration. The network of immigration liaison officers illustrates a new feature of "fortress" Europe.

The entire set of restrictive measures has not yielded the expected results in terms of preventing illegal immigration. On the contrary, as stated by ECRE "ever stricter control measures have not only obstructed the right of asylum seekers to access to the territory of Europe but have also forced people to resort to illegal entry and rely on criminal networks" (2002). This is probably the most striking paradox of EU immigration policy: by giving the highest priority to the fight against illegal migration, it fostered the problem it was initially supposed to tackle. Kjærum insists that "the sharp increase in human trafficking is a direct result of the restrictive policies and the lack of alternatives measures" (2002, p. 517).

This restrictive trend observed in immigration policy had another direct consequence on the asylum issue. Beside the impediments in terms of access to the procedure, a number of member states took restrictive measures within the asylum policy itself, using this protection instrument as a tool for migration management. This is replicated at the European level in a number of proposals.

The search for efficiency of the emerging EU asylum policy

A detailed examination of the critical aspects of the emerging asylum regime is beyond the scope of the present paper. The risks raised by the use of the notions of *safe third country* or *safe country of origin* and the Dublin Convention or the readmission agreements have already long been discussed (CREPEAU, 1995). I will only review here two recent proposals which illustrate the search for increased efficiency in the processing of asylum claims, and which may undermine protection standards for asylum seekers: the amended proposal for a Council directive on minimum standards on asylum procedures[3] and the recent proposal of the British government to create "Transit Processing Centres" in third countries. These two texts are partly based on the assumption that the asylum regime would be subject to repeated abuses from illegal economic migrants and that further steps should be taken to identify these bogus refugees as quickly as possible.

The amended proposal for a directive on asylum procedures

Pursuant to the Conclusions of the Justice and Home Affairs Council held in December 2001, the Commission was invited to modify the initial proposal of a directive on asylum procedures (COM (2000) 578, 20 September 2000). The structure of the new text has been significantly changed. The distinction between admissibility procedures and substantial examination procedure disappeared. The admissibility procedure (isolated in Chapter III of the preceding text) is now incorporated in the chapter on accelerated procedures.

The major change regards the increase in cases in which asylum claims can be processed under an accelerated procedure (Art. 23). In addition to the cases of inadmissible applications (Art. 25), the manifestly unfounded applications (Art. 29) and the other cases under the accelerated procedure (Art. 32), two new types of asylum claims are included in this category: the subsequent asylum application (Art. 33) and the asylum application made at the border (Art. 35). Surprisingly enough the regular procedure is defined in relation to the accelerated procedures: paragraph 2 of Article 23 states that all other procedures shall be considered as regular procedures. Given the extensive number of cases under accelerated procedures, the scope of the regular procedure seems to be rather limited.

This departure from the initial proposal clearly demonstrates the will to increase the efficiency of the management of asylum seekers in order to prevent abuses (for a complete analysis, see LAURAIN, 2003). This extension of accelerated procedures raises major concerns since the suspensive effect of the appeal proceeding against decisions taken

---

3 Amended proposal for a Council directive on minimum standards on procedures in Member States for granting and withdrawing refugee status, COM(2002) 326 final, 18 June 2002.

in this type of procedure is subject to further exceptions in comparison to the rules applicable to the regular procedure. In both procedures, national legislations may provide that the applicant for asylum is not allowed to remain on the territory of the Member State concerned awaiting the outcome of his appeal or review. In that case, "the Member States shall ensure that the court of law has the competence to rule whether or not such an applicant may, given the particular circumstances of his/her case, remain on the territory of the Member State concerned (...)". No expulsion may take place until the court of law has ruled on this right to remain. In the regular procedure, the proposal allows the Member State to provide for only one exception to this prohibition: when grounds of national security or public policy preclude the applicant for asylum from remaining on the territory of the Member State concerned. By contrast, in the accelerated procedures, the text allows for a wider range of exceptions. Expulsion may take place (Art. 40):

—where it has been decided that the asylum application is inadmissible;
—where the applicant has not submitted new facts after a court of law has aleardy rejected his/her claim to remain on the territory of the Member State concerned;
—where it has been decided that a subsequent application will not be further examined and
—where it has been decided that grounds of national security or public policy preclude the applicant for asylum from remaining on the territory of the Member State concerned.

These restrictive provisions on the suspensive effect of the appeal proceeding must be analysed in relation to the norms contained in the relevant international instruments and especially the *non refoulement* principle set up explicitly in Article 33 of the 1951 Geneva Convention and in Article 3 of the 1984 Convention against Torture, or implicitly in Article 3 of the European Convention on Human Rights (NOLL, 2002, pp. 3-5). Pursuant to these texts —which are legally binding for all EU Member States[4]— the expulsion of an asylum seeker to another state where there is a risk for his/her security is prohibited. Therefore, it can be questioned whether the proposal is fully consistent with this obligation (LAURAIN, 2003, pp. 2-6).

In addition, the new proposal allows for a wider use of detention. The previous limited list of cases which could justify the detention of an

[4] Except for Ireland and Belgium which have not yet ratified the Convention against Torture and Other Cruel, Inhuman or Degrading Treatment or Punishment.

applicant for asylum is now replaced by two general provisions (Art. 17.2): these clauses allow derogation of the prohibition of detention when it is considered as "objectively necessary for an efficient examination of the application" or "necessary for a quick decision to be made". A guarantee of maximum duration (two weeks) is only specified with regard to the second justification.

Besides, a series of limitations of minimum standards has been introduced in the proposal concerning certain procedural rights which must be normally guaranteed to the applicant for asylum. The right to an individual interview, access to legal advice or access to an interpreter are subject to certain restrictions.

On the basis of this brief analysis of the content of the amended Directive proposal on asylum procedure, it can be argued that the emerging asylum policy is increasingly designed to regulate the flow of asylum seekers, especially through a more efficient and accelerated scrutiny of their claims.

The British proposal for Transit Processing Centres

The recent proposal of the British government to create "Transit Processing Centres" in the third countries pursued the same goal. This initiative was presented in a letter sent by the British Prime Minister to his EU partners on 10 March 2003. The reasons for this proposal mainly lay in the need to decrease and better share the cost paid for each refugee received in Europe, the emphasis on the illegal channels the asylum seekers resort to in order to gain access to the EU territory, the low number of decisions granting protection to these people and the difficulties the Member States are facing to process the asylum claims (see MARIANI, 2003, pp. 75-80). This initiative consist in the creation of "Transit Processing Centres" in the third countries located on asylum seekers' routes where they would be transferred when arriving in the EU territory. Those applicants granted asylum would be reinstalled in a Member State whereas the others would be directly deported back to their country of origin.

This new proposal must be analysed in the context of the externalisation of the asylum regime (LAVENEX, 1998; LAVENEX/UÇARER, 2002) which aims at shifting away from the EU external borders the burden of the asylum seekers through the clauses of *safe third country* or first country of asylum and the development of readmission agreements. The British initiative marks a crucial turning point in this process: it suggests a complete transfer of the responsibilities of processing the asylum claims from the EU Member States to the third countries regardless of the type of countries the asylum seeker transited through. The impact on the common asylum policy would be drastic: if such a system were to be implemented, it would merely make the new European asylum regime irrelevant since most of the asylum claims would be examined outside the EU.

This initiative is already highly criticised by NGOs dealing with human rights and refugee protection (MARIANI, 2003, p. 78). It was discussed at the informal JHA Council in Veria on 28 and 29 March 2003. Member States invited the European Commission together with UNHCR to prepare a joint report to be examined at the 5-6 June JHA Council and at the 20-21 June European Council in Thessaloniki.

Attention must be drawn to these measures taken under the immigration policy framework and under the asylum policy framework which are motivated by the management of flux in general and the fight against illegal immigration in particular, regardless of the protection needs of the persons concerned. As far as the asylum procedure is concerned, priority is given to efficiency and the limitation of costs over substantial rights.

A more balanced approach is highly needed between the immigration and asylum policies on the one hand and within each of these policies on the other hand. This is a prerequisite to ensure the coherence of future EU common policy in these areas.

Positive prospects for a more balanced immigration policy

The intrusion of the restrictive immigration agenda into the asylum negotiations leads Member States to focus on the procedural aspects of the asylum regime with a view to fighting subversion of the procedure by economic migrants. Suspicion of "bogus" asylum seekers seems to be supported by statistics which indicate a significant drop in acceptance rates of refugees. In reality, this figure is also due to a narrower interpretation of the refugee definition of the 1951 Convention (BOUTEILLET-PAQUET, 2001, p. 21). As a result, it seems that the "spectre" of the abuses is somehow overestimated. However, it would be a mistake to deny it. It must be considered as a key factor in analysing the possible use of asylum policy as a tool for migration management. Moreover, it should be taken into account in order to reconcile asylum and immigration as two "separate but closely related issues". Since these abuses of the asylum system partly stem from the absence of alternative avenues to gain legal access to the EU territory, a more balanced EU immigration policy might lift the pressure on the asylum regime.

"I believe (...) the moment has come to acknowledge that we in fact need legal immigration" António Vitorino, EU Commissioner for Justice and Home Affairs, stated in his closing speech at the Conference on the role of Civil Society in promoting Integration held in Brussels on 10 September 2002. A number of directives recently adopted or under discussion in the Council seem to make this commitment. These texts aim at establishing legal channels of labour migration and promoting the integration of third country nationals legally residing on EU territory. The purpose of this paragraph is neither to give an extensive description of all the relevant instruments in the field of immigration, nor to discuss the different views concerning the need for immigration as "a complementary labour market strategy" (NIESSEN, n.d.). These issues are better addressed by other contributors in this book. My option is rather to point out a few elements which have a direct impact on the asylum regime itself in the sense that they may contribute to lift the migratory pressure and restore the specificity of the protection mechanism.

The Directive proposal on the conditions of entry and residence of third-country nationals for the purpose of paid employment and self employed economic activities provides for a coherent set of minimum standards.[5] This text aims at establishing a uniform application procedure and a common legal status for migrants admitted in the EU. My first assumption is that the proposal provides the EU with a real opportunity to counterbalance the emphasis on the fight against illegal migration. It lays down common criteria for admitting third-country nationals to employed activities and self-employed economic activities. It is not argued that the issue of fighting illegal immigration will disappear from the European agenda. Nonetheless, the harmonisation of the ways to regulate migration for economic purposes may contribute to a better distribution of the flow towards the EU. However, as stated by Vitorino, the proposal is based on a considerable degree of flexibility to adapt to the national and regional needs of the labour market. Therefore, the Member States may choose to further develop a migration scheme under specific conditions focusing on high skill workers and depending on the changing needs of the labour market (WEIL/LOCHAK, 2002, p. 49). It has also been questioned whether or not immigration could be an option to address the demographic changes in Europe (NIESSEN/SCHIBEL, 2002). In reality, "migrants cannot be thought of as a panacea for all ills" (LEWIS/ABBING, 2001-2002, p. 508). The risk of

---

5 Proposal for a Council Directive on the conditions of entry and residence of third-country nationals for the purpose of paid employment and self employed economic activities, COM(2001) 386 final, 11 July 2001.

instrumentalising the migrants pursuant to conjunctural factors is pending. With regard to asylum, this possibility would hardly fulfil the expectations of the migrants themselves who would probably continue to resort to the asylum procedure to gain access to the EU territory. However, this proposal has to be analysed in relation to two other proposals concerning the social integration of economic migrants in the receiving country.[6] These texts could indeed favour long term migrations and therefore initiate a structural change in the migration policy of the EU.

Conclusion

The Green paper on a Community return policy of illegal residents presented by the Commission on 10 April 2002 argues that, "as part of a comprehensive immigration policy, the adoption of common procedures for labour migrants could to a certain extent also reduce pressure on channels for humanitarian admission and that illegal migrants would be further deterred by more effective joint action against smuggling and trafficking" (COM (2002) 175 final, p. 7). This approach clearly demonstrates that the immigration and asylum policies of the EU are increasingly thought of in a complementary way instead of the contradictory way which long prevailed. Putting a stress on the positive interdependence of these two issues would potentially allow for a more coherent EU policy in the field of forced and voluntary migrations. The condition for successfully implementing this new approach is to guarantee the distinction between illegal migrants and asylum seekers. This is precisely what the Commission points out in this Green paper on return in order to ensure that no expulsion will take place before the need of any form of protection has been examined.

Reconsidering the impact of immigration policy on the asylum regime also requires developing a set of rights for the immigrants themselves. The recent EU initiatives aiming at combating smuggling and trafficking of human beings must be welcome. They seem to initiate a change in the conception of the migrant, who is no longer seen merely as a smuggler but as a victim entitled to certain rights.

---

[6] Amended proposal for a Council directive on the right to family reunification, COM(2002) 225 final, *Official Journal C 203 E,* 27August 2002, pp. 136-141.

References

BOELES, P. (2001): "Introduction: Freedom, Security and Justice for all." In: *Implementing Amsterdam: immigration and asylum rights in EC law*, ed. E. Guild and C. Harlow. Hart, Oxford.

BOUTEILLET-PAQUET, D. (2001): *L'Europe et le droit d'asile*, L'Harmattan, Paris.

CDR (2002): "The migration-development nexus." In: *Aid policy and practice*, Centre for Development Research, Copenhagen.

COM (2000): Communication from the Commission to the Council and the European Parliament on a Community Immigration Policy, COM(2000) 757 final, 22 November.

COM (2001): Communication from the Commission to the Council and the European Parliament on a Common Policy on illegal immigration, COM(2001) 672 final, 15 November.

CRÉPEAU, F. (1995): *Droit d'asile: de l'hospitalité aux contrôles migratoires*, Bruylant, Université de Bruxelles, Coll. Droit international.

ECRE (2002): Press Release, "Seville Summit: blocking access to Europe is not the answer", 17 June 2002, available at <http://www.ecre.org/> (visited 27 January 2003).

GOODWIN-GILL, G. S. (2001): "The individual refugee, the 1951 Convention and the Treaty of Amsterdam." In: *Implementing Amsterdam: immigration and asylum rights in EC law*, ed. E. Guild and C. Harlow. Hart, Oxford.

KJÆRUM, M. (2002): "Refugee protection between state interests and human rights: where is Europe heading?" In: *Human Rights Quarterly*, 24(2), pp. 513-536.

LAMBERT, H. (1995): "Seeking asylum: comparative law and practice in selected European countries".

LAURAIN, M. (2003): "Vers des normes minimales européennes concernant la procédure d'octroi et de retrait du statut de réfugié. Réflexions sur une proposition de directive." In: *Actualité et Droit International*, available on <http://www.ridi.org/adi>.

LAVENEX, S. (1998): "'Passing the buck': the European Union refugee policies towards Central and eastern Europe." In: *Journal of Refugee Studies*, 11(2), pp. 126-145.

LAVENEX, S.; UÇARER, E. (eds.) (2002): *Migration and the externalities of European integration*, Lexington Books, Oxford.

LEWIS, R.; ABBING, F. R. (2001-2002): "An asylum and immigration policy for the European Union." In: *Law and European Affairs*, 5, p. 508.

MARIANI, T. (2003): *Quelle politique d'asile pour l'Europe?*, Rapport d'information de l'Assemblée Nationale, n.° 817, mai 2003, pp. 75-80.

NIESSEN, J. (n.d.): "Changing the terms of the debate: immigrants and Europe's future", Speech of Mr Niessen, Director of Migration Policy Group, available on <www.ecre.org>

NIESSEN, J.; SCHIBEL, Y. (2002): *Demographic changes and the consequences for Europe's future. Is immigration an option?*, Migration Policy Group, available on <www.migpolgroup.com>

Noll, G. (2002): *Fixed definitions or framework legislation? The delimitation of subsidiary protection ratione persone*, UNHCR Working Paper No. 55, available on <http://www.unhcr.ch>

Noll, G.; Fagerlund, J. (2002): "Safe avenues to asylum? The actual and potential role of EU diplomatic representations in processing asylum requests", The Danish Centre for Human Rights and UNHCR, available at <http://www.unhcr.ch/> (visited 30 August 2002).

UNHCR (2002): *UNHCR's Observations on the Communication from the European Commission on a common policy on illegal immigration COM(2001) 672 final*, UNHCR, Geneva.

Weil, P.; Lochak, D. (2002): "Quand l'Europe choisit ses immigrés", *Alternatives internationales*, Septembre-Octobre, p. 49.

Belgian immigration policy[1]

Marco Martiniello

Belgium is one of the most multicultural and multiracial countries of the European Union. Today, the population of immigrant origin (about 900,000 foreign nationals and 300,000 with Belgian citizenship) represents about 12 % of the total population (about 10 million people). Unlike some neighbouring states, EU citizens (mainly Italians, French and Dutch) account for more than 60 % of the total population of immigrant origin. Outside the EU, Moroccans (more than 120,000 people) and Turks (about 70,000) are the largest groups but almost all the nationalities of the world are represented. The immigrant population is unequally distributed. In the capital city, Brussels, it composes more than 28 % of the population, whereas in Wallonia it is 10 % and in Flanders does not reach 5 %.

In 1974, the Council of Ministers took three important decisions. Firstly, it stopped officially any new immigration of workers. Secondly, it took measures to control clandestine immigration. Thirdly, it regularised a few thousand undocumented migrant workers. Since then and until very recently, the doctrine of zero immigration has dominated the debates and policy initiatives in this field. Even though immigration into Belgium has continued under different patterns (family reunions, free movement of EU citizens, foreign students, refugees and asylum-seekers, illegal immigration) and has contributed to the diversification of Belgian society, there has never been a proactive policy of immigration based on political acknowledgment of the fact that Belgium is indeed de facto a country of immigration. The stress has been on means to reduce immigration as much as possible, to prevent migration and to reverse it.

---

[1] This chapter was previously published in the *International Migration Review*, 27(1), 2003. It is reprinted here with the permission of the Editor.

Since 2000, a new debate has slowly been emerging. The impact of the report on replacement migration published by the Population Division of the UN has certainly contributed to put the issue of a partial reopening of the borders on the media and political agenda. The Belgian corporate world views immigration of highly skilled workers as a partial solution to the labour market shortages. But the government is reluctant to envisage a more open approach to migration in-flows. The logic of the markets and the logic of the state do not move in the same directions.

Furthermore, immigration policy, whether it deals with the regulation of migratory flows or with policies of integration of immigrants, is traditionally an exclusive right of nation-states. However, since the signing of the Treaty of Rome, the European construction has had an increasing influence on certain aspects of the migratory policies of the member States of the Union. While the latter try to keep control over these policies, the process of suppressing national boundaries within the European space and the free circulation of European citizens have produced a European convergence of national immigration legislation, which deals more with the control of migratory flows than with integration policies. The member states of the Union are no longer free to decide on their own what immigration policy to implement. In the field of integration, their margin of autonomy remains wider.

This paper addresses some of the key issues in Belgian immigration and integration policies today. It focuses on what is being done more than on what could and should be done in the fields of legal admissions, asylum, illegal immigration and the 'sans-papiers', integration policies, administration and relations with source countries.

Legal admissions

The decision taken in 1974 not to recruit any new migrant workers did not put an end to migration into Belgium. Even though the immigrant defined as a person who is entitled to live and work permanently in Belgium and eventually to become a citizen is not emblematic of the Belgian migration experience, there are legal gates for admission to the country, first temporarily and later, permanently. Leaving tourists aside, five main patterns of legal migration characterise the post-1974 era.

The mobility of EU citizens is the first source of legal admission. Under EU law, citizens' mobility within the member states is facilitated and even promoted. In public discourse, the issue of the free movement of EU citizens and the issues of immigration are increasingly separated, the latter being reserved for non-EU migrants. Meanwhile, the number of French and Dutch citizens who have decided to work and live in Belgium has constantly increased over the last ten years.

Family reunion is a second significant pattern of migration. Foreigners who are legally settled in Belgium have the right to bring in their spouse, children under 18, and in certain specific conditions, other members of their family. Family reunion is significant since many young people of immigrant origin marry a partner from their home country during vacation. It also concerns Belgian citizens or EU citizens who want to bring in their non-EU spouse or children. In 2000, 4,871 persons (out of 5,460 applicants) were granted the right to join their family in Belgium. This figure corresponds approximately to the average number of family reunion visas granted between 1995 and 2000.

Thirdly, Belgium grants temporary residence permits to foreign students. Some students from less developed countries receive a Belgian grant. Others come with their own resources. In theory, their residence permit expires at the end of their studies, but some overstay. Between 1995 and 1999 the number of permits granted each year did not exceed 1,665.

Fourthly, asylum applications are another important channel of legal admission in Belgium. This point will be developed in the next section.

Finally, specific categories of foreign workers receive each year the right to come and work in Belgium. There are two types of work permit for foreign workers. Work permit A is unlimited in time and is valid for all salaried jobs and professions. The applicant must prove either five years of legal residence in Belgium without interruption in the period before the application or four years of work without interruption and covered by a work permit B in the same period. Work permit B is limited to one year and is renewable under specific conditions. With a work permit B, the foreign worker is only authorised to work for one employer in cases of non-availability of Belgian or EU workers to fill a position. Between 1974 and 1984, 30,000 B permits were granted. Throughout the 1990s about 4,000 foreign workers received a B permit each year. Furthermore, there are other special categories of foreign workers such as au pairs, professional athletes and artists who are legally admitted each year.

These data illustrate the fact that there has never been a proactive planning of immigration in Belgium. They also clearly demonstrate that the ending of immigration in 1974 is a myth. By and large, the demographers agree that yearly legal admissions since 1962 have never dropped below 35,000. The patterns of migration and the profile of migrants have changed over the years but legal immigration has continued. Pro-immigration groups tend sometimes to overestimate the restrictive character of Belgian immigration policy. But Belgian officials overestimate the openness of the same policy. Even though there are in theory several ways to be legally admitted to Belgium, it has in practice been increasingly difficult to do so. Most of those who would like to migrate legally to Belgium are not allowed to do so.

Refugees and asylum seekers

Since the mid-eighties, asylum policy has become more and more clearly a matter of intergovernmental cooperation on a European and even greater international scale. Belgian sovereignty in matters of asylum, like that of its EU partners, has progressively been eroded. However, it would be incorrect to claim that the member states have lost all autonomy in their application of the general principles regulating asylum. Each state enjoys a relatively large freedom of interpretation in the definition of examination and application criteria for asylum requests. Thus national sovereignty is not entirely replaced by the European framework.

Asylum policy in Belgium has evolved considerably over the last 15 years. Asylum procedure has been modified several times between 1987 and 2000. The decisions made by Belgium were often influenced by European constraints and by the European debate on asylum and refugees. The 1987 Belgian initiative to impose sanctions on transporters who bring asylum seekers without papers onto Belgian territory, for example, preceded by a few weeks a decision by the European ministers charged with immigration affairs. Similar decisions were made in several European countries at about the same time. Belgium could not hesitate to follow the direction of its European partners. Such was also the case for the provisions of 1991, 1993 and 1996. These texts reflect some common concerns of EU member states. They also take up provisions introduced in previous legislation by other European states.

Between 1988 and 1999 more than 180,000 people applied for asylum in Belgium. In 2000 alone, more than 42,000 asylum applications were lodged. In the end, the rate of acceptance as refugee as defined by the Geneva Convention rarely exceeded 5-10 % of the total applications. Those whose application is rejected must in theory leave the country. Those whose application is not even taken into consideration are deprived of their liberty in closed detention centres in which they wait for repatriation.

During the 1980s and 1990s examination of these applications was very slow. This has been a major concern for Belgian policy makers and for asylum seekers themselves, who often have to wait for more than two years, and sometimes up to seven years, for a decision on their application. In most cases it is rejected. While waiting, they now receive material aid instead of financial support, as was the case before 2000, and they are not entitled to work. The length of the procedure is a dramatic problem since it leads to the expulsion of people who had plenty of time to integrate into the Belgian social fabric. Many other rejected applicants opt for the clandestine life and become undocumented. There have been discussions within the government to completely reform the procedure but so far, no agreement has been reached on how to deal with this complex and divisive issue.

Illegal immigration and the 'sans-papiers'

As in other countries, there are endless discussions between specialists about the vocabulary to be used in order to describe accurately phenomena related to migration. But the general public does not seem to make any difference between illegal, clandestine, and undocumented migrants and often also asylum-seekers. This is not the place to discuss the important issue of categories. It nevertheless seems clear that people enter Belgium illegally, that some people work clandestinely in the country and that others overstay after their legal document has expired. Unfortunately nobody has clear figures for this very versatile reality, which is not new at all.

Furthermore, Belgium is also a transit country for migrants who want to reach the United Kingdom and from there, North America. People smugglers operate by boat on the Belgian coast, helping migrants to cross the North Sea for a huge payment. Others are offered a passage on board one of the thousands of lorries that cross the Channel every month. In 2002, the tragic death of 58 young Chinese in a refrigerated truck bound for Dover, England, probably revealed just the tip of an iceberg. Policing this traffic is not an easy task. It implies cooperation with neighbouring states, some party to the Schengen agreement and some not. This cooperation is far from always being harmonious.

At the end of the year 2000, the Belgian government also launched a major campaign to regularise undocumented migrants (called in French *les 'sans-papiers'*) for the second time since 1974. After the tragic story of Semira Adamu, a young Nigerian rejected asylum seeker who died by suffocation during her deportation by the Belgian gendarmerie, the NGOs mobilised for amnesty and supported the independent organisation of the undocumented themselves, who occupied churches and even universities. After months of discussion and political negotiations, a law on regularisation of aliens present on the territory before 1 October 1999 was passed on 22 December 2000. In order to be regularised, applicants were required to fulfill one of the four following conditions: having been engaged in the asylum procedure for an abnormally long period without having been informed about the decision on their case (four years in general, three years for families with minor children); not having the objective possibility to return to one's country, for example because of a war; suffering a serious illness; having lived in Belgium at least six years without having received any official notification to leave the country during the last five years. This last category of potential applicants is considered to be integrated in Belgium.

More then 36,000 applications were submitted during the period of three weeks dedicated to the first phase of the regularisation campaign. In fact, the applications concerned more than 50,000 people from 140 nationalities, among whom the Congolese and the Moroccans were the largest groups. There is also reason to believe that the regularisation campaign did not touch all the undocumented living in the country. Firstly, some of them could not fulfill the conditions established by the law. Secondly, some of them did not really trust the whole process and feared expulsion if they applied. This one-shot campaign has so far not been completed. Thousands of people are still waiting for a decision about a year after having submitted their application.

Integration policies

Facing at the same time a migration situation and a post migration situation, Belgium has to design integration policies for newcomers as well as for the second and third generation. Integration policies developed quite late because until the 1980s, there was a hidden consensus on the provisional character of immigration: both the migrants themselves and the host institutions seemed to consider immigration simply as a temporary addition to the labour force.

Most issues linked to integration (education, health, housing, partly employment) are dealt with either by the communities or by the region, i.e. the federated entities of the Belgian state. Therefore, there is no national model of integration. Historically, different approaches developed in the North and in the South of the country. To put it very superficially, Flanders' approach was for a long time inspired by the Dutch multicultural model whereas Wallonia was more attracted by the French republican model. Declared multicultural policies were designed in Flanders whereas the Walloon government opted for general anti-exclusion policies. Things have started to change in the mid-nineties. Wallonia slowly opened up to issues linked to cultural diversity whereas Flanders, like the Netherlands, gave more weight to social and economic considerations in its integration policies. It remains the case that integration policies are often different in the north and the south of the country. Even the vocabulary used in legislation is often not the same at all. The region of Brussels, a crossroads between Belgian national groups, newcomers and "old" migrants is trying to develop its own approach by combining elements from the available models.

At the federal level, access to citizenship has been seen as a means to stimulate integration. Belgian nationality law has changed several times in the past 15 years. The most recent change took place in March 2000. The new nationality law presents three main novelties. Firstly, the acquisition of Belgian citizenship by a simple declaration is now open to foreigners who have legally resided in Belgium for seven years with an unrestricted permit. Secondly, access to naturalisation is made easier. Three years of legal residence for foreigners and two years for refugees are required to apply for naturalisation. The procedure is free. Thirdly, the notion of willingness to integrate has been suppressed as a basic condition to be granted naturalisation. It is fair to say that Belgium has one of the most liberal laws on nationality in the European Union. However, the implementation of the law is highly problematic. It seems that the administration often privileges a very restrictive interpretation of this liberal legislation, resulting in a growing backlog of applications.

Administration and relations with governments of source countries

In an extremely complex federal state like Belgium, the administration of immigration policy is highly problematic. Immigration matters are dealt with by several federal ministerial departments: Economics which hosts the National Institute of Statistics, Social Integration, Interior which hosts the opaque Foreigners' Office, Foreign Affairs and Employment. Even though the possibility of discussion within an interdepartmental conference exists, there are problems of communication and sometimes, different approaches between the various departments which hinder the development of a coordinated and coherent immigration policy, not to mention the gap between policies and their implementation.

Another crucial problem is the lack of accurate and up-to-date statistics. This is probably partly linked to problems of communications between ministerial departments but also to an underfunding of statistical tools. The current government has decided to create an observatory of migration flows, which is located at the Centre for Equal Opportunities and the Struggle against Racism, but it has not decided to invest in constructing adequate statistics.

As to relations with the governments of source countries, a distinction should be made between cooperation in the field of development and forms of cooperation aiming more directly at preventing inflows or reversing migration trends. Firstly, Belgium is engaged in various forms of cooperation with numerous source countries. It is often naively hoped that development will slow down departures. Secondly, there have been negotiations with Central and Eastern Europe governments to sign readmission agreements for dismissed asylum-seekers and illegal migrants in Belgium

Conclusion

In July 1999, the federal government presented its programme in the field of migration. Five main objectives were targeted: the creation of a status for persons displaced by war, the reduction of the length of the asylum procedure, a reform of nationality law to encourage the integration of migrants, launching a campaign of regularisation and expelling the undocumented migrants not admitted to regularisation, reforming administration and institutions dealing with immigration.

The government has certainly made progress on some of these key policy areas. But, it has not so far advanced significantly towards a more proactive immigration policy. A major European policy conference on immigration coordinated by the Minister of the Interior is scheduled for 16 and 17 October 2003. Optimists like to believe that during its presidency of the EU, Belgium will seize the opportunity to propose guidelines for a common proactive immigration policy. Pessimists say that no advance will be made for a long time. Realists wait and see.

Immigrants and minorities in Finland: problems and challenges

Matti Similä

Finland shares many things with the other Nordic countries, also when it comes to immigration policies. But Finland is also in many ways very different from the other Nordic countries and as regards immigration it also has some matters in common with Spain!

The commonplace that Finland belongs to the periphery of Europe is a truth in need of some qualifications. Historically, Finland is best described as an *inter-face-periphery*, a region between and dependent on the two centres of Stockholm and Petersburg as has been shown by KLINGE (1975) and ALAPURO (1980). Contrary to what has sometimes been alleged, Finland did not so markedly differ from the rest of Europe, except for the Finnish language.

In comparison with its Scandinavian neighbours, four Finnish features are worthy of note. A first distinguishing feature is the violent history of the recent past (the civil war following the Declaration of Independence and the Second World War). A second is the central position of agriculture until very recently, and the resulting impact on Finnish politics of what was earlier the Agrarian Party and is now the Centre Party, as well as the non-existence of a strong liberal party. A third is the heavy emigration to Sweden in the 1970s. Finally, a fourth distinguishing feature is the furious speed of structural changes in the 1970s, which made Finland more similar to its Scandinavian neighbours. As regards the distinctive features related to migration, I will come to them a little later, but as is well known, immigration to Finland started later and the number of immigrants is much smaller.

The Finnish nation state

Finland is a young nation and the nation building process started after a period of 600 years as part of the Swedish Kingdom. During the period 1808-1917 Finland was an autonomous Grand Duchy under the Russian tsar and this was the period of nation building and the development of the Finnish language. As a young nation with a history of being dominated by two of its present neighbours, it is perhaps tempting to classify Finland as a "nation-state" rather than a "state-nation". This could be said about Norway too, while Denmark and Sweden belong to the old states of Europe. According to some theories, young nations put more emphasis on cultural differences, while older ones stress the ideals of citizenship coming out of the French revolution (see for instance BRUBAKER, 1990).

However, while it is true that Finland is a young nation state, Finland is also a Nordic Welfare State. This means that there is an emphasis on universal values and rights and on equality and sameness. This model has its strength in safeguarding social security for all inhabitants, regardless of citizenship, but maybe also builds on a strong assumption of sameness, which can cause problems. I will come back to this issue.

Finland as a country of emigration and immigration

In sharp contrast to other Nordic countries, Finland has mainly been a country of emigration. Between 1946 and 1980, 610,000 persons emigrated from Finland of whom about 50 % returned to Finland. This means that Finns emigrated to Sweden at the same time as many Western countries attracted labour migrants to their factories and later to the service sector. For Sweden, the Finnish group was —and is— the biggest of these labour migrants. For Finland, this means that this labour market immigration never happened. The history of having been a country of emigration until very recently puts Finland in the same group of countries as Portugal, Spain, Italy and Greece, despite all other differences.

A short look at history

In a longer perspective, a comparison of Finland with the other Nordic countries reveals that although Finland has been a country of emigration, emigration has not been a very distinctive feature. Emigration to America in the 19th century was clearly lower from Finland than from the other Nordic countries. Between 1850 and 1910, 7.7 % of the population in Finland emigrated, compared to 17.5 % of the population in Sweden. So, Finland was a country of emigration, but the really big waves of emigration occurred as late as 30 years ago.

During the first three decades of this century Finland was both a country of transit and a country of permanent residence for refugees, especially after 1917, when many refugees from Russia arrived in Finland. The peak was in 1922, when the number was 33,500. From 1930 on there was a hesitant attitude to refugees from Central Europe in all the Nordic countries —Austrians, Sudeten Germans, Czechs and Jews. Finland took the smallest number of refugees from these areas, only about 200-300 (ENGMAN, 1989).

During the war years 1943-1944 63,000 Ingrian Finns were moved to Finland. In the Peace Treaty Finland bound herself to send back the Ingrian Finns "who had been interned and forcibly brought to Finland". About 8,000 stayed in Finland, of whom 4,000 left for Sweden for fear of being sent back to the Soviet Union. 55,000 were sent back. These events have an impact even today, since the Ingrian Finns are presently regarded as "return migrants" and are thus given a special status with right to "return" to Finland.

The greatest population movement in Northern Europe came about as a consequence of the territories lost to the Soviet Union after the war. 417,000 people —11 % of Finland's population— moved from the lost areas to the rest of Finland. The integration of these people was very successful. There were never any refugee camps; instead, special laws were instituted signifying that landowners had to give a piece of land to the refugees. This was possible thanks to the strong feelings of solidarity with the refugees. A great number of small farms were thus established, which postponed the structural change in agriculture in the countryside until the 1960s and 1970s, when the postponed changes came with brutal rapidity, creating new waves of migrants to the cities and abroad to Sweden.

In the period after the war, Finland was in some respects on the periphery, being a Western country, neutral and with an Agreement of Friendship and Co-operation with the Soviet Union. Asylum seekers from the Soviet Union were neither in the interest of our Eastern neighbour nor in the interest of Finland. The border was very well controlled from both sides, and Finland developed a special unit for border control directly under the Ministry of the Interior. The change occurred at the end of the 1980s with a clear increase in the foreign population; this development was advanced by the collapse and disruption of the Soviet Union, Somalia and former Yugoslavia.

Finnish minorities

Finland is fairly homogenous with only a few endogenous, nation specific minorities: the Sámi (about 6,000), the Roma (about 9,000), the Jews (less than 2,000) and the Tatar (less than 1,000). In some respects the Swedish speaking population (*ca.* 300,000) can be regarded to be a *de facto* minority, but in a legal sense it is not a minority, but a nationality with equal status. Finland is sparsely populated and the total number of inhabitants is about five million people. Besides the two official nationalities —Finnish speaking Finns and Swedish speaking Finns— the Sámi people have an official status with linguistic and cultural rights within the Sámi territory. Other minority groups do not have official rights in the same respect, but Finland has ratified the Human Charter for the Protection of Regional or Minority Languages.

Language

Finland is a bilingual country where the Finnish and Swedish nationalities are regarded as equal in the constitution, although, as stated above, in practice the size of the Swedish population —5.7 %— makes it a minority in many respects. The local rights of the language groups are connected with the municipalities and language relations within the municipality, based on censuses every tenth year. Municipalities can be Finnish, bilingual or Swedish, depending on the relative size of the two groups. The status of a municipality changes if the language relations change, which has consequences for the local administrative service, day-care centres and schools, etc., in Finnish and Swedish respectively.

Another case is the Åland Islands, which are defined as a monolingual Swedish *territory*, which has a considerable amount of self-government. The population amounts to about 25,000 people.

Religion

Finland is predominantly Lutheran, and the Lutheran church is a National church and a State church. Over 86 % of the population belongs to this (bilingual) Lutheran church, while about 12 % do not belong to any religious association. The Orthodox Church is historically well established in Eastern Finland, but in fact less than 60,000 people belong to it. Other groups are even smaller, like Catholics or the Jewish and Islamic congregations.

Background to the present handling of immigration issues

When analysing the situation and the politics as regards migration it is clear that some important changes in Finland took place fairly recently. The end of the cold war and the breakdown of the Soviet Union were obvious factors of relevance; others were membership of the European Council, the EEA agreement and membership of the EU. These developments led to the present situation.

The laws as regards immigration and rights of foreign citizens are harmonised with the EU. Being a Nordic welfare state means that laws on social security in most respects are very close to the rules in the other Nordic countries with which Finland has had so much co-operation since World War II.

The present situation as regards immigration in general terms

From having been a country of emigration, Finland now has a surplus of immigrants. Besides the Ingrian Finns, many are asylum seekers. Although the figures are very modest, the *relative* increase some years ago was quite substantial and led to new demands on the administrative agencies handling visas, work permits, and the integration and support of refugees and other immigrants.

The special features in the case of Finland as regards immigration can be summarised as follows:

—The number of immigrants is still very low in a Western European context.
—Many immigrants are returning migrants with Finnish ancestry, mostly from Sweden.
—Finland has never had flows of labour migration.
—Finland has its special composition of immigrants as regards country of origin (the importance of Russia, Estonia and the Ingrian immigrants)
—Because of the earlier flows of immigration mainly through marriage with a Finnish citizen, a rather high proportion of the foreign population is married to a Finn even today.
—And, of course, Finland has no colonial past.

One other difference from many other countries is the low proportion of illegal immigrants, due to a traditionally strong border control on both sides of the Russian border. There is illegal labour in the sense of people coming on tourist visas and working within the construction sector, agriculture or as prostitutes. Most of these people come from

Russia or Estonia. But there are no large numbers of illegal residents living permanently in the country.

Earlier, immigrants came to Finland in very small numbers, for instance as a consequence of marriage to a Finnish citizen. *Only during the last ten years* have greater numbers arrived as refugees and asylum seekers. This increasing number of refugees has, of course, led to further immigration in terms of family reunification. This means that

—Most immigrants have lived in Finland *for a very short time.*
—The increase in immigration happened in a period when Finland was struck by a very heavy depression in the early years of the last decade.
—Therefore, it seems to be too early to assess the success or failure of the present integration policy

The low number of immigrants is, of course, not just a coincidence. Besides the fact that other countries have attracted more immigrants and asylum seekers, Finland has traditionally tried to limit the influx from abroad. In fact there has been a long trend of homogenisation during the last century. At the beginning of 1900 there were 13 % Swedish speakers in Finland and, as said earlier, after the Russian revolution there was an influx of Russian refugees. The trend thereafter went towards homogenisation, which reached its peak in the 1980s. Migration since then has really had a very limited effect, as the percentage with Finnish as mother tongue has decreased from 93 % to 92.6 %.

The Ingrian Finns

A special group of immigrants are the Ingrian Finns, who are considered "return migrants" due to their Finnish roots. In practice, many Ingrian Finns, and especially when including all family members, are Russian speaking. As Annika Forsander has suggested, this may be seen not only as a special form of ethnomigration, but perhaps also the first attempt from the Finnish side to allow for a small scale labour migration. With an ageing population, this issue will be challenging in the future, because it will call for a radical change of contemporary attitudes (FORSANDER, 2000).

Attitudes, media, discrimination and racism

The fact that new immigrant groups arrived at the time when the recession was deepest is one probable factor behind resentful attitudes among Finns. Magdalena Jaakkola has made several studies on attitudes in the Finnish population, the latest published some years ago. In a summarising article she concludes that attitudes are more positive than during the deepest recession. The attitudes towards foreigners were more negative during the time of widespread unemployment in 1993 than before (1987) or afterwards (1998-99). A strong economy and good education seem to be two important factors connected with more tolerance towards immigrants. Contacts with immigrants also correlate with more positive attitudes. Those with little education, pensioners, the unemployed, men, supporters of the Central Party and those living in rural areas had more negative attitudes. In 1998 over a third of the young men living in the countryside supported the actions of skinheads against immigrants (JAAKKOLA, 2000).

The role of the media is another factor that has been studied. REKOLA (1996) and RAITTILA/KUTILAINEN (2000) have studied the Finnish press and its representation of immigrants, refugees and minorities, and a recent study has looked specifically at the same issues in the Swedish press in Finland (SANDLUND, 2000). Also, a recent dissertation has studied the parliamentary debate around immigration issues, with a special focus on differences of opinion as regards Ingrian Finns and Somalian refugees (LEPOLA, 2000).

Lepola's study is about the debate in Finland on immigration and foreign residents during the period 1988-1999 and what this debate tells about Finns' perceptions of Finland and Finnish identity. During the 1990s multiculturalism became a fashionable term in policy regarding foreign residents. In practice multiculturalism has been considered to be an issue directly related to immigrants: firstly as being a consequence of their presence, and secondly as giving them the responsibility to learn Finnish customs and the Finnish language, while preserving their own culture.

The conceptual boundary between a Finn and a foreigner appears on the basis of this research to be virtually insurmountable. Immigrants are left fundamentally outside the idea of a Finnish identity, with the exception of the Ingrian Finns. Whether foreign residents in Finland will ever actually be regarded as Finns will depend on whether Finnish identity stresses ethnic origins or Finnish citizenship, residence in Finland and participation in the Finnish society.

In 2002 a dissertation by Annika FORSANDER analysed the situation for the immigrants on the labour market and connected the situation to the specific qualities of the Nordic welfare state model. She concludes that the position of immigrants in the society is determined by the structure of the receiving society, and that the Nordic Welfare State is based on the ideal of national homogeneity. Therefore, social structures do not adapt easily to respond to the growing diversity of life-styles. In the Nordic societies the threshold to labour market inclusion is high, which keeps unemployment high among immigrants. In spite of this, the Nordic Welfare State has been successful in rejecting poverty, though the danger of ethnification of poverty exists. She also found that the region of origin was the factor best explaining unemployment among immigrants. The labour market status of refugees and those who immigrated from developing countries is weakest, whereas it proved strongest among Asians and especially immigrants from Western countries. This pattern could only partially be explained by educational background. The majority of the immigrants were in an unstable or marginal position in the Finnish labour market or outside the labour force.

A weak attachment to the labour market causes dependency on social income transfer. In 1997 61 % of immigrants received social income transfers, most typically unemployment benefits. Forsander notes that there is an increasing emphasis on cultural and social knowledge in the labour market, alongside traditional human capital, such as education, work experience and language skills. This development is problematic for the immigrants. In the present situation very many of them are extremely vulnerable to the labour market effects of economic trends and changes in production structures (FORSANDER, 2002a and 2002b).

According to the 1997 Eurobarometer, Finns consider themselves very racist somewhat more often (10 %) than in EU on average (9 %). Also, while on average 34 % of all Europeans felt they were not racist at all, only 22 % of the Finns say so. Finally, in 1998 2 % fully accepted skinheads' activities against foreigners, while 7 % in part accepted their actions.

It may be noted, though, that no groups on the extreme right wing have been able to register as parties, because of lack of support. This certainly is a positive fact in comparison with many other European countries. But although the attitudes of regular Finns have become more positive, Finland too has seen the number of racist crimes double between 1997 (194 cases) and 1998 (414 cases). (SISÄASIAINMINISTERIÖ, 1999). The more positive attitudes towards refugees from Kosovo suggest that plenty of information about the background of the refugees, the situation in their home country, their distress and need for aid, combined with political leaders' stress on Finland's international obligations, may have positive effects on opinions about refugees.

Foreigners are generally well come as tourists, experts/scientists, students and language teachers, but not as "economic refugees" and neither are they very welcome as musicians, restaurant owners or jobseekers. On the other hand, attitudes towards jobseekers are more positive now than earlier during the recession.

As regards refugees, the Kosovo refugees accepted in 1999 were accepted with much more positive attitudes than quota refugees were. A reasonable hypothesis is that the information about the war made people regard them as "real" refugees to a larger extent than otherwise.

As regards attitudes towards different groups, there seems to exist a Nordic/Western/ethnic dimension, with most favourable attitudes towards Norwegians, Ingrian Finns, and English, Danish, Swedish and American citizens. Most negative attitudes are directed towards Somalians, Arabs, Russians and Kurds.

A comparative study of Kurds in England and Finland by Östen WAHLBECK (1999) describes the Kurdish communities abroad as diasporas. Despite the large differences between England and Finland, Wahlbeck finds many common features, such as the Kurds' wish to return, their feeling of displacement and various psychological problems owing to their refugee experiences. All the Kurdish refugees, regardless of country of origin or of exile, also created and maintained transnational social networks. These networks included contacts with Kurds in Kurdistan and in the world-wide diaspora. As for the country of settlement, he further found important differences as well. Wahlbeck argues that neither country has fully understood the specific nature of refugee migration, although they approach the issue from totally different perspectives. The UK adopts a traditional communitarian and multicultural approach, while in practice Finland has a more assimilationist resettlement policy.

There were notable differences between the two countries in terms of practical problems experienced by refugees. In Finland, the official resettlement programmes and the structure of the welfare state greatly diminished the practical problems related to housing, education and income support. The refugees in Finland even experienced fewer problems connected with language than did the refugees in England. In London, however, the strong Kurdish communities and the Kurdish social networks were important resources for the refugees. The refugees were more isolated and their associations were not as well organised in Finland as in England. The ethnic labour market in London was often able to facilitate the refugees' employment. However, the only jobs available were poorly paid with bad working conditions. In Finland, the severe unemployment situation in practice excluded refugees from the labour market. Xenophobia and racism were also more visible features of society in Finland than was the case in the multicultural environment of London. Resettlement policies were widely different. The Finnish policy was to resettle refugees in small groups dispersed all over the country, while in Britain almost all Kurds lived in London. This led to notable differences in the social networks and types of social integration.

Regarding the present situation of immigration issues, it is noteworthy that there is no political party in Finland which could be labelled racist or xenophobic. There may, however, be a similarity common to all Nordic states, which could be described as an uncertainty about how to combine the values of universalism and individualism of the Welfare State with the new demands for coping with diversity due to immigration. At least, immigrants in all Nordic countries show a very high rate of unemployment and the debate on how to integrate immigrants is lively.

One possible future development is connected with the enlargement of the European Union. The near future will change the situation for Finland, when the Baltic States become members of the EU. The Estonians in particular, who not only live very close to Southern Finland, but whose language is also closely related to Finnish, will probably find the Finnish labour market attractive. On the other hand, at that point the limited, but existing problem of illegal labour migration from that area will cease to exist.

Migration and migration policy today

The present situation as regards immigration and immigration policy can shortly be described in the following way.

Statistics

The number of *people residing in Finland* is a little over 5 million. In 2001 145,000 (2.9 %) were *born abroad* and 98,000 (2.0 %) were *foreign citizens.* (In 1990 the corresponding figures were about 65,000 born abroad and 25,000 foreign citizens.)

The biggest immigrant groups are from the former Soviet Union, especially Russia and Estonia. Immigrants from Sweden are also relatively many, mostly Finnish remigrants. Other groups worth mentioning are from Somalia, former Yugoslavia and Iraq.

The Ingrian Finns are estimated to be around 23,000, family members included. They come from Russia or Estonia and are included in the figures above.

Table 1

Foreigners in Finland by country of citizenship, 2001

Russia	22,724
Estonia	11,662
Sweden	7,999
Somalia	4,355
Yugoslavia[1]	4,240
Iraq	3,222
United Kingdom	2,352
Germany	2,327
Former Soviet Union	2,249
Iran	2,166
USA	2,110
Turkey	1,981
China	1,929
Vietnam	1,778
Bosnia and Herzegovina	1,668
Thailand	1,540
Ukraine	1,133
Others	23,142
Total	98,577

[1] Former Yugoslavia and Federal Republic of Yugoslavia.

Source: Statistics Finland, Demographic statistics

The total number of refugees since 1973 (including those granted residence permits based on need for protection or on humanitarian grounds and also including persons received through the family reunification programme) is 21,000.

The number of *undocumented persons* in Finland is, of course, not known. It has been estimated that there may be 10,000 illegal immigrants in Finland per year (SORAINEN, 2002). Yet, this is not to say that 10,000 persons are living *permanently* and illegally in Finland. Rather, people come on tourist visas and work illegally, for instance in the construction sector, agriculture, cleaning, nursing and child care sectors (and as prostitutes). The illegal immigrants are mostly people who have entered legally, but whose residence permit, visa or visa exempt period of residence has expired. Entry of permanent illegal residents is not a big problem in Finland. They have quite aptly been labelled *working tourists* (FORSANDER, 2002a). Yet, the problem may be growing and should still be taken seriously.

The number of *asylum seekers* were 3,170 in 2000 and 1,651 in 2001. Since the processes are slow, it is not possible to say how many will be admitted into the country, but very few of those who are admitted to stay are given a Convention status. It seems clear that although Finland follows the same rules as other countries in the EU and Western Europe, the interpretation and implementation leads to a very restrictive policy *de facto*, with only 0.2 % of the applications granted Convention status as a refugee. The figures for the two last years are the following:

Table 2

Total number of applications decided and the statuses accorded

Statuses	2000		2001	
	Number	%	Number	%
No status awarded	2,121	58%	1,083	49%
Convention status, status A3	9	0.2%	4	0.2%
Need of protection, status A3	248	7%	347	16%
Status A4	199	5%	427	19%
Residence Permit, status A5	—	—	47	2%
Annulment	1,049	29%	300	14%
Total decisions	3,626	100%	2,208	100%

Source: Directorate of Immigration

Most applicants in 2001 came from Russia, Ukraine, Iraq, Former Yugoslavia and Turkey. Compared with 2000 there was a decrease in applicants from Poland, Slovakia and the Czech Republic, due to the introduction of accelerated asylum procedures and obligatory visas for Slovakia (the applicants were virtually all Roma).

In 2001, the intake of *quota refugees* to Finland were 647, mostly from Afghanistan, Iran, Sudan, Croatia and Iraq. In addition, 100 Iraqis and Iranians from Turkey were selected by the Finnish quota refugee mission, but were given a negative report by the Finnish Security Police. They are still in Turkey, since the Directorate of Immigration could not grant asylum for them.

The number of *unaccompanied minors* in 2001 was 32 (not an official number).

Asylum seekers may *withdraw* their application. If the decision is likely to be negative, withdrawal may prevent getting a prohibition of re-entry. Statistically, the Directorate of Immigration does not separate cessations and withdrawals. In the year 2000 the number of annulled applications was 1,049, in 2001 only 300.

Number of work permits: In the year 2000 there were 15,000 work permits granted of which about 5,000 were extensions

Deportation statistics: In 2001 altogether 108 persons were returned on grounds of "safe country". The countries considered safe (one should bear in mind that many applicants belong to minorities, as for instance the Roma people, etc) were: Algeria, Ethiopia, Lithuania, Morocco, Slovakia, Czech Republic, Turkey and Estonia. 122 persons were returned on Dublin Convention grounds.

No figures for 2001 are available for *expulsion/deportation* of asylum seekers. Normally rejected asylum seekers are *expelled*.

According to the Ministry of Labour there were 37 refugees who received a return allowance.

Detention of non-criminal immigrants: Asylum seekers whose identity and travel route cannot be verified are often detained upon arrival in Finland. Detention is also used in order to prepare for the expulsion of rejected asylum seekers. Annually, approximately 10 to 15 % of all asylum seekers are detained.

Overview of immigration laws

The legal basis: The Geneva Convention and New York Protocol, The Aliens Act of February 1991 (will be reformed and has recently been presented to the Parliament), The Aliens Decree of 1994, The Act on the Integration of Immigrants and Reception of Asylum seekers of April 1999 (The Integration Act), The Dublin Convention and The Schengen Agreement.

Work permits: According to Sorainen, the statistics have not been reliable, but it seems that labour immigration is rising. Several groups of foreigners are exempt from work permit procedures. This includes foreigners with permanent residence permits, students in regard to part-time work and holiday jobs, refugees and people receiving residence permits due to need for protection, asylum seekers who have been in Finland for at least three months, entrepreneurs, and teachers and researchers at universities (SORAINEN, 2002).

Family unification: Refugees and people who have permission to stay in Finland on grounds of need for protection can ask for family unification. Those accepted as family members are spouse and underage unmarried children. The process is very slow and often lasts several years. According to the change in the Aliens Act in 2000, the relation to the family may be proved by a DNA test. Most tested persons come from Africa. In 2001, 105 families (581 persons) were offered the test and 73 (389) were tested. The Directorate of Immigration makes the decision on family unification. As for minors who have applied for asylum, there has been a possibility to seek family unification too. In the proposal for the new Aliens Act, the Government wants, as a rule, to send the child to the country where its parents reside.

Asylum: *Convention Status* was only given to 0.2 % of the applicants in 2001 and 2000 (9 and 4 cases respectively). Convention status is granted in the form of a so-called A3 residence permit. Recognised refugees are entitled to permanent residence after two years.

A residence permit based on the *need for protection* may be issued. This residence permit is considered to be a de facto status. Holders are entitled to family unification and the same social benefits as Convention (and quota) refugees. They also are entitled to permanent residence after two years. In 2001, 16 % of the applicants got a residence permit on these grounds.

Until May 1999 it was also possible to grant residence permits on humanitarian grounds.

Role of the police: The police have normally been interviewing asylum seekers. In 2001 the Directorate of Immigration started to conduct asylum interviews. However, the police still do most of the interviews. The asylum interviews will gradually be transferred to the Directorate of Immigration by 2004. (The police will still, however, investigate the identity of the asylum seeker and the travel route.) The objective is to speed up the process.

Assistance programmes: Since Finland is a Nordic Welfare State, it is hard to cover all the components in the battery of support that can be given to immigrants, since the idea of universal rights for all residents applies to immigrants as well as to all other residents. There are, of course, also many special programmes aiming at facilitating the integration process, such as labour market training, special education programmes, and programmes in schools for young immigrants.

Trends

Illegal immigration may be increasing, but not dramatically. It is still a small problem, compared with what many other countries experience.

On *asylum policies*, legislation is "liberal", but practice is restrictive. It remains to be seen how the new version of the Aliens Act will differ, but radical changes will hardly occur.

Detention: A new law on the establishment of a detention centre for foreigners taken info custody under the Aliens Act came into force on 1 March 2002. Before that, detained asylum seekers were kept in police cells and county prisons together with common criminals. The detention centre was opened in July 2002. However, the capacity of the centre is only 30, so detained asylum seekers are still kept in police cells in some parts of Finland.

Labour issues: need for foreign labour? The procedures for work permit options changed on 1 April 2001. From this date an alien who has lived in Finland for three months as an asylum seeker is allowed to work without a work permit in accordance with more precise orders from the Ministry of Labour.

There will be a need for foreign labour, as the population gets older. In ten years the point where the population starts to decrease will be close. The proportion of retired people increases and the proportion in the active ages decreases. However, a change in national policy is not foreseeable for the moment, but the pressure to open up to labour migration will increase in a longer perspective. The enlargement of the union will also probably lead to increased immigration. However, it is not probable that immigration will reach such levels that it could provide a long-term solution to the structural problems of the Finnish labour market.

The question remains: If in the future there will be a growing need of labour migrants due to demographic developments, is it then possible to pursue a restrictive policy as regards refugees with a systematic intake of labour migrants without problems? What is the relation between immigration rules and the possibilities of integrating immigrants? Another question is how it will be possible to change attitudes in a country where people have tended to see foreigners as a potential threat, rather than a potential resource?

References

ALAPURO, R. (1980): *Finland: an interface periphery*, Research Group for Comparative Sociology, University of Helsinki.

BRUBAKER, W. (1990): "Immigration, citizenship and the nation state in France and Germany: a comparative historical analysis", *International Sociology*, 379-407.

ENGMAN, M. (1989): "De förflyttade karelarna: evakuering och integrering" (The transplanted Karelians: evacuation and integration). In *Nordisk flyktingpolitik i världskrigets epok* (Nordic refugee policy in the epoch of the second world war), eds. R. Johansson and H.-A. Persson. University of Lund.

FORSANDER, A. (2000): "New trends in migration and ethnic relations in Finland", A country report presented at the EUROFOR Annual Conference, Brussels, 22-27 November 2000.

FORSANDER, A. (2002a): *Luottamuksen ehdot. Maahanmuuttajat 1990-luvun suomalaisilla työmarkkinoilla* (Conditions of trust: immigrants in the 1990s Finnish labour market), Väestöliitto, D 39 2002, Diss.

FORSANDER, A. (ed.) (2002b): *Immigration and economy in the globalisation process: the case of Finland.* Sitra Report Series.

JAAKKOLA, M. (2000): "Finnish attitudes towards immigrants in 1987-1999", *Yearbook of population research in Finland,* 36.

KLINGE, M. (1975): *Bernadotten ja Leninin välissä. Tutkielma kansallisista aineista* (Between Bernadotte and Lenin: a study on national matters), Porvoo.

KOSKIMIES, S. (2000): *Experiences of ethnic and racial discrimination in Finland: a presentation of NEON material, 1998-1999*, Swedish School of Social Science, University of Helsinki. Centre for Research on Ethnic Relations and Nationalism (CEREN).

KUUSISTO, P. (2000): *Ethnicity in print. Implicit linguistic manifestations of the construction of ethnicity in British and Finnish newspapers. Pragmatics, Ideology and Contacts.* Monographs 1. Department of English, University of Helsinki. Diss.

LEPOLA, O. (2000): Ulkomaalaisesta suomenmaalaiseksi (From foreigner to "Finlander"). Helsinki: SKS. Diss.

PENTIKÄINEN, J.; HILTUNEN, M. (1995): *Cultural minorities in Finland: an overview towards cultural policy.* Publications of the Finnish National Commission for UNESCO, No 66, Ministry of Education.

RAITTILA, P.; KUTILAINEN, T. (2000): *Rasismi ja etnisyys Suomen sanomalehdissä syksyllä 1999* (Racism and ethnicity in the Finnish press in autumn 1999), Journalismin tutkimusyksikkö, Tiedotusopin laitos, Tampereen yliopisto, Sarja C31/2000. Tampere.

REKOLA, J. (1996): *Excluding the minorities: ethnic representation in the Finnish press.* KEPA Reports No 10/1996. Service Centre for Development Cooperation.

SANDLUND, T. (ed.) (2000): *Rasism och etnicitet i den finlandssvenska tidningspressen*, SSKH (Racism and ethnicity in the Swedish press in Finland), Meddelanden. Nr 57.

SIMILÄ, M. (2002): "Integration and multiculturalism: key concepts in the age of globalisation." In: *Reflections on diversity and change in modern society. A Festschrift for Annick Sjögren,* eds. N. B. Gomes *et al.*The Multicultural Centre, Botkyrka.

SISÄASIAINMINISTERIÖ (1999): *Polisin tietoon tullut rasistinen rikollisuus Suomessa 1998.* (Racist crimes known to the police in Finland 1998), Poliisihallinon julkaisu 11.

SORAINEN, O. (2002): "Finland." OECD Sopemi. *Trends in international migration*, 2001 edition, Ministry of Labour, Finland.

WAHLBECK, Ö. (1999): *Kurdish diasporas: a comparative study of Kurdish refugee communities,* Macmillan, Basingstoke.

Statistical data, legal and administrative issues and trends have been sought from various Ministries, The Refugee Advice Centre ECRE, Statistics Finland, the Institute of Migration and Annika Forsander's EUROFOR report. Special thanks to Annika Forsander at CEREN and Reetta Helander at the Refugee Advice Centre.

French immigration policy during the last twenty years

Emmanuel Ma Mung

The historical context

The history of migration in France is noticeably different from that in other western European countries: it is not a country of *emigration* to "new countries" as was the case with northern and southern European countries in the last few hundred years. French emigration to the New World and the colonies was far less substantial than in other European countries: on the contrary, the particularity of France is that it has a long history of *immigration*. For example, in the 17th century, Colbert, a minister under Louis XIV, recommended bringing in tinplate workers from Koblenz to work in French factories in order to compensate for the shortfall in labour force. This characteristic distinguishes it markedly from other European countries (SIMON, 1995).

For several centuries France has had a demographic deficit, hence a long-term trend of encouraging labour immigration with the authority to stay in the country and have the effect of boosting the population. It can be said that immigration has always been implicitly thought of as a permanent settling of people who are to become French, hence the nationality code developed during the 19th century to facilitate the acquisition of French nationality. The integration of foreigners has been —and still is— thought of as the integration of future nationals rather than the integration into society of people who retain their foreign character. This is illustrated by the French model of incorporation into the nation based on the integration of individuals and not groups, whether religious, regional or ethnic (SCHNAPPER, 1994). For this reason, the image of the foreigner is ambivalent: it is positive when the foreigner is thought of as an individual who will become a national and thereby lose his/her extraneous nature; it is negative when the foreigner remains a foreigner. The foreigner is tolerated only on condition that he/she disappears —not physically by returning to his/her country of origin, for example, but one could say semantically, by abandoning his/her foreign character (see LACROIX, 2002). Hence the strength of the concept of immigration/incorporation in the nation which characterises immigration policy. Thus, immigration in France has two dimensions which persist today: an economic dimension, through making use of a workforce which originates outside the country, and a demographic dimension through the need to boost the French population.[1] The trend of encouraging immigration for the purposes of labour and populating the country has however seen significant variations over time and it has undergone a profound transformation with European integration and the change in international migratory trends.

Fluctuations in immigration policy

From the 19th century up to the Second World War, immigration originated mainly from Germany, Belgium and Switzerland and thereafter Poland, central European countries, Italy and also Spain (resulting from the war against the Republicans). A lower rate of immigration can be noted from France's colonies in North and West Africa which only became extensive from the 1960s.

The "trente glorieuses" and the 1974 crisis: from "laisser-faire laisser-passer" to closing down the borders

In the post-war years, national reconstruction and the "*trente glorieuses*" (thirty years of economic growth) meant that as far as immigration was concerned, there was ever greater call on colonial labour (mainly from Algeria) and foreign labour mainly from southern Europe (Italy, Spain and Portugal). During this period, 80 to 90 % of the workers who entered France bypassed the legal entry procedures and the immigration policy consisted in facilitating the entries as far as possible by relaxing the controls and encouraging immigration to meet industry's growing need for labour. Bilateral agreements were signed with the countries of origin as and when the need arose, but no measures were taken towards an overall organisation of immigration (COSTA-LASCOUX/WEIL, 1992).

---

[1] For a history of the construction of French immigration policy and the regulation of the foreign presence based on the analysis of the administrative structures which managed them, see the outstanding work by Vincent VIET (1998).

1975: halting labour immigration and establishing an integration policy

The mid 1970s marks a turning point in France's immigration policy. Like the other major immigration countries, this involved the sudden cessation of labour immigration. Incentives were brought in to encourage immigrants to return to their home countries, but they had a very limited effect and involved only a few thousand people. At the same time, measures were taken to favour family reunion and bring in the spouses and children of immigrants already established in the country. Immigration has continued at a rate of several thousand people per year, but it is no longer labour immigration, but rather to boost the population, as was the case for most immigration in the preceding decades and the last century. Between 1975 and 1998, the average number of immigrants per year was 73,000, with variations between 55,000 in 1985 and 118,000 in 1998. The total number of immigrants during this "closed" period was 1,760,000, while in the period 1950 to 1974 when immigration was encouraged, the total amounted to only 1,330,000 (see Table 1). In 1999, there were 4,310,000 immigrants in France according to INSEE, making up 7.4 % of the population of metropolitan France.[2]

It was at this time that the subject of integration (in the sense of incorporation into the nation) grew in the public mind and the media and in the arena of research on international migration (see GAEREMYNCK, 2002). Despite the significance of this debate in all spheres of social and political life, specific measures centring on foreigners are rare. The most important of them concerned the bringing together of families, which was intended to favour the integration of immigrants who had already settled. On the other hand, a "city policy" was gradually implemented in the 1980s in urban areas facing social difficulties such as unemployment, housing and delinquency —where immigrant families were also to be found. This policy was not directed specifically at immigrants, but rather "problem populations" of which the immigrant populations were assumed to be a part. Given that the target of the measures was not specifically immigrant families, the significance of the French model of republican integration remains paramount, involving the integration of individuals rather than groups. Indeed, measures for populations chosen according to their ethnic or national

---

[2] For INSEE (French national institute of economic and statistical information), those counted as immigrants are people who are foreign or naturalised French, born outside the national territory. A French person by blood but born in another country is not recorded as an immigrant, as for a person with a foreign nationality born on French territory.

Table 1

Immigrants in France in 1999 by country of origin

Total	**4,306,094**	**100.0%**
Total Europe	**1,934,144**	**44.9%**
Total European Union	**1,629,457**	**37.8%**
Germany	123,186	2.9%
Belgium	93,622	2.2%
United Kingdom	75,020	1.7%
Spain	316,232	7.3%
Italy	378,649	8.8%
Netherlands	25,419	0.6%
Portugal	571,874	13.3%
Other EU countries	45,455	1.1%
Other European countries	**304,687**	**7.1%**
Poland	98,571	2.3%
Romania	23,270	0.5%
Switzerland	45,065	1.0%
Former Soviet Union	26,009	0.6%
Former Yugoslavia	75,262	1.7%
Other countries	36,510	0.8%
Total Africa	**1,691,562**	**39.3%**
Total North Africa	**1,298,273**	**30.1%**
Algeria	574,208	13.3%
Morocco	522,504	12.1%
Tunisia	201,561	4.7%
Other countries of Africa	**393,289**	**9.1%**
Cameroon	26,798	0.6%
Congo	35,449	0.8%
Ivory Cost	29,885	0.7%
Madagascar	28,091	0.7%
Mali	35,534	0.8%
Mauritius	28,220	0.7%
Senegal	53,762	1.2%
Congo (Rép. Dém., ex-Zaïre)	23,747	0.6%
Other countries	131,803	3.1%
Total Asia	**549,994**	**12.8%**
Cambodia	50,675	1.2%
China (PRC)	30,932	0.7%
Laos	36,838	0.9%
Sri-Lanka	24,613	0.6%
Turkey	174,160	4.0%
Viet Nam	72,237	1.7%
Other countries	160,539	3.7%
Total America and Oceania	**130,394**	**3.0%**
USA	29,396	0.7%
Brazil	14,600	0.3%
Canada	12,058	0.3%
Haïti	19,131	0.4%
Other countries	51,005	1.2%

Source: INSEE, Census 1999.

origin would revert to designating groups to be integrated rather than individuals and would contradict this model. During the same period an institution was established: the "Haut Conseil à l'Intégration" whose mission was to put forward proposals to favour integration.

A further debate developed: the right of foreigners to vote, which also involved the notion of citizenship. It is a debate which is periodically opened in the run up to elections. Those in favour see it as a measure which greatly favours integration for it confers on foreigners the quality of citizens: for them, a person who resides, works and pays taxes in the country has the right to have representatives elected democratically regardless of his/her nationality. Opponents object to it in the name of the nation's integrity and fall into two main camps: the first develops thinly disguised xenophobic arguments (or clearly affirmed in the case of the extreme right); the second opposes the right in the name of the defence of the republican model of integration. Citizenship —the most important expression of which is the right to vote— has a national character which has nothing to do with xenophobia (it is not denied that a foreigner may become French) but shows itself in the adherence to a community of values which founded the nation and the republic. This adherence lies in nationality and the acquisition of nationality expresses this adherence. It is necessary therefore to favour not only the concept of the right to vote but also the acquisition of French nationality which brings with it the right to vote. Attributing the right to vote to foreigners from a European Union country complicates the task of those who are against foreigners having the right to vote, but to date, the ban remains in place for other nationals.

The 1990s saw a significant shift in integration policy with the appearance of the theme of discrimination. In the public sphere, this led to the creation at the end of the 90s of GELD ("*Le Groupe d'Etudes et de Lutte contre les Discriminations*"). This organisation was state financed and its mission was to identify and analyse signs of discrimination in access to work, housing and leisure activities and put forward proposals to fight against it (an anti-discrimination law was passed in 2001). This shift is important as it can be seen as a recognition of the fact that integration measures have to be aimed at groups rather than individuals. Indeed, recognising that discrimination is exercised against individuals because they belong to a racial, ethnic or religious group clearly means the recognition of the sociological existence of such groups. And the fight against this discrimination with a view to integrating individuals leads on to working for the integration of the groups to which they belong.

The 1990s: immigration policy toughens

In 1993, a right-wing government came to power. From the first few weeks in office, the Balladur government put forward bills which became "les lois Pasqua" (the Pasqua laws), named after the Minister of the Interior of the time. They marked a turning point, but were nonetheless a continuation of projects initiated by the previous government. Discussions had already been taking place among the political classes —both left and right— for some years.[3] Furthermore, these policies were not called into question when the left returned to power in 1996. There has therefore been a continuity in the major trends in French immigration policy during the last twenty years, regardless of which government was in power. And the Pasqua laws are not only the culmination of internal development in France, but also the effect of recommendations made by the European authorities within the framework of the Schengen Agreement and the Maastricht Treaty (COSTA-LASCOUX, 1993). One can consider that they mark the beginning of the end of the particular character of French immigration policy to boost the population, and the move towards a gradual alignment with a European conception,[4] which, on the contrary, was preoccupied for historical demographic reasons with overpopulation.

These measures illustrate a hardening of French immigration policy and aim to limit the presence of foreigners. They also aim to fight against illegal immigration, which had been tolerated and even encouraged during the years of economic growth when workers entered the country without having to go through the normal legal entry procedures. Furthermore, the question of integrating foreigners, which has always been posed as a compensation for restrictive policies, does not result in supplementary measures to favour integration. The debate on integration which emerged in the 1970s and 80s also hardened. The generalisation "foreigner = criminal" grew along the chain of meanings "foreigner / irregular / clandestine / delinquent / criminal" and gave substance to the authorised deportation of foreigners in an irregular situation.[5] With the turning tides of the 1990s, deportation,

---

[3] In 1990, Socialist prime minister Michel Rocard declared: "France cannot open its arms to all the world's miseries." Even though it was not the minister's aim, this statement was considered as a sign of a toughening approach towards immigration.

[4] For Vincent VIET (1998), the Pasqua laws symbolise the end of decolonisation and the special relations France enjoyed with its former colonies which were a specific sign of the French immigration problem.

[5] Charles Pasqua, Minister of the Interior, chartered a plane to return Malians to their home country who were in an irregular situation.

which had until then been considered an extreme measure, became part of the immigration policy (MARIE, 2002).

The Pasqua laws concerned three domains: the nationality code, the control of immigration flows (conditions of entry, reception and residence for foreigners) and identity checks. Each clause taken in isolation does not violate constitutional principles or basic liberties. However, considering them together —in a climate of mistrust towards foreigners— leads to disproportionate repressive attitudes with regard to the situation of the vast majority of immigrants living in France (COSTA-LASCOUX, 1993).

The reform of the nationality code is the measure which has given rise to the most controversy, for it broke with the tradition of automatic entitlement to French nationality once people met certain prerequisites. Thus children born in France of foreigners who were formerly able to obtain French nationality through the principle of *jus soli* (the right of the soil) would now have to demonstrate their commitment to doing so. This reform which —more in intention that in fact— limited access to French nationality is a clear break with the French tradition of integration since foreigners no longer had the automatic entitlement to become French. Equally, as foreigners, they could be requested to leave. However, the obligation to prove a clear desire to become French was annulled in 1998. The unexpected result of the Pasqua Laws was a noticeable increase in the number of naturalisations, which grew from an average of 70,000 per year at the beginning of 1990s to 100,000 at the end of 1990s.

Controlling the inflow of immigrants also led to much controversy, concerning the rules for foreigners to be allowed entry; the requirements for issue of residence permits; bringing in family members; the right of asylum and ever more stringent identity checks. The rules for foreigners to be granted entry remain basically the same, but their implementation has become more stringent and pernickety: control of entries has been reinforced by way of rules and laws already in place. On the other hand, concerning residence permits, more modifications have been introduced which aim to restrict the conditions under which both temporary and permanent (10-year) permits are issued and they are becoming increasingly difficult to obtain. Moreover, it is now possible to withdraw the permanent residence permit of a polygamous foreigner who did not declare his situation at the time of issue. This measure has led to numerous contradictory debates on the subject of polygamy.

The conditions under which immigrants may bring in other family members to join them are becoming more restrictive and have a dissuasive effect. To the existing requirements (such as having sufficient resources to support the family and suitable living accommodation) have been added new elements, such as requiring the approval of the mayor in the *commune* of residence. This opens up the possibility for arbitrary decisions (the elected representatives on the far right will make the most of such provisions), the obligation of a minimum period of residence on the part of the foreign applicant and, in the case of a polygamous family, limiting the family members who can join the immigrant to one spouse and the children of this same spouse.

As COSTA-LASCOUX (1993) points out, the essence of the restrictive policy of the Pasqua law resides in the measures concerning the bringing together of families. Coupled with the clauses on the right of asylum, the dissuasive effect is further strengthened. In a period of high unemployment and a crisis in social housing, the administrative conditions are strengthened to create obstacles which are difficult to overcome.

The 1990s also marked a turning point in the policy on asylum insofar as it became a party to the treatment of the immigration issue.[6] Formerly clearly separated from the immigration problem, asylum policy has increasingly become one of the elements in immigration policy. Asylum policy was strongly marked by the context of the cold war but since the implosion of the Soviet bloc, the political and geopolitical challenges of asylum policy have disappeared for western states (LEGOUX, 2002a). The treatment of political asylum has conformed to the line of immigration. The right of asylum has become limited. Asylum seekers are suspected of being economic migrants and of using the procedure to circumvent border closures for economic immigration. New measures have been planned to allow for the refusal of permission to stay, but above all asylum seekers have to provide very specific proof of individual persecution —not just collective persecution. Those who flee their country because they consider themselves persecuted for their political, religious or ethnic convictions, but who have not been personally and directly implicated (for example through imprisonment or violence to the person), may be refused entry and have to leave the territory within one month. Indeed, the rejection rate for asylum requests increased noticeably between 1990 and 2001, with 83 % of requests turned down. The implementation of the right of asylum in France has evolved towards a restrictive interpretation of the Geneva Convention, notably on the fact that persecutions carried out by agents operating

---

[6] The colloquium *"la place de l'asile politique dans l'immigration"* (The place of political asylum in immigration) (Poitiers 4-5 February, 2000), the wording of which is revealing, dealt with this issue at length. The proceedings are to be published in 2003.

outside the parameters of any state control are beyond the bounds of the Convention. An effect of this in France has been to refuse refugee status to Algerian intellectuals who had fled their country because they were under threat from Islamic terrorists. In France, as in other European countries, there has been a passage from the "right to leave" to the "right to stay in one's country", in the words of LEGOUX (2002b). A preoccupation of asylum countries which would be very noble if it was not hidden behind the preoccupation of limiting the numbers of asylum seekers coming to the country. The current crisis in asylum policy in France, as in other European countries, has resulted in the obstruction of procedures; a noticeable lengthening of procedures; an extremely high refusal rate and the establishment of sub-statutes for refugees which maintain people in forms of "institutional illegality" (LEGOUX, 2002a). This situation has given rise to phenomena such as the Sangatte refugee camp where almost 40,000 asylum seekers passed in transit wishing to settle in Britain. The way in which the problematical situation at Sangatte was resolved is a good illustration of this evolution, since the issue of refugees and asylum seekers was treated as an immigration problem, without taking into account the political protection of the asylum seekers, or if so, only in a subsidiary fashion.

The Pasqua laws gave rise to numerous objections when they were promulgated but we are forced to note that they have undergone no fundamental modifications by subsequent governments. Some polemic minds even asserted that the "Chevènement laws", named after the Minister of the Interior in the Socialist government which followed, simply modified them slightly while keeping to the same original spirit.

2000 and the resumption of labour immigration

In October 2000, the Paris Chamber of Commerce and Industry announced that it lacked 200,000 workers to meet the need for labour in the construction, catering and clothing sectors in the Paris region. It suggested that the shortage could be solved by resuming immigration. In contrast with the preceding years when, as in other European countries, there was talk of the lack of skilled and highly skilled labour in different sectors (especially computing), this concerned *unskilled* labour. Since then, people have talked more and more openly about the resumption of immigration, a subject which was still taboo in the late 1990s, but which now seems to be acknowledged, if not by public opinion at least by the political class, with the obvious exception of the far right. The target of "zero immigration" has now been abandoned.

The right-wing Minister of the Interior N. Sarkozy, in a television programme broadcast in December 2002, judged it to be unrealistic, just as prime minister J.P. Raffarin has done in several declarations.

In October 2002, J.P. Raffarin presented his immigration policy at the re-election of the "Haut Conseil à l'Intégration". The choice of venue was clearly symbolic. He came down against the right of foreigners to vote and took a stance in line with French tradition: maintaining the national character of citizenship (for non-EU citizens), but encouraging the acquisition of French nationality and with it the right to vote: "Let us not open the door to the right to vote for foreigners and close the door giving access to nationality. That would go against our tradition [...] There are currently 100,000 naturalisations per year in France. This figure shows that naturalisation is a real possibility in our country." According to his declarations, his policy is to be organised in three main themes: a policy of accepted immigration; a project of renewed integration and a reworked campaign against discrimination. *Le Monde* of 24 October 2002 summed up the main points of the policy thus:

> The government's plan aims to develop a positive immigration in France. According to Raffarin: "necessary immigration control" will result in a reform of the asylum procedure, setting up statistical analyses needed for a "detailed assessment of the situation" and the efficient organisation of the policy "to send people home, whether on a forced or voluntary basis." He added: "Immigrants who are accepted and welcomed on arrival will spare us distressing immigration problems in the future that we have experienced before."
>
> Conversely, the reception of legal immigrants is a "national question". The prime minister continued: "It concerns taking in with dignity the 100,000 legal immigrants who arrive in our country each year." The reception contract planned by the government will offer these immigrants opportunities for language training, guidance on vocational training and access to state controlled employment. In exchange, the candidates will have to take on civic commitments. He stressed: " A public policy of integration has first and foremost a political objective to ensure that children of immigrants living in our country all have the same rights and duties."
>
> The third pillar in the integration policy aims to campaign effectively against discrimination. Mr. Raffarin hammered out: "Several generations of young people 'born of immigrants' have full French citizenship —which some people still seem to find difficult to grasp."

This policy can be interpreted as an incentive for immigration while maintaining strict entry controls as well as a policy of integration based on the principle of incorporating foreigners in the nation and relying on a campaign against discrimination. All things considered, the policy is in line with French tradition as to the relationship of the nation with foreigners: they are destined to become French nationals. However, the policy also raises serious questions about immigration control. How will the policy of sending people back be carried out —especially when it must be done by force? And in particular: how will the reform of the right of asylum take shape, since it is not the situation in the asylum seekers' country of origin that predominates, but the immigration situation in the country of arrival?

Conclusion

Over the long term, there has been much continuity in the principles at the basis of France's immigration policy coupled with much fluctuation in its implementation. The short period of the last twenty years is a good illustration of this continuity and fluctuation. The principles have remained the same: labour immigration to boost the population and as a consequence, integration in the nation. However, in practice, this has moved from a period when borders were closed to labour immigration while immigration to bring family members together increased —the attempt to limit this in the 1990s had little effect as the figures show— to an open resumption of labour immigration policies.

However, it is not certain that this immigration policy will maintain its principles for much longer because of two phenomena: European integration and the new forms of international migration. The harmonisation of immigration policies required by European integration are inevitably affected by the founding principles of the member nations as concerns the relations between individuals and the nation as a community. And these vary significantly from one European country to another. Transformations are appearing in Germany in particular where the nationality code has recently been substantially modified in its form and bases. Unless French national principles are transposed on a European scale, they will probably undergo significant changes. Furthermore, these principles are no longer suited to the pattern of international migrations today. As several works have shown (CHAREF, 1999; DORAÏ/HILY/MA MUNG, 1998a, 1998b; MA MUNG 1996; PERALDI, 2001; TAPIA, 1996; TARRIUS, 2002), attachments to nation roots have become more elastic because of the growth in migratory movement and peoples' mobility. Specific allegiances to the country of settlement or the country of origin —formalised by the principle of mono-belonging in the nation-state— have multiplied and interwoven, helped by the increase in immigration.

Immigrants are now increasingly demanding multiple belonging, not being *either* from here *or* over there, but from here *and* over there (TARRIUS/MISSAOUI, 1995). Integration can no longer aim at incorporation into the nation French-style, or no more than —in the British and American fashion— incorporation into communities in multicultural societies which is the other face of the principle of mono-belonging at the base of stato-national societies. The forms of international migration invite us to rethink our relations with the foreigner, otherness and exteriority: in other words, with the world.

References

CHAREF, M. (1999): *La circulation migratoire marocaine un pont entre deux rives*. Edition Sud Contact, Rabat.

COSTA-LASCOUX, J. (1993): "Continuité ou rupture dans la politique française de l'immigration: les lois de 1993." In: *Revue européenne des migrations internationales,* 9(3), pp. 233-261.

COSTA-LASCOUX, J.; WEIL, P. (1992): *Logiques d'Etats et immigrations*. Kimé, Paris.

DORAÏ, K.; HILY, M.-A.; MA MUNG, E. (1998a): "Bilan des travaux sur la circulation migratoire. Rapport final pour le Ministère de la Solidarité et de l'Emploi, Direction de la Population et des Migrations (DPM)" MIGRINTER, CNRS - Université de Poitiers.

DORAÏ, K.; HILY, M.-A.; MA MUNG, E. (1998b): "La circulation migratoire." *Migrations études,* 24, pp. 3-19.

GAEREMYNCK, J. (2002): "De l'immigration à l'intégration." *Cahiers français,* 307, pp. 66-76.

LACROIX, T. (2002): "La politique migratoire de la France: l'usage politique de l'altérité au sevice de la nation." In: *Quand l'altérité se fait en-jeux*, ed. Ludovic Joyeux. Paris: L'Harmattan. pp. 23-56.

LEGOUX, L. (2002a): "La crise de l'asile en France: des droits de l'Homme à la raison d'Etat." In: *Immigration, marché du travail, intégration*, ed. François Héran. Paris: La Documentation Française. pp. 273-284.

LEGOUX, L. (2002b): "Vers une redéfinition du droit d'asile." *Cahiers français,* 307, pp. 77-86.

MA MUNG, E. (ed.) (1996): *Mobilités et investissements des émigrés: Maroc, Tunisie, Turquie, Sénégal.* L'Harmattan, Paris.

MARIE, C. V. (2002): "Les politiques européennes de gestion des flux: contrôle et restrictions." *Cahiers français,* 307, pp. 57-65.

PERALDI, M. (ed.) (2001): *Cabas et containers: activités marchandes informelles et réseaux migrants transfrontaliers.* Maisonneuve et Larose, Paris.

SCHNAPPER, D. (1994): *La communauté des citoyens: sur l'idée moderne de nation*. Gallimard, Paris.

SIMON, G. (1995): *Géodynamique des migrations internationales dans le monde* (1re éd. ed). Presses universitaires de France, Paris.

TAPIA, S. DE, (1996): "La circulation migratoire dans les diasporas ouvrières de la Méditerranée. Turquie Maroc. Rapport final d'une recherche pour le Ministère de l'éducation nationale et de la culture" MIGRINTER, CNRS - Université de Poitiers.

TARRIUS, A. (2001): "Au-delà des États-nations: des sociétés de migrants." *Revue européenne des migrations internationales,* 17(2), pp. 37-62.

TARRIUS, A. (2002): *La mondialisation par le bas, les nouveaux nomades de l'économie souterraine*. Balland, Paris.

TARRIUS, A.; MISSAOUI, L. (1995): *Arabes de France dans l'économie mondiale souterraine*. Ed. de l'Aube, Paris.

VIET, V. (1998): *La France immigrée, construction d'une politique, 1914-1997.* Fayard, Paris.

Germany - still a reluctant country of immigration?

Wolfgang Bosswick

Introduction

At the beginning of the 1990s, the American scholar Phil Martin characterised Germany as being a "reluctant country of immigration" (MARTIN, 1993). This characterisation encompasses two aspects: firstly, that Germany had become a de-facto country of immigration, a fact which was fiercely ignored by official policy at this time, and secondly, that German politics refused to deal with the consequences of being a country of immigration. How much did this situation change with the profound developments in political discourse and legislative initiatives which took place during the last decade?

In 2001, the President of the German Bundestag, Wolfgang Thierse, stated that he is happy «that we do not anymore eschew the insight of being an immigration country» (THIERSE, 2001). This insight meanwhile seems to be shared by the overwhelming majority of the German public and politics, acknowledging the facts discussed in many publications and officially made public by the report of the Commission on Immigration in 2001: During the five decades after the foundation of the Federal Republic of Germany, a total of approximately 31 million people migrated into Germany, while 22 million left in this period; the net gain of 9 million people includes an annual net immigration average of 200,000 foreign citizens (ZUWANDERUNGSKOMMISSION, 2001, p. 15). At the end of the millennium, more than 40 % of the foreign population had been living in Germany for more than 15 years (LEDERER, 1997, p. 86). In many metropolitan areas, a large share of the population are foreign citizens (p. 100); even in cities which are not major centres of foreign immigration such as Köln, Frankfurt, Stuttgart or München, approximately one third of the population are first or second generation migrants (Bosswick 2000, 86). The fact of being a country of immigration today is not only a matter of statistics, but results in daily experience of profound and visible changes, especially in the metropolitan areas.

Nevertheless, politics has remained reluctant to deal with the consequences of this situation. The discourse on immigration stays within the national frame of reference, to a large extent ignoring the growing global interdependence and its impact on migration patterns and regimes. The discourse usually focused on small sectors of the overall migration situation such as the question of political asylum. It was only after the change of the German government to the Red-Green coalition in 1998 that core questions of immigration policy and citizenship became intensively discussed in public, and the German discourse on immigration reached a new level. Notwithstanding, the conflicts within the political spectrum on admission policy as well as on the concept and implementation of integration policies persist, and political action in the field of migration policy has to a large extent been paralysed by the blockage of the conservative CDU/CSU opposition.

Thus, the 1990 characterisation by Phil Martin still seems to remain valid, at least as long the conservative mainstream refuses to support the development of a modern migration policy. This paper gives an overview on the historical background of this situation and discusses current perspectives.

Immigration to Germany

Germany has a long-standing experience of immigration and labour migration. In the aftermath of the devastating depopulation of large areas during the Thirty Years War 1618-48, several emperors of the 17th and early 18th century intentionally settled migrants from abroad. A prominent example is the settlement of Huguenots from France and refugees from Switzerland and Austria by Friedrich Wilhelm, emperor of Brandenburg-Prussia. In the Edict of Potsdam (29 October 1685), the emperor guaranteed the same civil and economic rights to the settlers as held by the indigenous population (BIRNSTIEL/REINKE, 1990, p. 47). At that time, increasing the local population by settling immigrants was usually considered as being a benefit to resources and economic development, a strategy which had also been followed by Central and Eastern European emperors, resulting in a period of emigration from Germany to Russia during the late 18th century (CONZE, 1993). With the population increase during the 19th century, this emigration expanded to the USA, and contributed to an increasing demand for labour during the industrialisation of Germany in the late 19th century. In the mid-1890s, Prussia installed a strictly controlled rotation system for agricultural labourers from continental Europe, i.e. occupied Poland. Migrant labour was not only demanded by the agricultural sector, but included recruited settlement of ethnic Polish miners of Prussian nationality from the Upper Silesia coal mine area to the West German Ruhr and Emscher coal areas from 1870 onwards. The temporary labour migrant system for Polish workers in the agricultural sector and Italian workers in the construction sector contributed to an increase of foreign nationals in Germany from approximately 207,000 in 1871 to 1.26 million in 1910 (BADE, 1983, p. 29). During World War I, the rotation system practised mainly by the Prussian state was suspended, and the foreign labourers in the agricultural sector were forced to stay; their work force (approx. 374,000 at the end of World War I) was supplemented by forced labour by prisoners of war (approx. 900,000 at October 1918), both being an important factor for the war economy (BADE, 1983, p. 47). Following the restoration of the Polish state after World War I, a considerable return migration to Poland took place. During the Weimar Republic, the employment of foreign labour in 1922 became centrally controlled on the national level by the semi-official German Labour Centre (Deutsche Arbeiterzentrale), which determined the quota for seasonal labour from Central Europe in cooperation with the regional labour authorities. This pattern continued after the reform of the national labour administration in 1927 (Reichsanstalt für Arbeitsvermittlung und Arbeitslosenversicherung) which issued visas only if the labour demand could not be met by Germans. Consequently, the numbers of workers admitted closely followed economic developments during the Weimar Republic, decreasing to less than a quarter of the pre-war levels.

Other than the policy of German emperors before the 18th century who usually considered population growth and foreign settlers as a gain for their territories, the attitude of the labour migrant rotation system of the 19th and 20th century was best expressed in 1918 by the later president of the Weimar Republic's labour office.

> Without doubt, the German economy draws a high profit from the labour force of foreigners who are in their prime, while the country of origin had to raise the costs of rearing them to working life. But even more important is the expulsion or reduced recruitment of foreign labourers in times of economic depression... If employment of foreign labourers is unavoidable, it seems —with regard to social political questions— necessary to allocate them to the lowest sectors of the economy not requiring any education, and to employ them at

> lowest wages; thus, for the native labourers arises the remarkable advantage that their rise from ordinary low paid day-labourers' jobs to qualified and well-paid skilled workers' jobs will be facilitated (SYRUP, 1918, p. 297, quoted in TREIBEL, 1999, p. 120. Translation by the author).

Regardless of the general economic growth during the 1930s and the increased labour demand in Germany under the Nazi dictatorship, the employment of foreign labour remained on a very low level until 1939 (less than 500,000 in 1939), although agreements with Italy, Hungary, Poland, Czechoslovakia and Yugoslavia on hiring foreign labourers had been contracted (BADE, 1983, p. 53). But immediately after the German occupation of Poland in September 1939, Polish labourers for the agricultural sector were deported on a large scale (560,000 by May 1940, up to a total of 1.8 to 2 million by the end of the war). The deportation of forced labourers from all occupied territories and the forced labour of prisoners of war in Germany led to a peak of 8.5 million foreigners in 1944 (PROUDFOOT, 1957, p. 81), a figure not exceeded since then. In several sectors such as agriculture, mining and the chemical industry, the share of foreign labourers grew up to 40 % in 1944 (BADE, 1983, p. 56). This brutal forced labour system, even aiming at extermination for some groups such as Russian prisoners of war and concentration camp inmates ("Vernichtung durch Arbeit"), cannot be compared at all to forced labour during World War I and even less to the seasonal labourer system under Prussian rule. Nevertheless, it was implemented on the ground in agriculture, the construction sector and industry by farmers and regular civil employers who often actively hired forced labourers from the labour administration or the SS. With the exception of the depression during the 1920s and the national autonomy policy of the 1930s, in several sectors of the German economy there was a continuing structure of foreign labour employment which shifted increasingly to the German industrial sector by the massive use of forced labour in World War II. This continuity of employment of foreign labour in German industry and the construction sector was only interrupted during the chaotic situation after 1945: 43.7 million refugees and expelled ethnic Germans from Central Europe immigrated to the three Western Zones of Germany by 1949 (BADE, 1983, p. 59), when the post-war period began with the currency reform of 20 June 1948, and the foundation of the Federal Republic of Germany in 1949.

Immigration and migration policy in the Federal Republic of Germany

Until 1960, the first year of full employment of the labour force in Germany, a large share of the demand for labour could be met by returning German prisoners of war (4 million up to the end of 1950), German refugees from Central Europe (4.7 million) and migrants from the German Democratic Republic (1.8 million up to 1961, BADE, 1987, p. 60). Nevertheless there was regional demand in some sectors; the first Italian guest workers were employed in 1952 by South West German farmers regardless of an overall unemployment rate of 9.5 % (see HECKMANN, 1981, p. 149f).

In 1955 at the very beginning of the guest worker programme, an important decision was made when the government, the employers' associations and the unions agreed upon full integration of the labour migrants into the social security system (MEHRLÄNDER, 1980, p. 77ff). Since then, the German social security system does not differentiate between foreigners and German nationals. The guest worker programme responded to the increasing demand in construction and industry —partly due to the setting up of the German armed forces in 1956— and encompassed active recruitment of foreign workers by agreements with several European countries: 1955 Italy, 1960 Spain and Greece, and 1961 Turkey. These agreements were not only in the German interest; several sending countries intervened to increase the migrant numbers or to be included in the guest worker programme (STEINERT, 1995). After the erection of the Berlin Wall and the closure of the GDR border in 1961, further agreements with Morocco, Portugal, Tunisia and Yugoslavia were signed by 1968.

Until the halt on recruitment in 1973 in the context of the oil crisis, the number of employed foreign workers rose to 2.6 million, the most prominent groups being Turks (23 %), Yugoslavs (18 %) and Italians (16 %) (LEDERER, 1997, p. 52). This foreign work force compensated for demographic developments and the decreasing economic activity of natives (women, common prolongation of educational career). Although it led only to a minor increase in the total work force supply, it contributed considerably to the general economic growth (HECKMANN, 1981, p. 152ff). The employment of the guest workers has been understood as being temporary usually by both the German host society and the migrants. Although the "rotating ex- and import of each time 'young and fresh' guest workers" was officially intended (Hans Filbinger, President of Baden-Württemberg 1966, quoted by TRÄNHARDT, 1984, p. 123), other than for the seasonal migrant workers before World War I there was no enforcement of a rotation scheme. On the contrary, since the migrants were employed in unattractive sectors of industry (mining, construction, metals and textiles), employers were interested in keeping their trained workers. Nevertheless, the foreigners' law of 1965 which replaced the "Foreigners' Police Decree" of 1938 then still in force, placed the foreigner's stay within extensive discretion of the authorities (SANTEL/WEBER, 2000, p. 111).

By the early seventies, it was increasingly obvious that the rotation concept was not feasible; at the same time, the proportion of non-European migrants visible in public increased. With the 1973 halt on recruitment of non-EEC nationals in the context of the oil shock, the official rotation policy was replaced by a policy promoting voluntary repatriation. Since 1973, family reunion (spouses and children below the age of 16) has been the only possibility of immigration; in 1974, the high proportion of foreign families among the total births (20 %) was already being publicly discussed (HETTLAGE, 2001, p. 76). In an ambiguous policy with the official goals of stopping new recruitment, promoting voluntary return and integrating socially those who were unlikely to return (see HECKMANN, 1994, p. 161), in 1975 the government included resident foreign families in family allowance regulations, while at the same time, an interdiction on foreigners moving to several metropolitan areas was imposed until 1977. As an unintended side effect of the halt on recruitment, many foreigners preferred to stay since the option of return to Germany no longer existed. In 1978, the German parliament stated that problems of housing, medical services, schooling of migrant children and relations with the German population carried a risk of rising conflicts, and decided to establish the office of a "Commissioner for the Promotion of Integration of Foreign Employees and their Families", which was allocated to the Ministry of Labour and Social Affairs. In September 1979 the first commissioner, Heinz Kühn, former president of North Rhine-Westphalia, published a memorandum on the state of integration of foreign migrants which demanded an active integration policy for the immigrant population (GEIß, 2001, p. 128). The foundation of this office showed that the integration of migrants was officially recognised and defined as necessity (MAHNIG, 1998, p. 53). Nevertheless, the following two decades have been characterised by defensive and restrictive measures, while in the area of integration development has stagnated. In December 1983, a new law came into force which promoted voluntary return of migrants by financial support such as refund of the employees' share of pension fund payments in case of permanent return. About 250,000 migrants returned under this scheme, but the expectations of the government were not met: repatriation numbers were far below the intended figures, and it turned out that many of the returnees only accelerated their already planned return project in order to get the benefits of the programme (SANTEL, 2000, p. 112). After the programme's deadline, the repatriation figures dropped sharply compared to the level before 1983. While the intended result of the law had been very limited, its implicit message as "symbolic policy" both to the foreign population and the German public was crystal clear, thus counteracting the goal of social integration of settled migrants (MEIER-BRAUN, 1988, p. 69).

Although the halt on recruitment officially stopped demand driven immigration to Germany and the figure of employed foreign workers decreased from its peak of 2.6 million in 1973 to 1.6 million in 1984, approx. 3 million foreigners immigrated until 1980 via family reunion (LEDERER, 2001, p. 141). In addition to this mostly ignored family reunion, in the late seventies, a second side door for immigration became relevant: supply driven immigration via the asylum procedure according to article 16 (2) of the Basic Law. In 1980, asylum application figures peaked at 93,000, and the topic of asylum became prominent during the 1980 Baden-Württemberg election campaign and the national election campaign of 1981. Since then, the question of the right to asylum has been the focus of public discourse on immigration and of numerous legal initiatives and deterrent measures (BOSSWICK, 1997, p. 56f).

Faced with the settled guest workers and their families, during the eighties politicians and the majority of society realised that the population of foreign migrants in Germany was a long term fact which could not be dealt with only as a labour reserve or social problem. In addition to the structural integration of the migrants into the social security and welfare system, the large welfare organisations developed measures for social integration of the foreign migrant population. Religious welfare organisations (Catholic Caritas for Italian, Spanish and Croatian guest workers, Protestant Diakonie for Greeks and Yugoslavs) and the Arbeiterwohlfahrt stemming from the workers' movement (Turkish and North African migrants) were already offering counselling services for migrant workers during the sixties. During the eighties, these institutions faced increasing demand for broader social and educational services from the migrants' families. As a consequence, in 1984 the Federal Ministry for Labour and Social Affairs enacted a "Regulation for tasks, rules of operation and organisation for social counselling of foreign employees and their families" which set rules for social work with migrants and a guaranteed combined federal and state funding for the work of the three welfare organisations mentioned above. The traditional area of responsibility of the three welfare organisations according to ethnic origin was confirmed in the regulation (see BOSSWICK, 2001, p. 18).

The migrant population in Germany increasingly tried not only to cope with their precarious life situation but also to achieve a better social status, recognition and upward mobility. In intellectual circles, the former assimilative concept of integration was criticised and the idea of a multicultural society was —sometimes quite naively— discussed. Politics however moved increasingly towards a restrictive position. In the mid-eighties the Federal Minister of the Interior Friedrich Zimmermann (CSU) promoted a bill for a new foreigners' law which intended among other restrictive measures to lower the age limit for family reunification from the age of 16 to 6 years. This bill died when it was massively criticised by the churches, the welfare organisations and the labour unions which supported the resistance of Liselotte Funcke, the second Commissioner for Foreigners' Affairs (GEIß, 2001, p. 130). At the same time, public discourse became increasingly polarised by the dispute on Article 16 (2), the right to asylum. From 1984 onwards, asylum application figures rose again, and the question of asylum seekers framed by the pejorative term "Asylanten" (LINK, 1986, p. 55) was raised by the conservative parties as a main topic of several election campaigns. In the political discourse, it was asserted that economically motivated immigration was leading to an "abuse of the generous German right to asylum" by fraudulent asylum claims. As a consequence of growing internationalisation and air travel opportunities, asylum seekers increasingly came from non-European countries of origin (i.e. Sri Lanka, Iran and Lebanon, see LEDERER, 1997, p. 274). During the national election campaign 1986-87, the conservatives also claimed a serious threat to German national identity by multicultural foreign infiltration (see BOSSWICK, 2000, p. 46). During the same year, the number of violent attacks against asylum seekers and foreigners increased by 134 % to 117 cases (LEDERER, 1997, p. 167). The link between these xenophobic attacks and the heated public debate on asylum was quite obvious. Nevertheless, the government argued that the number of asylum seekers had to be reduced in order to reduce unrest within the German population and to combat this violence, thus legitimating the alleged causes for xenophobic attacks (BIELEFELD, 1993). At the end of the eighties, the discussion on integration of foreigners had been eclipsed in the political discourse by the predominant asylum issue; asylum seekers became the new bottom of the hierarchy of immigrants, while the presence of South European migrants in German society was meanwhile more or less accepted.

Notwithstanding considerable immigration via family reunion, asylum seekers and ethnic Germans from Poland and Romania during the eighties, the official position of the German government refused to develop an immigration policy; this position was explicitly stated by the former administrative regulations for the German naturalisation law: «The Federal Republic of Germany is not a country of immigration; it does not aim to increase intentionally its number of citizens by naturalisation» (Einbürgerungsrichtlinien 2.3, 7.3.1989, translation by the author). Although a large share of the migrant population had in fact settled permanently in Germany, many of them being already resident for more than two decades, naturalisation after a minimum stay of fifteen years was at the discretion of the authorities. This restrictive naturalisation law placed Germany after Ireland at the bottom of the list of naturalisations per foreigners in Europe during the decade between 1984 and 1994 (50 per 1000 foreigners), while in 1990, several rulings of high courts up to the Federal Constitutional Court denied foreigners the right to vote in local elections. Hammar coined the apt term *denizens* for this population with permanent residence status, but in Germany deprived of any political rights (HAMMAR, 1990). Until 1990, the strict *jus sanguinis* concept of German citizenship law remained in force. This dated back to 1913, when it was introduced to provide citizenship for descendants of Germans who had been permanently in the colonies, while excluding half-caste children of German colonial settlers (OBERNDÖRFER, 1989a, p. 7). This concept of an ethnic nation state, stemming from the German *Romantik* of the early 19th century in opposition to the French republican concept of nation during the occupation by Napoleon, had far reaching consequences: Germans in an ethnic sense, particularly German minorities in several Eastern and central European states, were entitled to German citizenship when migrating to Germany, while inclusion of migrants by naturalisation into a nation which understands itself as a community of descent and culture was denied or at least defined as an *exception to the rule* (HECKMANN, 2001, p. 16). Although the conservative mainstream still subscribed to the ethnic nation state concept and its myths, after the Nazi experience and the development of the Federal Republic it was replaced to a large extent by new concepts. The historian Mommsen described this situation in 1990 as follows:

> A new kind of national consciousness has developed in the Federal Republic. It is no longer under the influence of political and legal traditions of imperial Germany. This new national consciousness relates primarily to economic success and to the democratic and

> liberal political system. It is no longer in conflict with the political cultures of Western Europe and the U.S.A, as has been the case for so many years (MOMMSEN, 1990, p. 272).

However, the question of immigration, especially the problem of high numbers of asylum applications up to 1993, became a stressful test for this new concept of the German nation as well as for civil society. The fall of the iron curtain and German reunification eliminated a major migration barrier while at the same time, the civil war in Yugoslavia generated massive refugee movements which were hosted predominantly by Germany and Austria. These refugee migration movements culminated in 1992 at a peak of 438,000 applications, while the immigration of ethnic Germans —since 1990 predominantly stemming from the states of the former Soviet Union— peaked in 1990 at 397,000 immigrants. During 1992, reception facilities all over Germany had been stretched to their limits, and gymnasiums and schools had to be used for initial accommodation. While the immigration of ethnic Germans was still fully supported by the conservative government, the political conflict on asylum escalated to the end of 1992. The respective article 16 (2) of the German constitution *—politically persecuted persons enjoy the right to asylum—* was a prominent norm out of a republican tradition in the German Basic Law of 1948. Based on the experiences of German exiles fleeing the Nazi dictatorship, the article limited the sovereign nation state's control upon its borders; an asylum seeker had the right to enter the territory and to have his claim judged. For the liberal and left mainstream in Germany, this constitutional article was an important element of the German Federal Republic after the totalitarian Nazi state. For the conservative mainstream, the right to asylum was an unacceptable limitation of the nation state's right to control its border. These two positions had already clashed during the formulation of the Basic Law article in 1948, and the conflict continued until 1992 at varying intensity; a series of restrictive measures by the government and the administration since the seventies tried to limit the access to asylum while jurisdiction until the late seventies increasingly realised this institutional norm in their rulings (see BOSSWICK, 1997). Since 1987, the conservative government argued that the rising numbers of asylum seekers could only be stopped by an amendment to the constitution, and that the refusal of the opposition to vote for the required two-thirds parliamentary majority hindered the government from solving this serious problem. In face of the sharply rising application figures at the beginning of the nineties, the government and the media adopted an image of emergency. This situation contributed to a belief among some of the public that the people themselves had to take action, a development which Leggewie described as "violent plebejan activism" (LEGGEWIE, 1992, p. 59). From reunification in October 1990 until mid-1993, more than 5,000 violent crimes against foreigners were committed, resulting in at least 49 deaths. Facing increased political pressure within its own ranks from local communities which had to shelter incoming migrants, and in order to keep the asylum issue out of the headlines in the upcoming national election campaign, the Social Democratic Party agreed in December 1992 to a compromise for an amendment of article 16. Among other regulations, the right to asylum became restricted by the safe third country rule, the immigration of ethnic Germans became limited to 225,000 annually, and the citizenship law was amended. The numbers of asylum applications dropped sharply in 1993, stabilising since then at the levels of 1980; although this was widely perceived as impact of the constitutional amendment, it is likely that the practical implementation of acceleration measures in April 1993 and bilateral repatriation agreements for asylum seekers with several countries of transit or origin caused the decrease (BOSSWICK, 1997, p. 67). Although access to the asylum procedure was possible legally only via an airport (approx. 17,500 applications to end of 1999), in practice the vast majority of the 811,000 asylum seekers after the amendment until end of 1999 entered illegally and concealed their entry path, thus rendering the safe third country rule of the amendment quite ineffective. A consequence of this rule together with intensified border control has been an increasing market for professional smugglers which became necessary for crossing the German border. This development also contributed to a certain shift of the asylum discourse from the context of illegitimacy (fraudulent asylum seekers) to illegality, although illegal entry for asylum purposes is not persecuted yet.

The level of xenophobic attacks however remained high compared to the figures before the asylum debate escalated in 1990. In 1992, an arsonist attack on the home of a Turkish family in Solingen, killing the father and two children, finally awakened the German public. In response to a series of such attacks, a grass root initiative in Munich organised a large demonstration of approximately 400,000 people on 6 December 1992. While numerous earlier attacks against asylum seekers did not trigger major public worries and had been combated by the authorities with a certain restraint, the expansion of the attacks onto the Turkish guest worker minority raised the awareness that public order was in danger; a series of large demonstrations against right wing xenophobic violence took place in 1993.

With regard to the labour migrants, in January 1991 the conservative government enacted a new foreigners' law, replacing the 1965 regulations. The new law regulated family reunion and the legal status of immigrants under the family reunion scheme, replacing various Länder regulations and the hitherto wide discretion of the authorities. Further it guaranteed a return to Germany for foreigners with permanent residence status. Although the new law was heavily criticised for its restrictive tendency in many aspects (e.g. HUBER, 1992), it made a first breakthrough regarding German naturalisation law. For the first time, foreigners resident for fifteen years obtained a right to naturalisation which was not at the discretion of the foreigners' authorities (§§85, 86 AuslG 90), and naturalisation was made easier for foreigners aged 16 to 23 if they had stayed in Germany continuously for eight years. This introduction of *jus domicilii* into German citizenship legislation officially acknowledged the fact of long-term resident immigrant minorities, although the right was limited by a 1995 deadline. As part of the asylum compromise of 1992, the opposition succeeded in lifting this limitation and in changing the eased naturalisation for adolescents to a right to naturalise. These amendments for the first time introduced elements of the citizenship regulations of "classical" countries of immigration, although under quite restrictive conditions. Naturalisation was understood by the government as a *final step of a successful integration process*, a concept upheld by the conservative mainstream till today.

At the beginning of the nineties, two new schemes for immigration were introduced which raised little interest in public, but ended the policy of non-immigration adopted since 1973. The first door was opened by the last, already democratically elected government of the GDR in 1990 enacting a law which allowed immigration of Jewish persons from the former Soviet Union by a facilitated procedure. After the reunification in October 1990, the reunified Germany continued this practice. Although numbers have been comparatively low (120,515 by the end of 1999), this immigration had a large impact on the small Jewish communities in Germany which had serious difficulties with the task of integrating their new members.

More significant in ending the halt on recruitment, was the "Anwerbestoppausnahmeverordnung" (decree on exceptions from the halt on recruitment) enacted in 1990. It defined groups of labour migrants who are admitted. The most relevant groups are the "Werkvertragsarbeitnehmer" (contract labourers) and "Saisonarbeitnehmer" (seasonal labourers). Contract labourers are employees of foreign enterprises which are subcontractors of German enterprises, usually in the construction industry. These contract labourers may stay a maximum of three years; according to the labour market situation, each year quotas are determined by the Ministry of Labour and Social Affairs. Bilateral agreements on this programme had been concluded with several Central and South East European countries. Although contract labour had been possible since 1982 on a small scale of 10,000 to 20,000 workers, their number grew only during the nineties to a maximum of 95,000 in 1992. This programme was heavily criticised since these contract labourers —unlike the guest workers since 1955 and all other admitted groups of the nineties— were not integrated into the German social security system, but were subject to the social security regulations of their country of origin; the unions considered it as a pilot programme for lowering social standards. During the following years, the quota was no longer exhausted (LEDERER, 1997, p. 249).

Since 1991, seasonal labourers have been admitted for a maximum of three months per year, if the labour demand in certain sectors (farming, forestry, gastronomy) cannot be filled by Germans or EU citizens. Their numbers varied between 130,000 (1991) and 221,000 (1996).

The "Anwerbestopausnahmeverordnung" did not contribute significantly to the migrant population in Germany, although it regularised demand-driven immigration for the first time again since 1973. Notwithstanding the small numbers of admitted migrants, each of the nine doors for immigration (EU internal migrants, spouses and children of permanently resident foreigners, ethnic Germans, Jewish immigrants from CIS countries, asylum seekers and Geneva Convention refugees, temporary protection refugees, new guest workers (contract labourers etc.), foreign students and immigrating German nationals) is accompanied to a varying degree by irregular movements or employment. The supply-driven asylum system in particular became increasingly linked to illegal migration and human smuggling, or disappearance into illegality after an unsuccessful asylum claim. Out of the regular immigration, the family reunion scheme is the only one whose size can be estimated, since no central statistics are available. A calculation of the upper limit for family reunion immigration during the nineties, results in an annual average of 400,000 persons (LEDERER, 2001, p. 154). Although the unknown real numbers are lower than these upper limits, family reunion immigration is likely to be the most significant scheme, clearly exceeding all other immigration sources during the nineties.

In general, German policy on foreigners continued its restrictive course during the nineties, notably with an amendment to the foreigners' law in 1997 which invented visa requirements for foreign children coming unaccompanied from Turkey, former Yugoslavia, Morocco and Tunisia, and the requirement of an application for residence permit for already resident foreign children of parents from these states. The asylum and temporary protection regulations in particular became extremely restrictive, pushing the vast majority of civil war refugees from the Balkans into a "voluntary" return (BOSSWICK, 2000, p. 50).

On the other side, the social integration of resident labour migrants and the second generation was actively promoted by numerous institutions, namely the large publicly funded welfare organisations, the local communities and the local labour administrations (integration measures into the labour market). During the nineties, these programmes expanded to provide a broad scope of services for migrants such as community related social work, social educational counselling for migrant families and young migrants, health care, support for entry into the labour market, language acquisition, drug addict counselling, probation support for adolescent criminal offenders, counselling for schooling and educational career as well as for vocational training etc. In most cases, these services were not explicitly directed towards migrants, but in fact have a large share of resident migrant population among their clients. These programmes at the local level are an important contribution to the integration of the migrant population and the prevention of conflicts. An analysis of their extent shows that a minimum of 70 million Euro annual expenses (1999/2000) was spent on measures explicitly directed to the foreign migrant population and implemented by the large welfare organisations; the real efforts are considerable higher since this calculation could not include measures funded by the local communities and measures implemented by other organisations. The regulations for integration measures imposed a strict separation of the various immigrant groups; ethnic Germans received a broad range of services, while access for asylum seekers and de-facto refugees was heavily restricted. This traditional segmentation of federal and state funding schemes for integration measures according to the target groups ethnic German immigrants, foreign immigrants and refugees became permeable at the end of the decade; in practice, this strict separation was often circumvented by local institutions since it increasingly did not meet the practical requirements: The services became demanded by residents with a migratory background regardless of their legal status. The total volume spent by the welfare organisations alone for specific migrant integration measures only amounts to a minimum of more than 158 million Euro per year (BOSSWICK, 2001, p. 46).

These decentralised integration activities by welfare NGOs and local communities were widely ignored in the political discourse. Nevertheless, as a result of these massive efforts for the integration of migrants during the nineties, the state of social integration especially of the second generation of migrant youth is quite good compared to other European countries. As regards entry into the labour market, the German practice is comparatively successful, while legal and perceptional integration falls behind other European countries due to the restrictive citizenship practice (HECKMANN *et al.*, 2001, p. 16).

With the change in government in 1998, two decades of stagnation in official German migration and integration policy guided by the paradigm «Germany is not a country of immigration» seemed to be ended. As one of the first activities of the Social Democrat/Green coalition, the citizenship law was amended in May 1999, coming into force on 1 January 2000. The governing coalition introduced *jus soli* for children born to foreigners in Germany, who since 2000 automatically become German citizens if one parent has been resident for eight years and has residence right (Aufenthaltsberechtigung) or unlimited residence permit for at least three years. Children fulfilling these requirements and born in Germany since 1990 are entitled to naturalisation upon application. The residence time requirement of the *jus domicilii* regulation of 1992 was also reduced; after eight years of legal residence, foreigners are entitled to citizenship if they hold a residence permit, have no criminal record, are able to afford the costs of living for themselves and their family without social welfare benefits and have a sufficient command of German. Originally, dual citizenship should have been accepted as a rule for the first and second generation. This intended regulation was used by the conservative CDU in the 1999 election campaign of Hesse, starting a massive campaign against dual citizenship. This campaign, which raised a xenophobic mood in the population, contributed to the narrow success of the conservative CDU coalition with the liberals, consequently ending the previous Social Democratic/Green majority in the second chamber, the Bundesrat. Since the amendment had to pass this chamber, the dual citizenship regulation had to be taken out of the bill, resulting in an obligation for *jus soli* children to choose either German citizenship or the citizenship of their parents between the ages 18 to 23. The legal consequences of this rule are still unclear. Due to the compromise, naturalisations according to the *jus domicilii* regulation also excluded dual citizenship except in cases of hardship; in practice however, dual citizenship was accepted in about two thirds of the 143,267 naturalisations in 1999 (RÜHL/LEDERER, 2001, p. 80). This reform of the German citizenship law introduced the concept of *naturalisation as an important step supporting the integration process* into official policy and finally ended a situation in which the numbers of naturalisations during the first half of the nineties were exceeded by the number of foreign children born in Germany by more than 80 %, thus resulting in a foreign population which would grow even at zero net immigration levels.

The quest for a new immigration act

In response to increased demand for foreign specialists in the IT industry, in March 2000 the German chancellor announced the introduction of a so-called «Green Card» for the recruitment of foreign information technology experts. Although the proposed regulation was more like the US H1-B visa regulations and not comparable at all with the US Green Card, and although the new regulation did not exceed substantially the exceptions to the halt on recruitment in force since 1991, this proposal had a massive, presumably unintended side effect. Public discourse on immigration made a profound turn from the restrictive tendency and perception of immigration as a burden towards a connotation of immigration as an important resource in global competition. This unexpected development left the conservative mainstream in a quite precarious situation, requiring several substantial corrections in their hitherto very restrictive position, especially due to harsh criticism from industry which repeatedly stated the urgency of liberal immigration regulations. Under these circumstances, the Ministry of the Interior moved from former restraint to promoting a general reform of the German immigration and foreigners legislation and installed an independent commission on immigration (politicians, representatives of important institutions such as churches, unions, industry associations and experts) with the task of analysing the current situation in the field of migration and integration of migrants. The commission was to develop proposals for a general reform of the legal and institutional framework. Under the presidency of the former president of the parliament, Rita Süssmuth (CDU), the commission presented their results on 2001 July 4 in a comprehensive and well founded report (ZUWANDERUNGSKOMMISSION, 2001). In this report, the commission constituted a historic change in Germany's policies toward immigrants and foreign residents, concluding that immigration has become a necessity for economic as well as demographic reasons. For regulating migration inflows, the commission recommended a points system similar to the Canadian model, where points are granted according to migrants' age, language skills, qualification and other criteria; further proposals were a reform of the asylum system and coordinated integration measures for migrants.

Shortly after the presentation of the commission's report, the Ministry of the Interior Otto Schily presented a proposal for a new immigration and foreigners legislation. This proposal followed in some areas the commission's report and intended a complete restructuring of the foreigners' law (only two residence permit statuses instead of currently seven), but fell behind in several areas (especially in the field of asylum and the age limit for the immigration of children within the family reunion scheme). By such concessions to the conservative opposition, the government tried to gain the necessary support in the second chamber of the Länder which has to pass such legislation. Although a considerable part of the CDU opposition party was inclined to support the compromise bill which was passed by parliament on 1 March 2002, the conservative joint CDU/CSU opposition, ruled by the Bavarian prime minister Stoiber (CSU), the candidate for chancellor in federal elections of September 2002, decided to reject the law in the Bundesrat. Since the vote of the Länder governed by the opposition and by coalition governments with CDU participation constituted half of the votes, the federal government lacked the required one tie-breaking vote for passing and enacting the bill. In a unique clash in the Länder chamber after weeks of heated political debate, the SPD Prime Minister of Brandenburg (SPD/CDU coalition) broke the coalition agreement by overruling the vote of his Ministry of Interior (CDU). This act raised hitherto unsolved constitutional questions about procedure. These questions had been summarised precisely by the German President Johannes Rau in his official statement about his decision to sign the law on 20 June 2002 (RAU, 2002). The opposition immediately announced a constitutional plea at the Federal Constitutional Court, but did not file a plea for immediate action, preferring to avoid the high risk of a rejection during the federal election campaign. Candidate Stoiber's strategy has been to reserve the immigration issue as a campaign joker while primarily focusing on the economic and labour market situation. Thus, the dispute on immigration played a minor role during the campaign until the last week before election day. In the public and the media nevertheless, raising this issue was primarily considered as a last minute attempt of campaigning.

After the narrow success of the governing Red/Green coalition, the immigration act was scheduled to become law on 1 January 2003, but several Länder governed by a CDU or CSU majority (Baden-Württemberg, Bayern, Hessen, Saarland, Sachsen and Thüringen) filed a plea against the law in the Federal Constitutional Court, which finally decided to annul the immigration act due to formal faults in the voting procedure of the Bundesrat (decision of 18 December 2002, Az. 2 BvF 1/02).

The bill for an immigration act was intended to replace the Foreigners' Law (Ausländergesetz) of 1991 which had very complicated regulations by a new "law on stay, work and integration of foreigners" (Gesetz über den Aufenthalt, die Erwerbstätigkeit und die Integration von Ausländern im Bundesgebiet). The law was to reduce the hitherto seven different stay and residence permits to two permits, one for temporary residence and one for settlement. For the first time in Germany's legislative history, regulations for immigration, labour market access, the stay of foreigners and the integration of resident migrants would have been combined to an integrated legislative concept, differentiating according to the purpose of residence only. The bill intended a simplification of the hitherto parallel application process for a residence permit at the foreigners' authorities and a work permit at the labour authorities with its mutual interdependencies and bureaucratic overhead by a single procedure at the local foreigners' authorities ("one stop government"). For highly qualified personnel and specialists, an immediate settlement permit was intended, also covering core family members. Provisions were made for periods of labour market shortages, in which labour immigration based on a combined quota and point system (comparable to the Canadian regulations) was planned. With regard to refugees, the bill no longer referred to the right to asylum which carries a long history of political controversies, but regulated residence permits for political asylees as well as other refugees (Geneva Convention, de-facto refugees) under the common heading "Humanitarian Reasons", thus abolishing the discrimination against refugees who do not meet the narrow criteria for political asylum (BOSSWICK, 2000, p. 46). A completely new feature of the law was the inclusion of integration measures. For all newcomers, the federal state was supposed to provide basic language courses (300 hours) and basic orientation courses (30 hours). Further integration measures were up to the Länder, being regulated by a national legal frame.

Although the planned immigration act was intended to streamline the regulations for immigration and settlement, abolishing in many areas the restrictive regulations of the former legislation, it also had some very restrictive elements. Not all had been introduced by negotiations with the conservative opposition during 2001, such as the lowering of the regular age limit for immigration of children under the family reunification scheme from 16 to 12 years. The bill for the 2003 immigration act stated explicitly that its general aim is steering and limitation of immigration as well as the promotion of integration.

Conclusion

Germany —still a reluctant country of immigration? With regard to many sectors of German society, this characterisation has ceased to fit. Most important collective actors of German society —the employers' associations, the unions, both large churches, the majority of the political parties including the liberals— supported the initiative for a reform of migration and integration policy by the proposed new immigration act. Due to the tie in the second chamber, the conservative opposition was able to block this initiative. Nevertheless, in many areas considerable progress had been made in adapting the political, legal and administrative structure to the fact of an immigration situation. The changes in citizenship law especially are highly relevant for the future integration of resident foreign migrants.

Even the conservative opposition subscribed to the necessity of dealing with the consequences of immigration and supports the setting up of a coordinated integration programme for migrants. This current consensus on the necessity of an integration policy, however, covers up a hitherto obscured conflict upon some core questions: Integration into what, and how? This relates to the self-image of German society and related conflicts within the German political spectrum as well as to the resulting conception of «integration».

One can expect that within the European unification process which increasingly shifts the decisions on migration and integration policy from the national to the European level (TOMEI, 2001), further major changes to German society and its relation to immigrant minorities will take place. This process carries serious risks. Of course, migration processes raise practical problems such as the demand for resources and socio-economic conflicts. Both were evident during the precarious situation of German reunification and contributed to the escalation of the conflict. But also important is another aspect: The dispute within German society on the question of asylum in the context of the reunification process can also be interpreted as an internal conflict on the self-understanding and self-identification of German society. Migration processes always require a process of adjustment by the receiving population and often a restructuring of the consensus and the self-understanding of the society. This process is not easy and is often projected onto the migrants who are the *strangers*, the "*other*", reflecting conflict lines within the receiving society. European societies should be aware that the growing together within Europe might be also a risky process and that politicians have a special responsibility to deal appropriately with migration processes and their political consequences.

References

BADE, K. J. (1983): *Vom Auswanderungsland zum Einwanderungsland? Deutschland 1880-1980.* Berlin.

BIELEFELD, U. (1993): "Die institutionalisierte Phobie." In: Otto, Hans-Uwe / Merten, Roland (eds.): *Rechtsradikale Gewalt im vereinigten Deutschland.* Bonn, 34-42.

BIRNSTIEL, E.; / REINKE, A. (1990): "Hugenotten in Berlin." In: Jersch-Wenzel, Stefi and John, Barbara (eds.): *Von Zuwanderern un Einheimischen. Hugenotten, Juden, Böhmen, Polen in Berlin.* Berlin, 13-153.

BOSSWICK, W. (1997): "Asylum policy in Germany." In: Muus, Philip (ed.), *Exclusion and inclusion of refugees in contemporary Europe*. Utrecht, 53-77.

BOSSWICK, W. (2000): "Multiculturalism and cities in Europe: Nürnberg, Germany." In: Turton, D. / González, J. (eds.), *Ethnic Diversity in Europe: Challenges to the Nation State*, Bilbao, 83-102.

BOSSWICK, W. (2000): "Development of asylum policy in Germany." In: *Journal of Refugee Studies*, 13 (1), pp. 43-60.

BOSSWICK, W.; BRONNENMEYER, V. (2001): *Integrationsmaßnahmen der Wohlfahrtsverbände.* Expert opinion study for the Unabhängige Kommission "Zuwanderung", Bundesministerium des Inneren, Berlin.

CONZE, W. (1993): *Ostmitteleuropa. Von der Spätantike bis zum 18. Jahrhundert*. München.

GEIß, B. (2001): "Die Ausländerbeauftragten der Bundesregierung in der ausländerpolitischen Diskussion." In: Wunderlich, Tanja / Currle, Edda (eds.): *Deutschland - ein Einwanderungsland? Rückblick, Bilanz und neue Fragen*. Stuttgart, 127-140.

HAMMAR, T. (1990): *Democracy and the nation-state: Aliens, denizens and citizens in a world of international migration.* Avebury.

HECKMANN, F. (1981): *Die Bundesrepublik - ein Einwanderungsland? Zur Soziologie der Gastarbeiterbevölkerung als Einwandererminorität.* Stuttgart.

HECKMANN, F. (1994): "Is there a migration policy in Germany?" In: Heckmann, Friedrich / Bosswick, Wolfgang: *Migration policies. A comparative perspective*. Stuttgart, 157-170.

HECKMANN, F. (2003): "From ethnic nation to universalistic immigrant integration: Germany." In: Heckmann, Friedrich / Schnapper, Dominique (eds.): *The Integration of Immigrants in European Societies.* National Differences and Trends of Convergence. Stuttgart, 45-78.

HECKMANN, F.; LEDERER, H.; WORBS, S. in cooperation with the EFFNATIS research team (2001): *Effectiveness of national integration strategies towards second generation migrant youth in a comparative European perspective (EFFNATIS). Final report to the European Commission.* Bamberg.

HETTLAGE, R. (2001): "'Wem Gott will rechte Gunst erweisen...' Wissenssoziologische Auffälligkeiten im Rückblick auf 45 Jahre Migrationsliteratur." In: Wunderlich, Tanja / Currle, Edda (eds.): *Deutschland - ein Einwanderungsland? Rückblick, Bilanz und neue Fragen.* Stuttgart, 69-109.

HUBER, B. (1992): "Das neue Ausländergesetz: Mehr Rechtssicherheit für Migrantinnen und Migranten in der Bundesrepublik?" In: *Informationsdienst zur Ausländerarbeit* 1/92, Frankfurt, 21-25.

KOSLOWSKI, R. (2000): *Migrants and citizens. Demographic change in the European state system.* Ithaca / London.

LEDERER, H. W. (1997): *Migration und Integration in Zahlen. Ein Handbuch.* Beauftragte der Bundesregierung für Ausländerfragen (ed.), Bundesministerium für Arbeit und Sozialordnung, Bonn.

LEDERER, H. W. (2001): *Indikatoren der Migration. Zur Messung des Umfangs und der Arten von Migration in Deutschland unter besonderer Berücksichtigung des Ehegatten- und Familiennachzugs sowie der illegalen Migration.* Stuttgart (forthcoming).

LEGGEWIE, C. (1992): "Der rechte Aufmarsch." In: Nirumand, Bahman (ed.): *Angst vor den Deutschen.* Reinbek, 52-66.

MAHNIG, H. (1998): *Integrationspolitik in Großbritannien, Frankreich, Deutschland und den Niederlanden.* Research Report 10 of the Swiss Forum for Migration Studies. Neuchâtel.

MARTIN, P. L. (1993): "Germany: Reluctant Land of Immigration.".Conference paper from June 15, 1993. Revised version printed in: American Institute for Contemporary German Studies, *German Issues* 21, 1998, Washington DC. http://www.aicgs.org/publications/PDF/martin.pdf

MEHRLÄNDER, U. (1980): "The 'human resource' problems in Europe: Migrant labour in the Federal Republic of Germany." In: Ra'anan, Uri (ed.): *Ethnic resurgence in modern, democratic states: a multidisciplinary approach to human resources and conflict*, New York.

MEIER-BRAUN, K.-H. (1988): *Integration oder Rückkehr. Zur Ausländerpolitik des Bundes und der Länder, insbesondere Baden-Württembergs.* Mainz / München.

MOMMSEN, W. J. (1990): "Die Idee der deutschen Nation in Geschichte und Gegenwart." In: *Gewerkschaftliche Monatshefte*, 5/6, pp. 263-273.

OBERNDÖRFER, D. (1989a): "Der Nationalstaat - ein Hindernis für das dauerhafte Zusammenleben mit ethnischen Minderheiten?" In: *Zeitschrift für Ausländerrecht und Ausländerpolitik* (ZAR) 9, p. 1.

OBERNDÖRFER, D. (1989b): "Bundesrepublik Deutschland - Vom Nationalstaat zum Einwanderungsland." Manuscript of a radio report on March 10, Süddeutscher Rundfunk, Stuttgart.

PRIES, L. (1996): "Transnationale soziale Räume. Theoretisch-empirische Skizze am Beispiel der Arbeitswanderung Mexiko-USA." In: *Zeitschrift für Soziologie*, 25 (6), pp. 456-472.

PROUDFOOT, M. J. (1957): *European refugees 1939-1952. A study in forced population movement.* London.

RAU, J. (2002): "Erklärung von Bundespräsident Johannes Rau zur Ausfertigung des Zuwanderungsgesetzes am 20. Juni 2002 im Schloss Bellevue in Berlin." See internet document http://www.bundespraesident.de/Downloads/erklaerung.pdf. Berlin.

RÜHL, S.; LEDERER, H. (2001): *Migrationsbericht der Ausländerbeauftragten im Auftrag der Bundesregierung*. Beauftragte der Bundesregierung für Ausländerfragen (ed.), Berlin.

Santel, B.; Weber, A. (2000): "Zwischen Ausländerpolitik und Einwanderungspolitk: Migrations- und Ausländerrecht in Deutschland." In: Bade, Klaus J. / Münz, Rainer: *Migrationsreport 2000. Fakten - Analsyen - Perspektiven*. Frankfurt/New York.

STEINER, J.-D. (1995): *Migration und Politik. Westdeutschland - Europa - Übersee 1945-1961.* Osnabrück.

SYRUP, F. (1918): "Die ausländischen Industriearbeiter (vor dem Kriege)." In: *Archiv für exakte Wirtschaftsforschung*, 9 (1918/1922), pp. 278-301.

THIERSE, W. (2001): "Rede des Bundestagspräsidenten Wolfgang Thierse anlässlich der Verleihung des 'Julius-Rumpf-Preises' am 7. September 2001 in Hermannswerder." See internet document: http://www.martin-niemoeller-stiftung.de/Projekte/Julius-Rumpf-Preis/2001/2001.html.

TREIBEL, A. (1999): *Migration in modernen Gesellschaften. Soziale Folgen von Einwanderung, Gastarbeiter und Flucht.* Weinheim / München 1999.

ZUWANDERUNGSKOMMISSION (2001): *Zuwanderung gestalten, Integration fördern. Bericht der Unabhängigen Kommission "Zuwanderung".* Unabhängige Kommission "Zuwanderung", Berlin.

Between guilt and gift: the politics of identity and immigration policy in Italy

Enzo Pace

Introduction

A recent survey, carried out by the Ministry of Education, into the presence of foreign students in every type and level of school in Italy shows with what speed and intensity Italian society is changing (MINISTERIO PUBBLICA ISTRUZIONE, 2002). In the school year 2000-2001, for every hundred students enrolled, two were foreign; ten years before, there were two for every thousand enrolled. It is not only the percentage that has changed but also the cultural composition of the school population. The new generation of foreigners has brought the number of different ethnic groups present up to 184. Alongside the main ones, Albanians and Moroccans in first and second place, there has been a marked increase in the presence of pupils from China, Rumania, Serbia, Peru, Macedonia, the Philippines, Tunisia and India (see Table 1) in our schools. These constitute the first ten groups in order of magnitude, but the list includes pupils from a vast range of origins: Sinhalese, Sikh, Ghanaian, Egyptian, Somali, Senegalese, Nigerian, Kurdish, Lebanese, Colombian, Ecuadorian and so on (PACE, 2002).

These figures highlight what can be described as the substantial avant-garde of a new generation of Italians, composite and multiethnic. In such a short time, Italy, a relatively homogeneous society, has, so to speak, *changed complexion*. The choice of metaphor is by no means casual. If you happen one day to visit a Catholic parish in the outskirts of a megalopolis like Chicago, the white American parish priest will show you how the demographic composition of his community has changed over the last twenty years: the white component is in sharp decline, the black component is stationary, and the Latin element is

Table 1

Foreign students by type of school and country of origin

Country	Primary school	Secondary school	Total
Albania	15,984	9,064	25,050
Morocco	14,993	8,659	23,652
China	4,558	4,100	8,658
Serbia-Montenegro	5,466	3,077	8,543
Romania	3,891	2,213	6,104
Peru	1,898	2,598	4,496
The Philippines	2,704	1,152	3,856
Macedonia	2,612	1,183	3,795
Tunisia	2,326	682	3,008
India	2,004	921	2,925

Source: Ministero Pubblica Istruzione, 2002.

strongly on the increase. The latter is a recent arrival from the less fortunate areas of the Latin-American continent, but it has only partially boosted the presence of Catholics at Sunday mass, since many have brought with them either the ancient Afro-American cults or the new, innumerable Pentecostal churches. A parish which changes complexion so quickly poses immediate and substantial pastoral problems: the language, mentality, and lifestyles of the new arrivals are very different from those of the longstanding parishioners and the parish priest.

We need not travel very far to have a concrete example of the phenomenon in question. Near at hand are the many global villages in the highly industrialised areas of the North East of Italy, typified by extremely specialised production, low technological content, and a powerful vocation for export. A visit to one of these would soon convince us that the problems of our Chicago priest are basically the same as that of a small municipality in the heart, for example, of the ski-boot manufacturing district. In the crèche attached to the parish, nowadays most of the children are Ghanaian; their families are usually Christian, but not Catholic (they belong to Protestant neo-Pentecostal churches, often with high ethnic homogeneity). So, what is to be done? Welcome them or draw a demarcation line between those who are Catholic and those of other religions? Would not a crèche closed to non-Catholics constitute, in the long term —also for practical reasons— an intolerable social surplus for the spirit of Catholicism and for the small local community called upon to receive the newcomers without conflict and trauma? The data on foreign pupils in Italian schools, together with the two examples of the changes within a parish (whether large or small the problems appear to be the same), will enable us to formulate the question we intend to analyse. We may put it in the following terms:

a) a society in which various different cultures coexist against the background of a dominant culture, for example Catholicism in Italy, will sooner or later be called upon to rewrite the pact for social and political solidarity which should, in theory, bind all who form part of it;
b) the rewriting of the pact for solidarity is necessary because the simultaneous presence of people of different cultures may give rise to conflicts of values and political competition for the recognition of cultural differences;
c) since both these types of conflict develop in the public sphere and involve the main public institutions (such as schools, hospitals, prisons, job centres and trade-union representation), the difference is not hidden, but emerges and is perceived by the culturally dominant majority, in the constituent stage of the multicultural society, as something extraneous;
d) there are basically two methods of dealing with cultural extraneity, if we turn to Todorov's theorem (TODOROV, 1992): either as something which may ultimately be assimilated, by projecting onto the Other the values (so perceived) of the majority, since the Other is imagined as being potentially the same as me, or on the other hand, as something which is radically different and therefore incompatible with my value system, something inferior and imperfect; luckily, between the dilemma of assimilating or recognising the difference, there are intermediate possibilities, but this does nothing to remove the social actors' difficulty in finding a point of balance to promote a new solidarity among foreigners (HABERMAS, 1997);
e) solidarity among foreigners is what is at stake in both real and symbolic terms, for so-called multicultural societies: it is a question of gradually drawing the social map of the conflict among actors (social, political, religious, trade-union and so forth) on the public stage, competing not only for material advantage, but also and in particular for the right of recognition for cultural differences, with all the normative corollary which that entails;
f) each recognition implies, on the one hand, the presentation and representation of different world views, on the basis of which value conflicts might (or might not) arise (on a continuum of

maximum to minimum negotiability) and, on the other, the will to act to reach a possible agreement between socio-linguistic evidence and different symbolic worlds («Should a traffic policeman giving a ticket be expected to take into account the socio-religious identity of a young Sikh riding his motor bike without a crash-helmet, which he cannot wear for religious reasons?»).

In a society, such as that of Italy, which is becoming multicultural, the fundamental sociological and political problem is the relationship between the majority culture (sociological Catholicism) and the "new entry". There is a growing perception in Italian society that a new pact for social solidarity must be drawn up. This conviction is gradually taking root in the collective consciousness, with ramifications in all walks of civil society (from businessmen to elderly people in need of domestic assistance; from Catholic voluntary organisations to the major trade unions). It also constitutes the mass of resistance to all those political and cultural tendencies which have no intention of extending the rights of citizenship to immigrants. The ideological conflict which has developed in Italy over the last ten years on the issue of immigration has, however, brought to the fore the question of Italian identity. An analysis of immigration policies reveals that we have passed from a *gift* policy, under the centre-left government, to a *guilt* policy under the centre-right. In the first case, the reception of immigrants is seen as a generous act of recognition of the Other as the holder of rights and bearer of legitimate cultural differences. In the second, it is viewed as a limited concession of rights to avoid jeopardising the Italian national identity, since each concession is seen as a guilty yielding of sovereignty "in one's own home". The presence of a substantial Muslim community in Italy (approximately 600,000 people) has become the centre of extreme ideological contrasts, especially since the events of September 11. In fact, Islam provides a pretext for many political and social forces to prevent policies of integration and the protection of immigrants' rights and to keep immigrants in a condition of legal and social inferiority.

Immigration policy in Italy

What are the features of the current policy on immigration in Italy? The pattern which emerges is that it is based, primarily, on the notion of the guest worker, though slightly different from the German *Gastarbeiter*: a guest under observation, seen as a potential deviant, since, if he should lose his job, his prospects are either to find another within six months or face repatriation. All the recent legislation on immigration suffers from the security syndrome. The main problem seems to be to show that we are able to combat the phenomenon of illegal entry, deliberately confusing the issue of integration for immigrants who have been part of Italian society for years and who, in point of fact, conduct themselves as citizens to all intents and purposes, on the one hand, with that of the repression of clandestine immigration. As has occurred in other countries in the European Union, the most recent election campaigns featured the theme of security and, within that, the issue of illegal immigration in somewhat xenophobic tones (if not racist, in certain cases), according to the various political leanings.

Secondly, the Italian model regulates access to citizenship according to the principle of *jus sanguinis* and not *jus soli*. Despite the reforms introduced in the early 1990s, there are severe restrictions on acquiring citizenship. This partially explains why a proposal to extend the right to vote at local administrative elections to immigrants was conveniently forgotten. Moreover, it explains certain violations of religious freedom and the right to worship carried out by the centre-right mayors of many cities in Northern Italy, by stopping the opening of mosques (on a variety of bureaucratic pretexts), and even banning prayer meetings for the end of the month of Ramadan. In the prosperous city of Treviso, the Northern League mayor refused worshippers the use of a hall to celebrate the end of Ramadan, so the chairman of Benetton (the clothing chain based in Treviso) let them use the local sports stadium (his property) and the local Catholic clergy willingly agreed (in open dispute with the mayor) to take part in the ceremony and address a message of reconciliation.

Thirdly, the Italian model gives the State control of the flow and regulation of access to the labour market, in open contradiction to the centre-right government's declared devotion to free market ideology and decentralisation. In other words, central government sets itself the task of laying down the annual entry quota and checking for the presence of irregular immigrants as well as forms of organised crime which exploit immigrant labour illegally (such as prostitution and drug-trafficking). However, this policy has by no means come up to expectations: illegal landings of immigrants continue and are on the increase; the government has had to introduce a mass regularisation of illegal workers of an unprecedented 700,000 people; neither for 2001, nor 2002 was the influx of immigrants fixed. Moreover, the fiscal crisis has pushed the government into moving the social costs for integration from the coffers of the State onto industry and private associations, such as voluntary groups, cooperatives, trade unions, and local churches, effectively shifting onto them the burden of the right to shelter and education.

The social conflict map and its actors

Our description of the Italian immigration policy model over the last few years shows the number and type of conflicts it has given rise to. The movements of the social actors on the public stage reveal the different, changing stakes. We can trace the outline of a map, identifying the interests and ideal perspectives which the actors, in their different ways, look to and defend. In this way we can also distinguish the rhetorical repertoires which show to what extent the immigration question is tackled with reference to an Italian ethnic/national identity. Below is a brief summary of the Italian situation with its complexity reduced as far as possible (see Figure 1 and Table 2).

+ACCESS	Interests and ideals at stake	–ACCESS
Recognition of citizens' rights and cultural differences on human rights grounds		Limited access to citizens' rights and limited recognition of cultural differences
Entrepreneurs →	Increasing manpower shortage/ better integrated, though culturally different, workers	↔ Many vote centre-right
Part of the centre-right with Catholic inspiration ↔	Defence of the rule of law against illegal immigration, assertion of Italian ethnic and cultural identity against foreign invasion	← Social and political forces of the centre-right
Catholic Church (the majority of the hierarchy and clergy and voluntary groups and associations) →	Assertion of their role, on the one hand, as repository of the national collective memory and, on the other, as controller of public ethics: welcoming newcomers but without casting doubts on the Catholic identity of Italians and defending it whenever it is attacked or threatened (e.g. the issue of crucifixes in schools and public offices)	↔ Wide variety of situations among local churches: some ready to welcome newcomers, others more cautious or even sceptical
Centre-left social and political forces (including trade unions of workers with Catholic or left-wing leanings →	Extension of citizens' rights, seeking to represent new subjects (immigrants), seen as the "new proletariat"	↔ In factories where the new proletariat form the majority there is no shortage of conflicts
→ indicates affirmative action		↔ indicates contradiction

Figure 1

Predominant poles in the social and political division on immigration

From the map, we observe that for some subjects the tension between immigration policy and identity policy is very low or even absent, whereas for others it is much higher. In the following table we summarise the degree of social anxiety caused by the presence of the Other among the various components of Italian society.

Table 2

Degrees of social anxiety for one's own national identity

Immigrants threaten the Italian national identity	Immigrants may threaten the cultural integrity of the Italian nation	Immigrants are an economic and cultural resource and do not threaten the Italian identity
Extreme right-wing parties (Northern League and Neo-Fascists)	Official Catholic Church	Employers' Associations
Neo-integrist Catholic groups Certain bishops of the Catholic hierarchy	Social and political forces of the Centre (including those of Catholic and post-Fascist leanings)	Social and political forces of the Centre-left (including trade unions and Catholic voluntary associations)

If we take a look at the surveys (FONDAZIONE NORDEST, 2001) which have been carried out repeatedly to monitor attitudes toward immigrants, statistics show a gradual shift over the last five years: fear and suspicion has been replaced among the majority by a tendency to live with the idea that immigrants constitute a resource. Only a minority (approximately 30 %) are convinced that immigrants constitute a threat to identity and the cause of evils such as unemployment and disruption in public order.

Conclusion

Again in Treviso, a city which is virtually a testing ground for the contradictions described above, the Northern League mayor ordered a number of slum dwellings to be knocked down in September 2002. They were council properties and had been occupied for years by 20 or so immigrant families, all of whom held valid stay permits and had legal employment contracts. Finding themselves suddenly on the street without notice, these families took refuge in the cathedral portico. The

Bishop of Treviso took up their defence, thus attracting the mayor's wrath, and undertook to persuade a group of local businessmen to provide money and shelter to cope with the emergency. The bishop's mediation was successful, thanks to the social pressure of certain movements of the civil society which moved to create a girdle of solidarity around the families. Faced with this unexpected turn of events, the mayor asked for the supreme authorities of the Church of Rome to intervene to call its priests to order, whom he accused of being excessively indulgent and yielding to those not belonging to the "race of the Piave" (i.e. local stock, the river Piave flows through the Veneto and has a special place in the historic memory of Italians, being the site of the last battle against the Austro-Hungarian Empire during the First World War; in the past, those who lived on the banks of this river felt proud to be the bearers of this patriotic memory).

This episode, which is typical of Italian provincialism and its unwillingness to accept changes, deserves little comment. It is nevertheless useful to illustrate the light and shadows of the Italian situation. The shadows are clearly visible: the stigmatisation of the Other as a guest "in our house", whom we tolerate temporarily produces feelings and attitudes of closure and xenophobia. As for the light: the civil society, rather than political parties, seems to be a vital force (including the economic world, voluntary organisations, as well as local churches, not only the Catholic Church but also the Protestant minority, and the Jewish community which has on a number of occasions come out against the new law on immigration passed in 2002). This welding together of such different interests and ideals is only possible at this level; politics is impaired by a logic based on ideological demarcation and the pursuit of consensus. In truth, it is no longer enough to seek consensus on the question of immigration. There is a tendency, chiefly (but not only) among centre-right parties in many European countries, to play to the anti-immigrant mood and fears which the majority of citizens are assumed to have. This leads them to make choices which curtail basic freedoms: for example, why should only immigrants be fingerprinted? Why stop people from burying their dead until they have a permanent stay permit? Why should a person be expelled from the country without a proper trial? Such restrictions may dignify a negative collective idea by feeding it with stereotypes and prejudice. There is always some political entrepreneur who tries to exploit it to gain political consensus.

We can only place our hopes in the movements of the civil society and groups which operate at the micro-social level (including in schools and at the work-place), to stem the sense of collective guilt which seems to affect the minority of Italians worried about losing their identity and about not doing enough to oppose foreigners who come here and take over streets, houses, schools and jobs. The feeling of guilt is difficult to remove because it involves resentment: one's own identity becomes an object of contention (between me and the Other). The only thing to do is to oppose this sense of gift —not ideologically, but through the concrete experience of everyday life. This is what Marcel Mauss (1950) has taught us to speak of in sociology: a gift creates a tie, it expects something in exchange. In political terms, it presupposes the rewriting of the pact for social solidarity, something which has to be done in the countries of the European Union, which have become multi-ethnic and muti-religious.

References

FONDAZIONE NORDEST (2001): *Rapporto sulal situazione sociale ed economica del Nordest*, Venezia.

HABERMAS, J. (1997): *Solidarietà fra estranei*, Milano, Guerini & Associati.

MAUSS, M. (1950) *Teoria generale della magia e altri saggi*, Torino, Einaudi.

MINISTERO DELLA PUBBLICA ISTRUZIONE (2002): *Rapporto sulla presenza di studenti stranieri nelle scuole italiane*, Roma.

PACE, E. (2002): "Conflitti di valore e riconoscimento delle differenze in un sistema educativo multiculturale", in R. De Vita, F. Berti (a cura di), *Dialogo senza paure*, Milano, Angeli, pp. 60-71.

TODOROV, T. (1992): *La conquista dell'America*, Torino, Einaudi.

Third country nationals and labour immigration in the Netherlands

Jeroen Doomernik

Introduction

The Amsterdam Treaty, which came into force in May 1999, potentially is to fundamentally change policy making in the field of immigration and asylum in all the member states of the European Union. As an important element of this Treaty, member states have agreed on the establishment of an area of free movement for all persons legally resident in the EU (be they nationals of member states or third country nationals) within the borders of the Union. In order to make this possible, and also as a goal in its own right, it was furthermore decided that the Union should within five years arrive at common immigration and asylum policies. In effect, by May 2004, all member states will have to surrender a key element of their national sovereignty, i.e. the right to decide whom they admit to their territory, to Brussels. As in most other countries, in the Netherlands this is considered to be a sensitive issue. Nevertheless, the Dutch government, together with all other EU governments, has clearly committed itself to the implementation of this element of the Amsterdam Treaty as became clear at the Tampere meeting in late 1999. Furthermore, the European Commission was requested to formulate an outline for such common policies. The responsible Commissioner, Antonio Vitorino, in November 2000 published his Communication from the Commission to the Council and the European Parliament on a Common Immigration Policy (COM(2000) 757 final). In the introduction, on page three, the following statement can be found:

> On the one hand large numbers of third country nationals have entered the Union in recent years and these migratory pressures are

> continuing with an accompanying increase in illegal immigration, smuggling and trafficking. On the other hand, as a result of growing shortages of labour at both skilled and unskilled levels, a number of Member States have already begun to actively recruit third country nationals from outside the Union. In this situation a choice must be made between maintaining the view that the Union can continue to resist migratory pressures and accepting that immigration will continue and should be properly regulated, and working together to try to maximise its positive effects on the Union, for the migrants themselves and for the countries of origin.

In this Communication member states are urged to come up with medium and long term analyses of their expected need for labour immigration and to re-evaluate current immigration policies. As to the concrete measures proposed, among these is the suggestion to introduce visas for prospective labour immigrants as part of the common immigration policy. This would, in other words, be a supply driven instrument. To discuss these suggestions and investigate their relevance and implications for the Dutch case an expert meeting was called, with input from employers and trade unions, several ministries (Employment and Social Affairs, Interior, Justice, Foreign Affairs), think tanks, and academia. The findings of this expert meeting were to serve the Cabinet in its response to the above-mentioned document.

At more or less the same time, in Germany, a country that in many respects can be considered the Netherlands' bigger brother, the government of Chancellor Schröder has proposed to completely and fundamentally rethink the country's stance on immigration. While until very recently, Germany was officially not a country of immigration, these days it is agreed to be one, even by the CDU, the party which loudest proclaimed *Deutschland ist kein Einwanderungsland*. It remains to be seen whether this change in rhetoric will indeed mean completely different types of immigration and immigration management or will boil down to the re-labelling of existing migration flows. Yet, even words have consequences.

The intimate relationship between the Netherlands and Germany has in the past always been very visible in the making of immigration policies. Few if any exceptions can be found to the rule that changes in admission policies (especially where they are aimed at restricting access for unsolicited immigrants) in Germany are copied in the Netherlands some time later. It is therefore the more remarkable that when in October 2001 the Dutch Cabinet responded to Vitorino's communication and made public the way it chooses to go regarding (labour) immigration this turned out be: let's keep things as they are. Four key arguments were put forward. First of all, the Netherlands is not yet facing a demographic need for (more) immigration. The Dutch population is relatively young, compared to Germany and especially to the Southern European states. Secondly, pension schemes in the Netherlands are, to a large extent, capital funded, making the ratio between those of working age and those who are retired a much less crucial variable than it is in a country like Germany. Thirdly, where necessary labour immigration is already possible. And lastly, the number of inactive people of working age is considerable. Among them are approximately 800,000 persons who are not employed because of physical or mental disabilities but used to be employed at one stage or another and could, and in the government's view should, therefore be reintegrated into the labour market. Satisfying labour market needs through more immigration would, according to the Dutch cabinet, permanently exclude those people (among whom are many previous immigrants).

The government is moreover of the opinion that a visa system accommodating the supply side on the migration market is not a very good idea as it fears an increase in illegal residents if those particular immigrants fail to find employment. However, and in contrast to German and Austrian proposals, the government has made public that it wants to immediately extend freedom of movement to citizens of Central European states once these have become full EU members.

Brief history of Dutch immigration

It was suggested above that Dutch and German developments in the field of immigration policies and experience have often been similar (this was different when it came to integration policies, see DOOMERNIK, 1998). From the early 1960s until the mid 1970s both countries recruited guest workers around the Mediterranean; Germany first and foremost in Yugoslavia and Turkey, the Netherlands mainly in Turkey and Morocco. Very dissimilar is the Dutch experience when it comes to the arrival of (post) colonial immigrants. Indonesian independence brought numerous people to the Netherlands who were labelled repatriates (most of whom where born in Indonesia) and who had served the colonial administration. Often these people were of mixed descent. When Surinam became independent in 1975 its citizens, until then Dutch nationals, were given the choice of becoming Surinamese nationals or remaining Dutch. Many preferred the latter and moved to the Netherlands. Between 1975 and 1980 Surinamese nationals could still opt for Dutch citizenship. Due to the fact that independence turned out to be fraught with problems, another influx of Surinamese immigrants took place shortly before 1980. In effect, around a third of the Surinamese population now lives in the Netherlands. Of the Dutch colonies today there is one left, or more accurately, the Dutch kingdom still contains the island of Aruba and the Dutch Antilleans. Its residents are thus still Dutch nationals and can freely move to and from the Netherlands.

Since the second half of the 1980s the Netherlands and Germany have shared the same experience again as they have been confronted with large numbers of unsolicited immigrants claiming asylum from seemingly random countries of origin. Meanwhile, as is discussed below, former immigration still has its after-effects in the form of chain migration of family members and spouses and of friends and acquaintances (often with an irregular residence position, see STARING, 2001).

Unlike in Germany, immigrants these days are usually not referred to as aliens or *Ausländer* but as allochthonous persons, meaning foreign born or the child of a foreign born person. The main reasons for not referring to them as aliens is that this would unduly stress irrelevant differences and because they are encouraged to naturalise and therefore many are indeed not aliens but Dutch nationals (or have always been Dutch nationals). Among those allochthonous persons certain categories are pinpointed for special attention: Turks, Moroccans, Surinamese, Antilleans and refugees. These are the target groups of Dutch integration policies. The category "refugees" is of growing importance as can be deduced from a close look at table 1. Immigrants from such countries as Afghanistan, Iran, Iraq and Somalia are clearly on the increase and the second generations are still relatively small.

Present Dutch immigration policies

In 2000 132,000 people immigrated to the Netherlands, while 80,000 moved elsewhere, resulting in a net gain of 52,000 persons. Broadly speaking half of all annual immigrants who arrive in the Netherlands are either Dutch nationals or citizens of another EU member state, many of whom can be considered labour migrants. The other half consists of third country nationals. Again half of those or less (or no more than one quarter of all immigrants) are asylum applicants. In recent years about 40 % of asylum applicants have eventually been granted some type of residence permit. Other third country nationals are admitted into the country for a number of other reasons (study, work, medical care, etc.) among which family reunification and education are prominent.

Table 1

Non-Western allochthonous population, all and (first generation) × 1000

	1995	1999	2000	2001
Afghanistan	3 (3)	16 (15)	21 (20)	26 (24)
China	22 (15)	28 (19)	30 (20)	32 (22)
Egypt	11 (8)	14 (9)	14 (9)	15 (9)
Philippines	7 (5)	9 (6)	10 (6)	10 (7)
Ghana	12 (9)	15 (10)	16 (11)	16 (11)
Hong Kong	17 (10)	17 (10)	18 (10)	18 (10)
India	9 (7)	11 (8)	12 (8)	12 (8)
Iraq	8 (7)	30 (27)	33 (30)	38 (34)
Iran	14 (12)	22 (19)	23 (20)	25 (21)
Cape Verde	16 (11)	18 (11)	18 (11)	19 (11)
Morocco	219 (140)	252 (149)	262 (153)	273 (156)
Dutch Antilleans and Aruba	86 (57)	99 (63)	107 (69)	117 (77)
Pakistan	14 (9)	16 (10)	16 (10)	17 (11)
Somalia	17 (15)	27 (21)	29 (21)	30 (22)
Surinam	276 (179)	297 (182)	303 (183)	309 (185)
Turkey	264 (166)	300 (175)	309 (178)	320 (182)
Vietnam	13 (9)	14 (10)	15 (10)	15 (11)
South Africa	9 (5)	12 (6)	13 (7)	13 (7)
Other	111 (78)	149 (102)	161 (110)	178 (122)
Total	1,129 (744)	1,346 (854)	1,409 (886)	1,483 (929)

Source: Centraal Bureau voor de Statistiek, 2001, p. 82 and 83.

Labour immigration

After the end of the guest worker era in 1973, labour immigration was subjected to a restrictive regime. Until then, the Dutch government was not overly concerned about immigrants who arrived illegally and only applied for a residence permit upon finding employment. In fact, approximately half of all guest workers arrived spontaneously instead of being recruited directly by employers (PENNINX *et al.*, 1993).

When the government decided that, in view of the economic downturn following the first oil crisis, further labour immigration was not desirable, it was more or less taken for granted that unemployed immigrants would return to their countries of origin, mainly to Turkey and Morocco. Even though some did return, most decided to stay in the Netherlands and gradually started to bring over their family members. This was the start of a long process of chain migration that by now has created ethnic communities broadly ten times as large as the original guest worker populations. Even though the government never pursued policies that would seriously curb this type of secondary immigration, it is clear that implicitly it was not welcomed either. This was especially due to questions as to what extent and how these newcomers could be integrated, for instance in the labour market. To this very day, but more markedly in the 1980s and 1990s, unemployment levels among former guest workers and their relatives have remained much higher then for the population at large (see DOOMERNIK, 1998 for details). This unforeseen outcome of the guest worker era has certainly contributed to the current restrictive policies when it comes to labour immigration and tends to taint any discussion on possible liberalisation of the current immigration regime.

Labour immigration in the Netherlands is regulated through the *Wet Arbeid Vreemdelingen (WAV)* (the Law on the Employment of Aliens). This law is entirely demand driven and allows an employer to recruit third country nationals not already legally resident in the country *only* when he can demonstrate that he made every possible attempt, within reason, to recruit a Dutch national, someone already legally residing in the Netherlands (excluding those aliens without a work permit like asylum seekers or students) or a national of one of the other EU member states. If this condition is met, the worker who is recruited will, as a rule, only receive a temporary work and residence permit (usually not exceeding a one year period). Once the employment period is coming to its end, the work permit may be extended provided the same conditions still prevail. After a three year period, a work permit is no longer required and the employee may seek employment with another employer if he so desires.

Labour immigrants are exempted from the integration courses (see below) most other newcomers are obliged to participate in. Where appropriate, they can be accompanied by their family members (spouse and minor children).

Table 2

Granted work permits, 1997-2000

	1997	1998	1999	2000
Work permits granted	11,065	15,181	20,816	27,678

Source: Tweede Kamer, vergaderjaar 2001-2002, 19637, nr. 616, p. 17.

The numbers of people granted a work permit under the WAV has in recent years seen a gradual increase and in the year 2000 stood at 28,000 (see table 2). This figure should not be equated with numbers of immigrants. First of all, many permits were given to workers who entered the country to take seasonal employment in horticutlure and agriculture. These people do not qualify for registration in the municipal population registry and hence should not be considered to be immigrants. The same applies if a permit is granted to an artist who comes to perform in a Dutch theatre or to someone who is to conduct an internship. Permits granted to workers already in the country and whose employment is extended are also counted. Asylum seekers and immigrants with temporary leave to remain (a category no longer in existence since a new aliens law was introduced in April 2001) can temporarily be employed (for asylum seekers a maximum of twelve weeks annually) but require a work permit. No good statistics are available but it seems reasonable to assume that in the end approximately 8.000 people who were granted a work permit during 2000 can be considered to be immigrants (officially: when the intended duration of stay exceeds four months of the first half year upon arrival (NICOLAAS/SPRANGERS, 2000 p. 10)). Sixty% of all permits have a duration of less than one year and just over 20 % are immediately granted for three years, the maximum duration possible under the WAV (Tweede Kamer, vergaderjaar 2001-2002, 19637, nr.616, p.17).

Among third country nationals who immigrate to the Netherlands to fill vacancies in the labour market, employees of multi-national companies are an important category. As a rule these are people who are regularly relocated to different offices around the world as part of their career. Of the approximately 6,500 WAV related immigrants from outside the EU in 1998, over 1,000 were US citizens and almost 500 were Japanese *(ibid.).* Who the other 5,000 immigrants were and where they came from is not easy to find out but they will have included IT workers (NICOLAAS/SPRANGERS, 2001) and others with very specialised professions like imams to serve the Muslim communities, soccer players, and chefs for exotic restaurants.

In the years 2000 and 2001 the WAV was also used to alleviate shortages in the medical sector, especially of qualified nurses. Several hundreds were reportedly imported from the Republic of South Africa and Suriname. In these countries Dutch, or very similarly Afrikaans, is the lingua franca, which is an obvious advantage in this type of job. Yet, in public discussions the recruitment of nurses from these countries is generally depicted as being fraught with problems. For one, the style of work these nurses were used to differs considerably from the Netherlands, especially with regard to South Africa, in dealing with patients and colleagues alike. Furthermore, many consider it unethical to recruit nurses from countries where medical staff and care are already scarce. It seems unlikely, therefore, that this type of labour recruitment is going to be continued to any extent.

Integration courses

Policy makers elsewhere in Europe, for instance in Germany and Austria, show considerable interest in the Dutch *Wet Inburgering Nieuwkomers (WIN)* (Law on the Integration of Newcomers). This law, which came into force in September 1998, makes it compulsory for newcomers to meet minimum standards in terms of language skills and general knowledge of Dutch society and culture. Upon admission to the Netherlands, an interview is held with the aim of assessing whether the immigrant already meets those standards and can be exempted from the WIN or, if not, precisely what type of course should be offered. Once this is established, a contract is drawn up in which both parties (the educational institution which provides the courses and the immigrant) commit themselves to the completion of the course. If the immigrant fails to comply sanctions may be imposed (administrative fines) and, furthermore, the same rules apply as those which govern school attendance for children of school age. Typically the key element of an integration course consists of 600 hours of language training.

It is interesting to note that the WIN is only applicable to immigrants who have been admitted upon an asylum request and those arriving for family reunification and marriage. EU citizens and labour migrants who enter the country under the provisions of the WAV are excluded. In contrast, the discussions in other countries, where similar policies are under consideration, tend towards integration courses for labour immigrants and not for immigrants who are admitted on humanitarian grounds. In the Netherlands, the idea has been that if an immigrant is allowed into the country because of his particular skills, integration —at any rate in the labour market— is guaranteed. Furthermore, the WAV is geared towards a stay that is of a temporary nature.

It is somewhat of a paradox to note that many, although it is unknown how many precisely, immigrants do not complete their course because they are lured into the labour market. The present labour shortage, in combination with the understandable desire among immigrants to earn their own living instead of depending on social security benefits, is the main reason for this undermining of the WIN. The sanctions that the authorities have at their disposal are too weak to counter this development: the administrative fines are defined as a small%age of standard social security benefits. Once in employment these fines hardly cause any pain. Moreover, local governments, who are responsible for the implementation of the WIN, do not seem to prioritise the imposition of sanctions. It remains to be seen whether those immigrants who do not complete their course will not be among the first to be made redundant once an economic downturn sets in.

Asylum immigration

Although immigrants who apply for asylum are not in any way screened for their skills and only for their humanitarian needs, once they are admitted into the country and have been granted a residence permit, at a certain stage they are likely to participate in the labour market. The annual inflow of asylum seekers varies due to the extent to which wars and persecution uproot people, the ability of those people to seek refuge in Europe in general and the Netherlands in particular, and as a result of policy responses in neighbouring countries. Nevertheless, the number of asylum seekers arriving in the Netherlands has during the past few years shown some stability and fluctuates between 35,000 and 45,000 persons (table 3).

Table 3

Number of asylum applications in the Netherlands, 1997-2000

	1997	1998	1999	2000
Total	34,443	45,217	39,299	43,895
Afghanistan	5,920	7,118	4,400	5,055
Yugoslavia	1,652	4,289	3,692	3,851
Iraq	9,641	8,300	3,703	2,773
Iran	1,253	1,679	1,527	2,543
Turkey	1,153	1,222	1,490	2,277

Source: Tweede Kamer, vergaderjaar 2001-2002, 19637, nr. 616, p. 21.

If we use past admission rates, this inflow annually adds approximately 15,000 to 16,000 immigrants to the legally residing population (and accounts for 0.01 % in population growth).

In the past, many asylum seekers were given a temporary protection status, instead of being recognised as a refugee. During the first two years this kept them from the labour market, unless they successfully applied for a work permit under the WAV. The Aliens Law that came into force in April 2001 no longer provides for this category of immigrants to exist. Anyone admitted as an asylum seeker, under the new regime, is granted all the rights previously reserved for recognised refugees. This includes the right to work.

The remaining asylum seekers, i.e. those who are not admitted, are, as a rule, not forcibly removed. Under the new Aliens Law rejected asylum seekers are granted a 28 day period in which to voluntarily leave the country. After these four weeks, all rights are retracted (where applicable the rental agreement is terminated, otherwise eviction from the hostel takes place, social security and other benefits are no longer available etc.) and the police will establish whether the person in question still resides at the last known address. If the answer is negative, the conclusion is that the former asylum seeker has left the country —at any rate administratively.

Currently about 85,000 asylum seekers are still awaiting the outcome of their application. As a consequence it can be expected that within the foreseeable future a large number of aliens are to be administratively removed.

Family formation and reunion

Immigrants who arrive in order to reunite with their family members or to settle with a (marriage) partner are numerous (see table 4) and, like asylum immigrants, also have labour market implications. Not all of those will become active on the labour market (among former guest worker populations labour market participation among women is still lower than the national Dutch average) and some are still of school going age, but many will want to be in employment. Following an integration course should enable those immigrants to become independent.

Table 4

Migration motives of third country nationals, 1998

	Asylum migration	Secondary migration	Labour migration	Study	Other	Total
Non-EU	17,300	32,000	6,600	4,300	3,200	63,600
Turkey	300	4,400	300	100	100	5,100
Morocco	300	4,400	200	300	100	5,300
Surinam	100	2,700	100	100	100	3,200
Afghanistan	3,300	600	0	0	0	3,900
Iraq	5,700	1,600	0	0	0	7,400
USA	0	1,500	1,100	200	300	3,100
Former SU	700	1,200	300	300	100	2,600
Others	6,800	15,600	4,600	3,300	2,500	32,800

Source: Tweede Kamer, vergaderjaar 2001-2002, 19637, nr. 616, p. 6.

In the Dutch labour market statistics it is not possible to discern the formal motive under which an immigrant is admitted. We can merely establish that immigrants who, in all likelihood, were admitted as secondary immigrants (family formation and reunion) are a) less likely to be in the active labour force, and b) if they are, are more likely to be unemployed. Among the explanations for this phenomenon, the most prominent is a mismatch between labour supply and current labour market needs. As a rule these immigrants lack the qualifications needed in a predominantly service based economy (DOOMERNIK/ PENNINX, 1999).

The net participation rate (in 1998) among Turks and Moroccans stands at 47 % and 44 % respectively, where for the native population the rate is 69 %. For the older cohorts the discrepancy is even more marked. Of people in the age bracket 55-64 the figures are 6, 16 and 27 respectively (MARTENS, 1999, p. 45). The unemployment levels for Turks and Moroccans in 1998 stood at 17.5 and 19.5 whereas for the native population it was a mere 3.6 % (p. 47). Meanwhile the demand for labour has further increased and the unemployment levels among former guest workers and their dependants have dropped further but remain approximately four times as high

Undocumented workers

Immigrants who work illegally are mainly found in those sectors of the economy known for their high level of informality: the catering industry, the cleaning business and horticulture. Virtually nothing is known about the numbers of people who are irregularly employed on the Dutch labour market. Only incidentally police raids on a particular company or area provide some insight. In early October 2001, for instance, a tomato farm was raided in the Westland (an area with dense horticulture near the Hague). Among the 170 workers present, 110 turned out to be irregularly employed. This amounts to 65 % of this firm's labour force.

Recently, the market for employment agencies has been completely liberalised, which fact has caused a mushrooming of such agencies in the larger cities. It is generally assumed that many of these act as brokers between illegal immigrants and employers. In other words, it is safe to assume that the Dutch labour market has a considerable, yet unquantifiable, need for unskilled, flexible and cheap work.

Not only is the demand for irregular labour given, the supply is present too. Again no reliable data are available but the estimates that have been made suggest that the number of immigrants who remain in the country without a residence permit is also considerable. ENGBERSEN/ VAN DER LEUN (2001, p. 82) refer to research done during the 1990s in the four largest cities (Amsterdam, the Hague, Rotterdam and Utrecht), which gave reason to suspect that, on top of the legally residing members of the traditional immigrant communities (Turks, Moroccans and Surinamese) another 7 % are illegal residents. This would roughly be equivalent to 63,000 people. As we saw in table 1, the total number of non-Western immigrants and their descendants stands at almost 1.5 million. Seven percent on top of that would mean a total of 105,000 persons. In addition, it can be safely assumed that a certain percentage of the administratively removed former asylum seekers mentioned earlier remain in the country. It is not known how many asylum seekers have needed the assistance of a smuggler on their way to the Netherlands but the immigration authorities estimate their number to be high (70 % is sometimes quoted). Nor is it known how much these migrants have needed to pay for these services. In spite of these uncertainties it seems safe to assume that many former asylum seekers will have invested their own money (or that of relatives and friends) and are unlikely to return before those investments have been earned back. Among them especially those who cannot fall back on the assistance of a large community of legally residing co-ethnics, are forced to accept any employment offer made if they are not to resort to crime. This assumption is supported by ENGBERSEN *et al.* (2002) who currently estimate the number of undocumented immigrants to lie between 112,000 and 163,000 persons, some of whom indeed have to resort to "survival crime".

At times it has been suggested to generously regularise illegal immigrants. Although this has been made possible for a very select number (those who could prove a long history of legal employment but without possessing a residence permit) the government fears the arrival of more illegal migrants (hoping for another pardon in the near or distant future) if it decided to do so.

Conclusion

We have seen that the international context, in which Dutch policy making in the field of immigration is taking place, has drastically changed during the past year or so. The European Commission has formulated a long-term vision of the future of labour immigration in the European Union, which dismisses fundamentally restrictive policies as a suitable answer to future demographic and economic developments. Also in Germany, the Dutch neighbour and a close relative, winds are coming from an entirely new direction. What both the Commission's and the German government's reasoning have in common is that labour immigration policies should not only address the demand side but should also include the supply side, for instance by means of quota systems (possibly including a point system like the Canadians use). To the previous, and present Dutch governments (which should leave office sometime this year) such an adjustment towards the incorporation of supply driven immigration, other than via the asylum channel, is clearly a bridge too far. Whether its successor will still be able and/or willing to maintain the status quo is, obviously, an open question. Yet, it is hard to envisage common EU policies in the field of immigration and asylum, to which the Dutch government unequivocally has committed itself, on the same basis as currently underpinning Dutch policies. It will therefore be interesting to see how the government which comes into office after the next elections is going to tackle this issue.

References

CENTRAAL BUREAU VOOR DE STATISTIEK (2001): *Allochtonen in Nederland 2001* Voorburg/Heerlen: CBS.

DOOMERNIK, J.; PENNINX, R. (1999): "Economische groei, werkgelegenheid en immigranten: veranderende verhoudingen?" in: J. Godschalk (ed.) *Die Tijd komt nooit meer terug. De arbeidsmarkt aan het eind van de eeuw.* Amsterdam: Het Spinhuis, pp.115-132.

DOOMERNIK, J. (1998): *The effectiveness of integration policies towards immigrants and their descendants in France, Germany and The Netherlands.* Geneva: International Labour Office.

ENGBERSEN, G.; VAN DER LEUN, J. (2001): "Uitsluiting van illegale migranten; risico's van het restrictieve vreemdelingenbeleid" in: *Justitiële Verkenningen* 27 (8), pp.80-90.

ENGBERSEN, G.; STARING, R.; VAN DER LEUN, J.; DE BOOM, J.; VAN DER HEIJDEN, P.; CRUIJFF, M. (2002): *Illegale vreemdelingen in Nederland. Omvang, overkomst, verblijf en uitzetting* Rotterdam: RISBO.

MARTENS, E.P. (1999): *Minderheden in beeld. SPVA-98* Rotterdam: Instituut voor Sociaal Economisch Onderzoek.

NICOLAAS, H.; SPRANGERS, A. H. (2000): "De nieuwe gastarbeider: manager uit de VS of informaticus uit India" in: *Maandstatistiek van de bevolking* nr.9, pp.9-12.

NICOLAAS, H.; SPRANGERS, A. H. (2001): "Waarom komen immigranten naar Nederland?" in: *Maandstatistiek van de bevolking* nr.1, pp.4-7.

PENNINX, R.; SCHOORL, J.; VAN PRAAG, C. (1994): *The impact of international migration on receiving countries: the case of the Netherlands* The Hague: NiDi.

STARING, R. (2001): *Reizen onder Regie. Het migratieproces van illegale Turken in Nederland* Amsterdam: Het Spinhuis.

Spanish immigration policies: a critical approach from a human rights perspective

Eduardo J. Ruiz Vieytez

Introduction

This paper aims to present a critical analysis of immigration policies in the Spanish State. The target of this critique is, fundamentally, the work of the state's central institutions, but also the role played in this field by Non-Governmental Organisations (NGOs).

With this aim, the presentation consists of four fundamental parts. In the first part, some basic information on the reality of immigration in Spain is presented. Secondly we approach the critical analysis of institutional policy on immigration, distinguishing four types of policy: normative, organisational, social and cultural. In the third section, we reflect on the responses of society, particularly the actions of NGOs. Finally, by way of conclusion, we will sketch a panorama of what, in our opinion, are the most relevant challenges in this area, and the strategies with which we should face them.

Immigration in Spain

Immigration from the countries of the South constitutes a recent phenomenon for Spain. Until the 1980s, Spain was traditionally considered to be an emigrant country. Even today, there are approximately twice as many Spanish resident abroad as foreigners resident in Spain. The total number of foreigners resident in Spanish territory is roughly one and a half million, out of a total population of approximately 40 million. The proportion of resident foreigners who are European citizens has been falling significantly during recent years, and they now form about a quarter of the total.

This means above all that the Spanish State still has an extremely low proportion of foreign residents in relation to its native population, compared with the proportions in the countries of central and northern Europe, which have two, three or four times the percentage of foreigners.

However it is also true that, though immigration is still a relatively minor phenomenon in Spain, in the last two decades it has appeared as a new and unfamiliar process for Spanish society. At the same time, it is a process subject to significant acceleration. The total number of foreigners is small, but even so, the population of foreigners legally resident in Spain in 1998 was ten times greater than in 1962 and twice that of 1992. At the same time, a qualitative change in the origin of migrants is evident in recent years. From 1998 to 2002 the increase in immigration from Africa and, especially, Latin America has been a very large proportion of the whole. Fifty years ago eight of every 10 resident foreigners in Spain were from developed (First World) countries, whereas at present they are at most three out of 10. All this has begun to influence the collective psychology of a society which has moved from being very homogeneous to experiencing plurality in a relatively brief space of time.

The location of non-European immigrants within the territory of the Spanish State is very unbalanced. In effect, from the geographical point of view, there is a clear trend towards the concentration of immigrants around Madrid and along the whole Mediterranean coast, from Catalonia to Andalusia. With less intensity, the Canary Islands and the Ebro Valley are also zones of attraction and concentration for non-EU immigrants. As regards the Basque Country, it has not in principle been an area of preference for socioeconomic reasons, but there has been a significant increase especially in the large cities and along the Ebro.

As regards the nationality of immigrants to Spain, far in the lead are the Moroccans, who comprise 40 % of non-EU foreigners. Further back, but still worthy of note, are immigrants from China and the Philippines, together with certain Latin American countries, principally Peru, Ecuador, the Dominican Republic, Argentina, Colombia and Cuba.

As regards gender, according to official sources, the ratio between men and women among legally resident foreigners is becoming more balanced, compared with the past. There is still a notable disproportion between the sexes, however, with respect to work permits and Social Security cards, which indicate lower participation by immigrant women in the labour market, at least formally. Within certain national groups, such as from the Dominican Republic, Equatorial Guinea, the Philippines, Colombia and Peru, however, women have more work permits that men. There is also a significant number of foreign minors in Spanish territory, of which approximately 40 % are of Maghreb origin. Within this group, there are an increasing number of unaccompanied minors who live under the actual or theoretical protection of Spanish institutions. As regards recognised political refugees, this group is very small in Spain. Half of asylum-seekers come from African countries, although applications for asylum diminished drastically with the entry into force of the Law of Asylum of 1994. On the other hand there are an increasing number of foreigners deprived of freedom in Spanish jails, who at the moment constitute roughly a quarter of the total prison population. As regards the number of irregular immigrants, the latest regularisation procedures have shown that there was a larger number than initially estimated. In any case, estimates of the size of this group are very approximate and subject to continuous variations over time, but we can say that at all times there has been a percentage of irregular immigrants at least equal to 15 % or 20 % of the total foreign resident population

It is also worth pointing out as initial descriptive information that most immigrants arrive in Spain by air or, failing that, land. The number arriving by irregular, seaborne routes is only a very small percentage of the total. From the legal point of view, probably the most habitual mode of access is with transit documentation (tourist visa) and, therefore, legally. Possibly this reality does not coincide with the average citizen's image of immigration, distorted by the mass media, which might lead one to think that the majority of immigrants arrive in open boats across the Straits of Gibraltar.

Finally, it should be emphasised when we talk about the reality of immigration in Spain, that the presence of foreign workers is economically very profitable for Spanish society. More than 800,000 foreigners make contributions to the Spanish Social Security system, while only a very small number receive unemployment benefit. On the other hand, in certain areas of work, principally those related ones to the primary sector and domestic work, the numbers of work permits granted demonstrates the need for foreign workers to maintain the respective economic activities.

Critique of public immigration policies

Normative policy: the law of immigration

The normative policy carried out in relation to immigration is condensed in the so-called Law of Foreigners or of Immigration (*Derecho de Extranjería*). By virtue of its content and the procedures followed in its preparation, the Law of Immigration can serve as a summary of the whole of public policy relating to immigration. As in other sectors of the law, the Law of Immigration simply reflects in legal language the political decisions taken in the area and converts them into coercive rules. In this way, the Law reflects a certain conception of foreigners, the public response to them and a certain idea (or lack of idea) of the future design of society.

In line with the novelty of immigration in Spain, the Spanish Law of Immigration is also a new law. It should be made clear that by the Law of Immigration we understand a set of rules that is coherent and displays a systematic pattern. In this respect, the Spanish Law of Immigration has its origin in the mid-1980s. From that point, in our opinion, three different stages or moments in the evolution of this Law can be distinguished:

1) The creation of the first generation of laws on immigration. This first generation of laws was approved in the mid-1980s. Thus, in 1985 the first Law of Immigration saw the light of day, with its corresponding regulation of development adopted in 1986. In parallel, the Law of Asylum was approved in 1984 and its regulation of development in 1985. To this regulation we must add the Royal Decree of 1986 regulating the situation of European citizens (so-called European citizenship did not then exist) and two important judgments of the Constitutional Court: 107/1984, relating to the fundamental rights of foreigners in Spain, and 115/1987, which resolved the charge of unconstitutionality levelled by the Defender of the People against parts of the Law of Immigration. This first generation of immigration laws marked the basic guidelines in the matter and the governing principles that would remain in force from then on. These laws as a whole clearly put the emphasis on the control of migratory flows, and the regulation of the requirements created by the presence of foreigners in the territory of the State, two particular classes of foreigners being established which were clearly favoured relative to the general case: citizens of European community countries, and asylum-seekers.
2) The second generation of laws on immigration. The origin of this stage is in a non-legal resolution adopted by the Congress of Deputies in 1991. As a consequence of this resolution, also in 1991 an important extraordinary procedure for regularisation of foreigners developed. From this moment, and after the entry into force of the Agreement of the European Union (by which European citizenship was created), the Law of Asylum was modified substantially in 1994 and its Regulation in 1995, as

well as the Regulation of development of the Law of Immigration, in 1996. The modification of the latter showed a greater interest in the regulation of aspects relating to integration of immigrants into society, without losing the basically controlling character of the regulation. At the same time, processes of participation for relevant social organisations were opened. Also in this period the first Plan for the Social Integration of Immigrants saw the light of day. By this time two important inter-governmental regulations had already been incorporated into internal Law: on one hand, the Dublin Agreement, relating to the regulation of asylum and its application procedures and, on the other hand, the Agreements for application of the Schengen Agreement regulating the disappearance of internal borders between a number of Member States.

3) The acceleration of the Law of Immigration. In the year 2000 we entered a phase of acceleration of legal reforms. This stage is articulated around two polemical reforms of the Law of Immigration, prepared over a longer space of time, but introduced in the short space of a year. The first reform, in force during most of the year 2000, marks clearly a more integratory intention and a desire to partially overcome the scheme of the Law of 1985. In this respect, the second Law of Immigration seems to mark a positive point of inflexion in the treatment of the phenomenon, both in its content, and in its mode of preparation which was plural and participatory, though without very substantial modifications in the underlying policy. The opposition of the Partido Popular (Popular Party) to this law, was translated into a swift reform of it in the same year 2000. This process of legal modification was rapid and with little dialogue, and concluded in December 2000 with the adoption of a new draft of many of the articles of the Law. In this case, the most evident trends appear in three directions: the legal status of irregularity became harsher; the regime of sanctions became harsher in both content and procedure; finally, the power given to the Executive to develop the content of the Law was increased enormously. From this base, the Government proceeded to approve in 2001 a new and extensive reform of the Law of Immigration, which followed the general criteria of the second reform and ended up constituting the bulk of the Spanish Law of Immigration currently in force.

Nevertheless, the acceleration in legislative reforms in this area, as in neighbouring countries, has not finished, since the Popular Party

Government itself has formally announced its intention of again reforming the Law of Immigration. Everything suggests that before long we will again see a new legislative modification with the basic aim of giving government more flexibility to act on immigration. It is interesting to remember in this respect that the current Law of Immigration is under appeal before the Constitutional Tribunal for supposed violation of the fundamental rights of immigrants, thanks to the decision adopted by the Parliament of the Basque Country in this regard.

This group of laws that we call the Law of Immigration can be condensed around two main governing principles, which in previous works we have come to call the principle of authorisation and the principle of viability. The principle of authorisation establishes that no foreigner can remain on Spanish territory without corresponding administrative or legal authorisation. From the breach of this basic principle is directly derived the existence of the legal category of illegality or irregularity, which characterises this normative group. As for the principle of viability, this implies the granting or recognition of authorisation, and with it the condition of legality, to those foreigners who can demonstrate the economic and social viability of their project of life in Spain. This viability is essentially accredited by a stable income, which could come from an employment contract, viable self-employment or from the availability of sufficient economic resources for maintenance. Together with these two governing principles, the Constitution proclaims, in a way that is more generic than real, equality of rights between Spanish subjects and foreigners, apart from political rights. Nevertheless, the excess of executive power that we have previously criticised as one of the basic characteristics of the law on immigration, goes a long way to dispel this illusion of equality, relegating the efficiency and effectiveness of this principle to a secondary level.

The possible critiques of the content of the Spanish Law of Immigration are numerous and affect both the regulation itself and the procedure by which it was prepared. Nevertheless, here we will focus on what we consider the fundamental conceptual bankruptcy or fracture of this Law. This fracture bears a direct relation to the existence of the legal status of illegality, an essential part of our Law of Immigration, as we have already explained. The incoherence of this section of the law on this point can be ascribed, in our opinion, to two reasons. On one hand, because the legal condition of irregularity in itself forms an important challenge to allegedly basic values of our political culture, such that we must weight the reality of such an administrative infraction against the supposed universality of the most basic human rights. On the other hand, because the mere existence of these irregular situations ends up contravening the logic of the system and makes it evident, reflecting the inadequacy of our laws when compared with the reality of our migratory environment.

In effect, the Law of Immigration is revealed as openly unsatisfactory in the social context in which it acts. Its governing principles make it chronically and permanently obsolete with regard to the reality that it seeks to legislate. To support this it is enough to remember that the number of foreigners in an irregular legal situation in Spain has varied considerably through period of existence of the Law of Immigration. Far from disappearing, the number of foreigners in an irregular situation has increased spectacularly on several occasions throughout these 17 years, and on others decreased, thanks to juridical procedures adopted to that effect. These cyclical variations in the size of the "irregular" group are explained from the legal point of view by the occurrence of "extraordinary" processes of foreigners' regularisation. In effect, in these 17 years of the development of the Law of Immigration in Spain, at least four "extraordinary" processes of regularisation of foreigners have taken place, implying the resolution of more than 400,000 cases. Besides these processes, there have been other normative mechanisms with the same purpose of regularising foreigners in an illegal situation: using the annual quotas of work licences for foreigners already present in the territory of the State, assignment of extraordinary permissions to those who enter the State by way of certain borders (fundamentally Ceuta and Melilla) and other, alternative mechanisms of documentation, such as the one developed in the year 2001 concerning the concept of "rooting".

All these procedures, then, qualified in principle as extraordinary, break with the logic of the system constructed around the previously stated principles of authorisation and viability. Nevertheless, if we look at the alleged "extraordinary" nature of the aforementioned normative mechanisms, we find that their quantitative effects have been as much or more than those of the permanent or ordinary procedures. If anything demonstrates this contradiction it is the evident insufficiency of these normative rules effectively to contain or to regulate the migratory process. With the accumulation of experiences in this respect, and with the acceleration of legislative reforms previously indicated, a high level of legal insecurity is created, and "call effects" (*efecto llamada*) are provoked that theoretically ought to be avoided.

The resulting panorama seems to be intended, in effect, to keep immigrants and social organisations "in suspense", thus eliminating or reducing the responsive capability of alternative proposals. The legal system in question is merely a pattern that is applied repeatedly in the short term, but which provokes contradictory effects in the medium and long term, probably with devastating consequences for social cohesion and certainly, for the human rights of the immigrants. Definitively, from a merely legal analysis, the system is today characterised by a notable absence of legal security in the regulation of immigration. This dynamic, in which the processes of regularisation are cyclical and dispersed, with regulations sometimes differentiated by geographical zones or by countries of origin of the immigrants and with more or less permanent messages of coming normative modifications, must be considered as opposed to the basic requirements of a constitutional state, in violation of the principle of juridical security. Not only ethical, but also utilitarian arguments in our opinion move us to make radical changes to this normative policy and to advance in the informed design of a consistent Law of Immigration for a multicultural social stage in the long term.

Organisational policy

According to the Spanish Constitution, the whole area, both decision-making and executive, relating to immigration, asylum, nationality, passports, borders and foreigners is the responsibility of the central bodies of the State. From the executive point of view, most of the competences have traditionally been distributed among the Departments of Interior, Foreign Affairs, Work and Social Matters. Since 1995 there is an Inter-ministerial Commission for Foreigners and in 1999 a new Secretariat of State (Government Delegation) for Immigration and Foreigners was created. This Secretariat, which constitutes the top governmental body for immigration, is under the Minister of the Interior, representing a vision of migration in which the police perspective predominates over that of social integration.

The Autonomous Communities and Municipalities participate indirectly in the area of immigration through the exercise of their competences in such matters as social well-being, education, health and housing. Certain differences exist in the policies of both in this regard. Since 2001 there has been a Higher Council on Immigration Policy, as the body for coordination between administrations. Nevertheless, it does not seem as if its work to date has served to shed excessive light on this panorama of general lack of coordination.

Among the Autonomous Communities which have expressed important differences with the restrictive policy of the central government, the Basque Country certainly stands out. The contradiction between the Spanish and Basque governments in this matter is testified to by the mutual battle of regulations in the courts. The Basque Government is currently in the approval phase of a very progressive Plan of Immigration, which undoubtedly contradicts the policy of the State on the matter.

As regards social participation in public policy, the principal institution to this effect is the Forum for the Social Integration of Immigrants, created in 1995 as the supreme consultative body in the matter. Public administrations, unions, representatives of business and NGOs, both native and immigrant, take part in this body. Its effectiveness, after seven years of existence, has in general been very limited. This is due, in our opinion, to three factors:

a) The manipulation of the organisation of the Forum by the Government
b) The lack of publicity for its meetings and decisions
c) The inability of the NGOs to carry out unified strategies.

As regards functional participation in the creation of institutional regulations or plans, this has depended basically on the political circumstances and, especially, on the political will of the acting government. In the 1990s there were positive experiences, which were sharply truncated by the legal reforms of 1999 and 2000. In recent years, the general policy of the central government in this regard has been one of scanty and fragmented dialogue: divide and rule. Unfortunately, the lack of political or economic independence of many organisations has facilitated this situation, in which the government seems to be comfortably installed.

Social policies

Regarding the social political for immigration developed throughout the last 17 years, we will synthesise our critique from four basic aspects:

1) Social policy has always been relegated to second place behind repressive control. We have already reflected on this idea, having defined the law in force as a Law of Foreigners and not so much a Law of Immigration.
2) The proliferation of agents that control social policy of foreigners, derived from the complex institutional organisation, which has provoked a great lack of coordination in the adoption and execution of policy. There are important differences between territories and areas of intervention.

3) The appearance in Spain of immigrants from the specific countries from which they have come, coinciding with periods in which the welfare state is being reconsidered in theory and practice. The treatment of immigration is a fertile field for new ideas. There has been a marked increase in participation by the social organisations in this area of public management.
4) A social, institutional and media trend exists linking immigration with social exclusion. This vision makes a blank slate of the enormous differences between immigrants and impedes the adoption of social policy of true integration, not mere welfare.

From the state point of view, two plans for social integration of immigration have been approved to date, in 1994 and 2001. The first served as a base for the creation of the Forum for the Social Integration of Immigrants and of the Permanent Observatory for Immigration.

In 2001 the "GRECO" Plan[1] was approved. This plan has as its central axes, border control, social integration and development cooperation. Nevertheless, many critiques can be made of this programme, which can be summarised as follows:

a) The plan was designed fundamentally by the Ministry of the Interior and not by the Ministry for Social Matters
b) The philosophy of the Plan centres on the control of immigration not on the social integration of immigrants
c) The plan does not contain money for its execution or development
d) Its preparation was accelerated and cryptic, without space for an authentic debate with other policy, institutional or social agents involved.

At present, it cannot be said that the GRECO Plan should be the document of reference for the social policy of immigration. Nor has the existence of regional immigration plans so far served to illuminate a clear and unanimous model of integration. On the contrary, immigration is related exclusively to the demand for work and is seen as a phenomenon of the moment. Social policy is definitively fragmented, ineffective and dispersed. Equally uncoordinated and dispersed are the auxiliary social services given by many social organisations in collaboration with the Administration.

As result of all this, basically the same social problems persist which were perceived in the first analysis fifteen years ago: difficulties in

[1] Global programme of Regulation and Coordination of Foreigners in Spain, whose application covers the period 2000-2004.

access to housing, scanty social or community participation of labour immigrants, precariousness and exploitation, etc. To these are added more recent social problems such as high rates of school failure, family precariousness, the complex situation of many unaccompanied minors or that of prostitutes who are the victims of networks of human trafficking.

Cultural policies

The processes of immigration increasingly raise challenges not only with respect to social integration, but also the need to articulate living together in cultural diversity, beginning by assuring the maintenance and potential development of the immigrants' own cultures. The cultural area affects basic elements of human dignity and, therefore, its treatment is also a requirement of the universal respect for human rights.

Nevertheless, in the Spanish State today cultural policy for immigration is practically nonexistent. Beyond occasional actions, there is no expression, however faint, within any institutional area of a cultural policy that calls for assuring the survival of other cultures, still less for achieving a final state of multicultural coexistence. The lack of a considered model in this respect is evident. The fundamental concern today is over controlling migration and, at most, over the consequences of migration, in terms of collective security. In the most optimistic vision, we run up against social policy of integration, but without knowing about the new cultural reality that appears to us.

Critique of social responses

The reaction of society

Based on analysis of the information offered by sociological studies, it seems possible to deduce that Spanish society has hardly reacted to the new situation. If we look at the evolution of the so-called index of xenophobia, we observe that for the period 1991-1997, there were only small variations and, in any case, a certain positive trend (DEPARTMENT OF WORK AND SOCIAL MATTERS, 1998, p. 14). Racist and xenophobic attitudes have retreated for the most part; but nor does Spanish society show a generous attitude, *a priori*, either to immigration or to the equality of foreigners with natives. In this respect, there is a predominant view that the arrival of immigrants can or should only be allowed inasmuch as the Spanish socio-economic situation permits. Thus, the majority is in agreement with proposals to admit immigrant workers when there are no Spanish workers to fill those jobs (ORIZO/ELZO, 2000, p. 73). This basic consensus can be extended to almost all social areas, though differences exist. Thus, the most open and progressive attitudes are abundant among young people (as opposed to older people), single people (as opposed to families) and those with university education (as opposed to those with a lower level of education). From the policy point of view, the most favourable attitudes to foreigners correspond to the voters of Izquierda Unida (United Left) and some nationalist parties of the Basque Country, Catalonia and Galicia. On the other hand, the voters of the Partido Popular show a clear trend to limit the entry of immigrants, an aspect in which they do not seem to differ significantly from the voters of the Partido Socialista Obrero de España (Spanish Socialist Workers' Party). As regards social participation in organisations related to immigration, it turns out to be almost irrelevant. Passive participation is very scarce, as is voluntary action, in these areas.

But it is relevant in this respect to state that immigration is seen today, from the point of view of public opinion, as one of main problems of the country. An important sector of society increasingly relates immigration to delinquency and the question of immigration is increasingly present in the electoral debate.

Finally, we must say that until now, topics related to immigration and multiculturality have not provoked a major theoretical debate in Spain. In recent years the number of publications, seminars and spaces for reflection in this area has increased, but this fact seems to be the result of a short-term fashion in policy more than the existence of an authentic, long-term profound reflection on the model of society.

Organised society: NGOs

Since the second half of the 1980s, associative voluntary movements with the aim of promoting the social integration of immigrants in Spain have begun to appear. In fact, social organisations dealing with migration did not make their public presence felt until the 1990s. Today in Spain there is a complex panorama of organisations working wholly or partly in this area. Their number has grown spectacularly in recent years. From the state point of view, we could classify these organisations as follows:

a) NGOs whose fundamental activity centres on the defence of immigrants' human rights. Some originated in groups formed within the Catholic Church, some of which have since become independent, including *Red Acoge* (Welcome Web), *Andalucía*

Acoge and *ACEM*.; other organisations focus on work with refugees (*CEAR*) or on campaigning against racism (*SOS-Racismo*).

b) NGOs focused generally on the struggle against exclusion, which devote part of their activity to immigrants: among them, fundamentally *Caritas* and the Red Cross.

c) Humanitarian aid and development cooperation NGOs which dedicate part of their activity in the fourth world to supporting immigrants: *Medicos del Mundo*, *Medicos sin Fronteras, MPDL*.

d) Labour unions that devote part of their activity to the specific defence of immigrant workers: within the area of the Spanish state, fundamentally *UGT* and *CCOO*.

e) Associations and organisations of immigrants and refugees. There are now numerous organisations of this type, both state-wide and local. Their representation of the respective groups is limited. Their purpose and principles of action are as diverse as those of the NGOs. Their structure follows a union model in most cases and they particularly defend interests of origin, depending on the national or cultural group that forms them.

We have already noted how the reformulation of the welfare state has legitimised the adoption by these organisations of a relevant role in the subsidiary execution of public social policy. In principle this phenomenon can be judged to be a positive channel for social participation in public management. Nevertheless, it had and continues to have its disadvantages.

In effect, this dynamic has negatively affected the development of several organisations, especially the development of united strategies of political pressure. From the organisational point of view, many organisations which initially consisted almost exclusively of volunteers now have a significant percentage of contracted personnel in order to provide services subcontracted or promoted by the administration. In many cases this has meant that the voluntary and ideological element of NGOs has moved into second place and, at the same time, they have become strongly economically dependent on the public administration. To this we must add the paradox that many of these organisations with humanitarian and socially responsible aims keep their own workers in precarious conditions which sometimes verge on the exploitative. This does not help them to provide quality services, let alone the truly transformative action which many NGOs should theoretically carry out. On top of this there is the lack of coordination with and between public bodies which has already been criticised.

Definitely, their substantial financial dependence on outside, specifically public, funding, tends in many cases to cancel out the transformative capacity of NGOs. We must add to this other elements which meet perniciously in our social movement, among which we would highlight:

a) The personal or partial interests that are frequently brought into the organisations
b) The absence of long-term strategic reflection
c) The absence of a culture of honest coordination of efforts and of work in networks
d) The weak international presence and work experience of Spanish NGOs.

In this respect, today we face a situation in which a dispersed and weakly coordinated group of social organisations end up supplying a few services to the powers that be. On many occasions this leads to inevitable strategic contradictions, since those who manage these organisations are habitually dependent on public funding through the programmes that they carry out. The administration thus also becomes the legitimating agent of many of their policies. The organisations that are highly professionalised and strongly dependent on external financing thus drastically reduce their transformative and critical capacity, serve the process of slimming down the welfare state and lengthen their life in an interminable process of managing increasing programmes (and consequently resources) that do nothing but provoke larger doses of dependence.

In this situation, the efficiency of NGOs should always be measured against their power to transform reality. Social movements should develop deeply political-ideological work, to the detriment of their resolutional work. Transformative action today demands the greater involvement of social groups in the area of social sensitisation and policy pressure, and a deep strategic redefinition. In this respect, it must be emphasised that other NGOs or social agents, not exclusively related to immigration nor necessarily Spanish, have initiated an appropriate strategy in this respect in our environment. Among these we could mention Human Rights Watch, Amnesty International, Jesuit Refugee Service and some academic areas.

Principal challenges for migration policy today

In conclusion, we will next present the most relevant challenges that we face today in relation to migration policy in Spain. This set of challenges can be synthesised, in our view, around three fundamental axes or processes: European construction, respect for human rights and social participation.

The process of European construction

The process of European construction is projected, certainly, based on the set of institutional policies on which we have commented. In the new and irreversible European reality accelerated by the entry into force of the Amsterdam Agreement, we must think about the following points:

a) The increasing weight of the European Union in decision-making on migration is balanced neither by mechanisms of control nor by a democratisation of community institutions. The centres of decision in the matter become more distant without the appearance of new mechanisms of democratic participation.
b) The institutions of the Union must construct social and cultural policy to accompany policy regulations. Common immigration policy cannot be reduced to the regulation of the phenomenon from the prism of control.
c) Development cooperation and co-development are concepts used rhetorically in many European documents relating to migratory flows. The definitive communitarisation of immigration should imply the same for this area of foreign policy.
d) The NGOs of the Spanish State lack international projection, contacts and experience. They must be prepared to urgently make the leap to the European area in their work of political pressure. The creation and consolidation of European networks of non-governmental organisations in this area is urgent.

Respect for fundamental rights

In this theory, the legal structure consists of a reference to collective safety in the face of the hypothetical arbitrariness of public power. Nevertheless, as we have previously indicated, in the area of immigration, the Law does not comply with the principle of legal security, and in reality integrates a system tending to the segregation of non-native persons. In this framework, it is necessary to attend to the following elements:

a) The Law of Immigration must be reformed in depth, even in its basic principles, in order to adapt to the social reality which it takes charge of controlling. Legal intervention in the migratory phenomenon must be fundamentally focused with regard to the human rights of migrants and not to their harsh control. First of all, the system must guarantee legal safety to the persons, institutions, organisations and bodies involved in the migratory process. The so-called extraordinary processes of regularisation cannot continue shoring up an essentially repressive system.

b) Respect for human rights also demands the disappearance of "dark zones" or "opaque zones" in which foreigners can be found and where most violations of human rights take place: borders, jails, centres of internment or detention, ships or aircraft in the case of human trafficking, and similar environments which the guarantees of a constitutional state hardly reach. The gravity of human rights violations in such areas demands a rethinking of the guarantees that the State must provide, which is translated fundamentally into a definite investment in suitable means, both from the economic and human points of view.

Social participation

Finally, it is in any case necessary to penetrate into the process of democratisation of the State inasmuch as it concerns the area of immigration. This process carries with it the need to contribute efforts in the following areas:

a) The creation of authentic participative conduits in public decision-making, which ensure the presence of effective and independent representatives both of the immigrants themselves and of the host society in the continuous definition and assessment of the development of public policy.
b) The promotion of the construction of social fabric, particularly among immigrant groups. This development of the associative movement should take place within cultural parameters which give priority to voluntary work and the independent criteria of the movements themselves.
c) The institutionally coordinated adoption of strategic plans in the long term with respect to the phenomenon of immigration. The plans must ultimately be adopted by the representative political level of our system, but avoiding the commercialisation of their content on the electoral market.
d) The creation of coherent policies of education and public communication with a positive vision of immigration and multiculturality. The role of the public mass media could be fundamental

for a suitable social interpretation of the dysfunctions that the process will inevitably produce, without ending up in dynamics of conflict or rejection.

e) A deep reflection on the role that the NGOs have played in this area in the last fifteen years. We need a change of course in the strategy of the social movement, and the assumption of social and political pressure as the fundamental area of action of organised civil society, rejecting their conversion into a mere complementary and cheap response that serves to mitigate the social dysfunctions provoked by the established system. On this level, we need to activate the organisation of qualified volunteers and achieve economic independence for the movement.

Definitively, the basic criteria that today orientate public policy relating to immigration in the Spanish State must be profoundly revised and reoriented. In this respect, it is urgent that social movements help to create the necessary conditions so that the above mentioned review can take place. It is also the responsibility of the committed academic area to stimulate and facilitate this dynamic as part of its contribution to a culture of human rights. Not without reason, it is in the area of immigration that Europe will live through its greatest conflict over human rights, at least in the first half of the 21st century.

References

Department of Work and Social Matters/Permanent Observatory on Immigration (1998): *Attitudes towards Immigrants*, Institute of Migrations and Social Services, Madrid.

Orizo, F. A.; Elzo, F. J. (eds.) (2000): *Spain 2000, between localism and globalism. The third European survey of values, 1981-1999*, Foundation Santa Maria / University of Deusto, Bilbao.

Contradictory dynamics within British multiculturalism: pursuing ethnic pluralism while excluding asylum seekers

Charles Husband

In this paper I want to track two contradictory strands in the politics of contemporary British multiculturalism, and explore their implications for immediate and future developments. One strand is the creep of progressive legislation and the attendant policy directives that are incrementally consolidating a distinctive commitment to a pluralistic multiculturalism. A striking feature of this process is the unusual political modesty with which the Government is pursuing this agenda.

The other strand is the pursuit of a politics aimed at deterring refugees and asylum seekers from considering Britain as a preferred place of refuge, and as a corollary of this to drastically reduce the number of asylum seekers who are granted refugee status. Unlike the former political initiative this policy is being pursued with a robust and explicit political rhetoric which panders to xenophobic and racist sentiments.

As any comparative analysis of European states' management of ethnic diversity would reveal, the history of their nation building and the particular construction of their distinctive political institutions, is always central to an understanding of any country's current politics of multiculturalism (KOOPMANS/STATHAM, 2002; GEDDES, 2003). Thus, I would like to initially provide a thumbnail sketch of key features of the British experience.

Firstly, in Britain there is a long history of the management of ethnic diversity. The United Kingdom itself represents a process of conquest and partial incorporation by the English of the Irish, the Scots and the Welsh: memorably described by HECHTER (1975) as Internal Colonialism. And, from COLLEY's (1992) influential account, the meshing of these national minorities together in armed struggle against "common" Catholic enemies in Europe helped to forge a British identity.

Externally the dual processes of colonisation and Imperial administration that were the weft and warp of the British Empire provided centuries of experience of the management of ethnic diversity overseas. The practice of Imperial management was, of course, accompanied by a complementary process of ideological justification. One core element of this was the progressive elaboration of race theory which developed in response to, and legitimated, British involvement in slavery and the expropriation of other peoples' lands and resources. A second ideological element which was central to early race thinking, until substantially overtaken by scientific racism, was Christian theology (JORDAN, 1969). In the late nineteenth century "muscular Christianity" provided a powerful underpinning to British expansionism in Africa and elsewhere. Race thinking (BARZUN, 1965) and Christian theology and idiom continue to exist in British life as two ideological strands in a national imagery woven together like strands of DNA, with the many bridging linkages being formed around specific issues in ethnic interaction. The growth of Islamophobia in recent years has been one such highly visible, and disturbing, linkage.

With this history the British, and perhaps particularly the English, are comfortable with the management of ethnic diversity. It is an established part of our political repertoire and has both the institutional structures and the conceptual language comfortably established as part of the national political fabric. Recognising ethnic diversity and managing ethnic relations does not embarrass the British either personally or politically.

A sense of how important this is can be gained by comparing Britain with France, where, as an on-going consequence of the Jacobin tradition of the French Revolution, the political system is deeply uncomfortable with recognising ethnic diversity. The concept of *laïcité* underpins a secular citizenship which is entire unto itself; not something to be fragmented by considerations of gender, religion or ethnicity (HARGREAVES, 1995). As struggles over the wearing of the chador in school by young Muslim women have revealed, a routine acceptance of cultural diversity and differential citizenship does not sit easily with French political tradition (GEDDES, 2003).

In Britain on the other hand, there is both a political capacity and a language for addressing ethnic diversity. It is the language of "race" and of colour. Early in the modern phase of demographic change through post-war migration of labour from the Commonwealth into Britain both of these languages became established as the norm. In the 1960s and 1970s it was through a discourse about "coloured immigration" that the British state and the British people developed their understanding of contemporary events (HARTMANN/HUSBAND, 1974); and the state apparatus rapidly developed a corpus of law and institutional practice based around a series of Race Relations Acts: 1965, 1968,1976 (SOLOMOS, 1993).

Thus, in the British political context we now have four decades of parliamentary policy formulation and highly contested public debate, in which the language of race and colour has been normalised as both unproblematic and acceptable. We should pause to consider the Promethean significance of this discursive practice. Firstly, we should perhaps reassert its fundamental factual inaccuracy and consequent political danger.

Race is a social construct, not a meaningful biological entity. Thus, as BANTON/HARWOOD (1975) noted:

> As a way of categorising people, race is based upon a delusion because popular ideas about racial classification lack scientific validity and are moulded by political pressures rather than by the evidence from biology (p. 8; see also MASON, 1986).

The danger, and error, in using the language of race is that it introduces a whole historically rooted mode of thought, of "race thinking" which makes rigid categorisation of peoples reasonable; and readily facilitates the routine utilisation of socially constructed stereotypes. Where "race" is used to "explain" social phenomena there is necessarily a distortion of understanding. This process of *racialisation* (OMNI/WINANT, 1986) excludes other modes of understanding and specifically denies acknowledgement of the complexity, flexibility and social nature of human identity and behaviour that is *potentially*[1] accessible through the alternative language of ethnicity.

However, if the historical experience of contact with people of other cultures has provided Britain with a cultural and institutional capacity to recognise ethnic diversity, and to manage it through a racialised understanding of difference, it has also laid down a quite different edifice of belief and value that is relevant to our current circumstances. The British have a strand of self-belief and self-stereotyping that can be found rooted in the collective sense of the long continuity of Britain as a Parliamentary democracy. In the creative acts of selective retention and strategic myopia that goes into the building of a national identity, and the "invention of tradition" (HOBSBAWM/RANGER, 1983), the British have come to see themselves as blessed with an inherent

[1] Ethnicity is of course itself capable of reduction to rigid and inflexible usage; especially where *essentialist* notions of identity generate powerful policing of the processes of inclusion and exclusion from membership in an ethnic group (ERIKSON, 1995).

decency. Notions of Britain the "mother of Parliaments", of being an historical haven for refugees and of having a distinctive capacity for tolerance, are part of this tradition (HUSBAND, 1974, 1987). That there *are* historical bases for these perceptions is important. Equally, a critical scrutiny of these claims would require a considerable exercise of qualification and suitable humility. However, the veracity of self-images is not the sole determining facet of their relevance. Their credibility is de facto more important than their truth, and their ubiquity as general ideas is more potent than knowledge of any supporting evidence. These ideas and values have in the past underpinned imperial expansion, as Britain "took up the White Man's Burden", and in the last decades they have been co-opted into the politics of negotiating the changing ethnic demography of Britain.

A recurrent theme in the political discourse of managing the changing ethnic diversity of Britain has been an explicit concern with "maintaining harmonious community relations". This liberal concern with guaranteeing tolerance and decency in inter-ethnic interactions both draws upon and sustains this notion of British decency. It was classically invoked in the 1960s when a Labour government sought to introduce immigration controls. In the 1965 words of the Labour politician, Roy Hattersley: "Without integration limitation is inexcusable, without limitation integration is impossible." This casuistry in which a tolerant concern for ethnic harmony can be invoked to justify discriminatory immigration legislation was not without its precedents; and has been much copied subsequently.

Notoriously, after Kristallnacht in 1938 Nazi Germany, the British Government understood the current and future circumstances of German Jews, and yet they assiduously endeavoured to limit the number of Jewish people who would be received as refugees in Britain. In the words of one commentator:

> ... one basic assumption emerged, whether all its implications were consciously understood or not. If more Jewish refugees meant, or might eventually mean, more anti-Semitism in host countries, then the cause of anti-Semitism was —the Jew. And since anti-Semitism, at least in its more virulent form, was clearly wrong and barbarous, the only course was to prevent any notable increase in our own Jewish population (SHARF 1964, p. 170).

Here we have a wonderfully corrupt rhetorical formula which in its essence states:

—as decent and tolerant people we are naturally opposed to any form of racism and discrimination and simultaneously

—we are committed to a harmonious society
—immigrants and ethnic minorities have a capacity to generate racial hostility and discrimination from the majority population
—consequently, in order to guarantee harmonious community relations we must rigorously control immigration; but not all immigration —just the immigration of categories of people who attract racist responses.

Consequently, Jews are responsible for anti-Semitism and "coloured immigrants" are responsible for creating racism and discrimination. The locus of this racism, and the access to discretionary power that permits discrimination remains an irrelevant penumbra in this formulaic rehearsal of British tolerance and decency. It is a formula that has been irresistible to successive Governments of the left and right in Britain. In 1973, after a Labour government had passed the deliberately discriminatory 1968 Immigration Act, and when the then Conservative government was pursuing rapid and extreme policies to stop the entry of East African Asians into Britain, the then Home Secretary, Robert Carr, asserted that:

> The Government therefore thinks it right, at this time, when we have just swiftly and honourably accepted the Ugandan Asian refugees and when there is no threat to UK passport-holders elsewhere, to make it clear that while we shall continue to accept our responsibility to UK passport-holders by admitting them in a controlled and orderly manner through the special voucher scheme, this is as much as it is reasonable and realistic for us to do if good community relations are to be maintained in Britain.

This mode of argumentation has been rehearsed by politicians advocating controls on immigration throughout the last four decades, and is amply present in the current politics of anti-Asylum seeker policy.

It is important to recognise the real double agenda in this rhetoric. Whilst its aim is to sustain illiberal and discriminatory border policies, it also *does* rehearse the British concern with tolerance and decency. Whilst efficiently legitimating racism it also asserts assumed common fundamental decencies. That unalloyed explicit racism has been defined as extremist and beyond the political pale is important. The existence of far right neo-Fascist parties, such as the National Front in the 1970s and the British National Party (the BNP) currently, is a potent complement to the rhetoric of generic tolerance and decency because they provide an entirely arbitrary, but politically expedient, definition of racism as extremism. If the BNP racists are extremists, then by definition the rest of us are moderates and reasonable citizens. Through this perversion of a commitment to decency, racist policies may be de facto pursued. And the mainstream steals the thunder of the explicit far right. Perhaps also the persistence of an extreme racist far right political movement in Britain makes a commitment to this fig leaf of decency for the majority routinely important.

As I proceed later in my argument I will return to this question in order to ask why these values are not equally available for co-option to support progressive political initiatives.

Having developed this brief historical context, let me now return to the two parallel processes I wish to examine. I will start with a selective account of two instances of progressive policy development. The first is an instance of primary legislation signalling a political will to pursue equity and social inclusion. From the 1960s British policy response to migration and a changing ethnic demography has contained two parallel agendas echoing Hattersley's formulation. Immigration legislation in 1962, 1968, 1971 and 1981 progressively restricted entry into Britain and attempted to close the boundaries of "Fortress Britain"; whilst in 1965, 1968, 1976 and 2000 Race Relations Acts sought to prohibit discrimination on the grounds of race, and set up institutional bodies —the Community Relations Commission and, subsequently, the Commission for Racial Equality— to promote equality and ethnic cohesion. The 1976 Act was particularly significant in its move away from conceptualising racism as merely a behavioural expression of personal prejudice. The 1965 and 1968 Acts were focused around direct discrimination. Critically, the 1976 Act introduced the concept of *indirect discrimination* which addressed situations where treatment is formally equal, but in its effect discriminates against a group defined in racial or ethnic terms. This removed the issue of intent from the process of demonstrating discrimination and opened up the exploration of *institutional racism* where the routine practices of an organisation *in their effect* are discriminatory (see, for example, CRE, 1999). From this perspective workplace cultures rather than individual actions become significant in exposing the discretionary powers of the majority in marginalising and discriminating against minority ethnic communities. Practically, it reveals the distressing truth that "nice people" can discriminate.

This Act provided a legislative environment in which no institution could take for granted the adequacy of its equal opportunities policy and practice. The absence of explicit racist behaviour was no guarantee of defending yourself against successful prosecution under the Act for procedural discrimination. The Commission for Racial Equality in its pro-active, educational mode published a framework for local authorities to guide their performance in race equality. This was entitled *Racial equality means quality* —a standard for racial equality for local government in

England and Wales. More usually referred to as "The Standards", these guidelines have been influential in informing policy and practice.

Currently the Government is implementing the implications of its Race Relations (Amendment) Act 2000 which came into effect this year. Section 71 (i) of this Act now imposes on every public authority (or organisation fulfilling public functions) a new general duty to:

> make arrangements to ensure that its functions are carried out with due regard to the need:
>
> (a) to eliminate unlawful racial discrimination
> (b) to promote equality of opportunity and good relations between persons of different racial groups.

This Act moves towards a proactive policy in which institutions must demonstrate that they have *anticipated* their capacity to respond to the cultural diversity that is present in the world in which they operate. Much will depend upon how this legislation is implemented and policed. But, it is potentially a significant shift in State intervention in regulating ethnic relations in Britain. It is at the very least an indication of a political will to confront racism and discrimination in the mundane practices of the majority and not just in the expressive extremism of the far right racists.

A parallel process of progressive Governmental intervention has proceeded through the policy initiatives of individual government departments where, through departmental directives and policy statements, significant shifts in practice have been promoted. I will illustrate this in relation to health and social care, where over the last ten years I have been actively engaged in policy related research and development.

Isolated grass roots commitment to recognising the distinctive health care needs, and health care beliefs, of minority ethnic populations has been present in the health care professions since at least the 1970s. But, this has very much been driven by the personal insight and commitment of isolated individuals. As recently as 1996, when with Kate Gerrish and Jenny Mackenzie (GERRISH *et al.* 1996) we published our extensive study of nurse education in Britain, the provision of training in transcultural health care practice was sporadic, excessively dependent upon minority ethnic professional initiative and frequently totally absent. And, in a recent study of how minority ethnic nursing staff achieved senior positions within the NHS, it was revealed that the supportive actions of isolated individuals was one of the key variables (ELLIOT *et al.* 2002). Equal opportunities and transcultural competence in nursing had not become addressed in a systemic manner. In effect, it was up to "nice people" to take responsibility for putting these issues on the professional agenda

Now, however, quietly and cumulatively the Department of Health has shifted the policy framework. There has been a considerable body of research on the inequality in access to care and discrimination within health care experienced by minority ethnic communities (AHMAD, 1993; NAZROO, 1997) and increasing awareness of the differing health care needs and health care beliefs of minority ethnic communities. These insights have been reflected in the recent policy initiatives of the Department of Health. For example, the 2000 Department of Health Paper *The vital connection* clearly stated the intention of the National Health Service to address the health care needs of minority ethnic users. And, the regulatory body of professional nursing, the UKCC, in its 2000 *Requirements for pre-registration nursing programmes* put transcultural competence onto the level of a professional requirement. And currently, as the NHS rolls out *National service frameworks* which provide clear guidance on health care provision and benchmarking of good practice for specific health care needs, issues of race equality have been explicitly included in these documents. And more recently, the Department of Health's (2002) *Essence of health: patient focused benchmarking for health care practitioners* continues the process in linking the benchmarking of clinical practice to the process of clinical governance. Clearly, the Department of Health has actively engaged with addressing the challenge of providing equality of care, and appropriate care, for the minority ethnic communities in Britain. It is important to recognise a key conceptual agenda that has been implicit in this process.

In recognising the demands of guaranteeing equitable treatment in the provision of health care to a diverse range of minority ethnic communities it has necessarily become apparent that "treating everyone the same" is not a viable option. The universalism of TAYLOR's (1992) *equality of respect* does not provide an adequate basis for responding to the different health beliefs and priorities contained within a multi-ethnic client population. Consequently, pragmatically, there has been a drift towards a necessary acceptance of Taylor's *politics of difference* with its powerful implication that "if you want to treat me equally you may have to be prepared to treat me differently". This could sit comfortably with the normative mantra of British nursing —"we deliver individualised holistic care"; but generic xenophobic and racist assumptions have also to be contended with within the profession.

Given the starting point of only a decade ago this transition within the British nursing profession constitutes a positive and important policy transition. It is in its infancy in its impact on actual practice; but it nonetheless represents a significant shift in policy.

For the purpose of my argument here, one of the most striking features of this transition in health care policy, and in the introduction of the Race Relations Act (Amendment) 2000, has been the relatively low profile these initiatives have occupied in the Labour Government's propaganda. At the last election the potential of the Race Relations Act as an explicit indication of the Government's commitment to equality and decency was not a major platform in the electoral strategy. And, it is likely that the expanding transcultural agenda within the NHS is unknown outside of the health care service.

It is as though the positive values that these initiatives articulate cannot be relied upon to generate an adequate political pay-off. It seems as though these values of decency, tolerance and equality are part of a national rhetoric of self-regard that can only be pressed into service when they are self-serving. Or put another way, these values are not so robust that they can effectively compete with other prevailing interests and values. We can pursue this question by turning our attention to the second major policy area of this address, namely border policy and asylum seeking.

In 1962, when a Conservative government introduced the first legislation to restrict immigration from the Commonwealth into Britain, the Labour Party were resolutely opposed to it. However, following the unambiguous electoral evidence of 1964, of how effective the "race card" could be in national elections, when Peter Griffiths won a seat for the Tories, against the national trend to Labour, with the slogan "If you want a nigger neighbour vote Labour", the Labour Party have pragmatically pandered to the racist sentiments of the electorate. The 1968 Immigration Act which was rushed through Parliament in three days in order to restrict Asian immigration from East Africa made some people de facto stateless and represented an explicit escalation in inter-party willingness to use racial antipathy for electoral gain. The process of inter-party competition resulted in a legislative progression through the 1971 Immigration Act until in 1981 under Margaret Thatcher, Britain had a new British Nationality Act. As GEDDES (2003, p. 37) observed: "The effect was that millions of people found their citizenship status amended to deny them access to the country of which ostensibly they had been citizens."

In effect, economic immigration of labour into Britain had exhausted its potential as a distinguishing feature of party politics. However, family renewal and asylum seeking remained potential issues for political contestation.

From 1990 onwards there has been an erratic, but consistent trend, of increasing asylum applications for entry into Britain: from 26,205 in 1990 to 71,700 in 2001. This demographic reality has fuelled a "moral panic" of classic proportions over the threat such immigration represents to British life and culture. This fed a political ferment to radically demonstrate that Britain was not generous to settling refugees. The Labour Government has applied itself with zeal to this task, perhaps succoured by their ideological flirtation with communitarianism. Through the prism of communitarianism the Government actively developed a discourse which favours a moral emphasis on communities; and specifically on the rights and obligations of individuals within them. This emphasis on "the community" has the capacity to extrude asylum seekers from domestic affiliation and render the moral claims of equality under international legal instruments appear flimsy and emotionally thin by comparison. Such sentiments would certainly be supportive of the Government's attempts to place asylum seekers outside of the normative circle of persons entitled to welfare benefits.

Whilst in opposition the Labour Party had opposed the Conservative Government's tough stance on asylum seeking. But, following their landslide election in 1997, they set about the task of reducing the number of asylum seekers entering the country. The 1999 Immigration and Asylum Act introduced vouchers for asylum seekers instead of cash benefits and introduced a national dispersal system to inhibit the concentration of asylum seekers in London and the South East. This Act has subsequently been superseded by the 2002 Nationality, Immigration and Asylum Act which, amongst other things, scrapped the vouchers that had generated a good deal of anger amongst Labour Party activists, and set up the system of rural accommodation centres to pursue their policy of dispersal of refugees and asylum seekers.

Additionally, the Government have been actively pursing a proposal to create "regional protection processing", which would be temporary holding centres for asylum seekers entering Europe; these would be within the European Union. This is itself a moderate variation of the ideas floated by the Blair administration to have "refugee transit processing centres" on routes of entry into Europe. These would be based outside the European Union in countries such as Albania. In these centres the asylum seekers would lodge their claims and be detained while they are being processed. One such camp is reportedly under construction at Trstenik near Zagreb in Croatia. These camps would be the United Kingdom's version of Christmas Island, and asylum seekers arriving in Britain and seeking to lodge a claim would no longer stay in Britain while their claims were being processed. They would instead be transferred to one of the camps outside the UK.

At the recent European Union Summit on 19 June 2003 these controversial plans for such "zones of protection" proposed by Britain and some other member states, were rejected. However, to the accompaniment of the sound of a pragmatic washing of hands, Britain was given permission to proceed on an experimental basis with pilot schemes. Perhaps the British historical experience of introducing concentration camps into South Africa during the Boer War has lowered our sensitivity to policies other member states find distasteful.

The frenetic pace of recent policy formation around asylum seeking and the accompanying assertive rhetoric of Draconian impacts on asylum seeking numbers can perhaps be better understood in the light of the press coverage of the issue. Whilst border policy and the policing of Fortress Britain has remained a recurrently popular theme in British media coverage of ethnic relations, in recent years the increasing number of asylum applications has been paralleled by an increasingly rabid media coverage of the issue.

Throughout 2000/2001 the "threat" posed by asylum seekers entering Britain through the Channel tunnel from a Red Cross reception centre at Sangatte in France provided a focus for a media neurosis. The perception was that Britain was seen as a "soft option" for refugees, with more generous welfare benefits than elsewhere. And media anger at the French Government was matched by a vehement populist campaign against asylum seekers. In January of this year, the *Sun* newspaper, a populist tabloid newspaper with the largest circulation of any newspaper in Britain, launched a "crusade" against what it called "Asylum madness". On 17 January, under the headline "Asylum Meltdown", it urged its readers to "Read this and get angry." At the end of the month the paper was able to claim that it had "touched a nerve in the nation" and that more than half a million people had signed its petition urging the government "to stop bogus refugees flooding the country".

Over the last six months the *Sun* has not been alone in pursuing this fetid agenda. The *Daily Mail*, the *Express* and the *Daily Telegraph* have similarly milked the issue of asylum seeking with a relish that has made a mockery of extant codes of practice for reporting ethnic relations. Asylum seekers have been painted as criminals, welfare scroungers and as occupants of extravagantly favourable housing at state expense. However, as if association with terrorism, malfeasance and unwarranted privilege was not an adequate stigmatisation of asylum seekers, they have also been accused in the press of being the vehicles for the entry into Britain of Aids, tuberculosis and Hepatitis B.

The language of this media assault has reminded me of the mindless venom unleashed against Germans during World War I. It is beyond any defence of relevant fact, it is deliberately emotive and extreme and it is calculated to engender hatred against a whole category of people. It is propaganda of the vilest kind that should shame British journalism. However, it does increase newspaper circulation.

In its Parliamentary existence as one of the most pressing policy issues and in its centrality to press reporting of ethnic diversity, the issue of asylum seeking has revealed a deep vein of xenophobia and myopic nationalism within British life. The ease with which government policies can render someone destitute, provided they are an asylum seeker, and the ease with which the media can maliciously vilify thousands of people, provided they are asylum seekers, must be challenged. That this should be so in a country that is simultaneously pursuing progressive multicultural initiatives adds an ironic and bitter twist to the current situation.

The reality is that in comparison with many other nation states in the European Union, and in the ten accession states of the expanding European Union, Britain has a much more extensive legislative and institutional framework aimed at challenging racism and at promoting ethnic equality within a pluralistic framework. Additionally, although evidence of discrimination, racial antipathy and, indeed, racial assault is not hard to find, judged against a benchmark of 1960, or 1970 the nature and extent of such behaviour has changed. And, undoubtedly Britain is a de facto multi-ethnic society in which ethnic diversity has been normalised in everyday life in a way that would have been unimaginable to the anti-immigrant lobby and the racist ideologues of the 1960s and 1970s. Minority ethnic communities and individuals are present in the everyday fabric of society in a way that demonstrates a progressive transition toward equitable pluralist multiculturalism. There is a long way to go; but, without an historical perspective the current racism and discrimination can seem inevitable and irresistible.

Thus, in this context the parallel politics of anti-asylum seeker malice and social exclusion, and the contradictory cumulative creep of progressive anti-discriminatory policy and practice, is both distressing and dangerous. And, I would like to conclude by offering a brief analysis of this scenario.

To return to my opening argument I feel it is necessary to locate aspects of the ideological environment which underpin the possibilities of both policies. Clearly, despite all the literature about globalisation and its post-modern social correlates, the nation state is far from being an obsolete organisational and political entity, and is still a viable element of collective identity construction. In the United Kingdom the recent history of extending the political autonomy of Scotland and Wales has, if anything, highlighted the English national sentiment and made national identities generally more salient within the United Kingdom. This, of itself, provides one vehicle for sensitising popular feelings about both shared identities and territorial integrity. We have seen pointed questions being put about the possible cultural criteria for entry to British citizenship, and strong border policies have a ready resonance with the wider population.

At the same time, as we noted at the outset, the British have a strong positive self-regard about their own decency. The language of tolerance has been invoked to sustain both the politics of progressive social inclusion and the discriminatory border policies. In terms of the internal politics of progressive multiculturalism, the language of tolerance necessarily places the majority ethnic population in a position of flattering moral virtue. For as I have argued previously:

> For tolerance to be necessary, there must be a prior belief that the person to be tolerated has an intrinsically undesirable characteristic, or that they are not fundamentally entitled to the benefits which are to be allowed them. Those to be tolerated, by definition, possess some such social stigma.
>
> Tolerance is the exercise of largesse by the powerful, ultimately on behalf of the powerful. It is the generous extension of forbearance toward someone who is intrinsically objectionable or not deserving of the privilege being allowed (HUSBAND, 2000, p. 228).

In the context of contemporary multi-ethnic Britain, promoting positive pluralistic social inclusion on the basis of majority tolerance fatally ignores a key reality of British ethnic demography: namely the very great majority of our minority ethnic population are full British citizens. They do not require the generosity of the majority to allow them the resources and freedoms they demand. They have these as of right as citizens. Minority ethnic communities do not seek privileges granted by a tolerant majority, they are demanding their rights. As long as large sections of the majority population hang on to the notions of national identity that render minority ethnic citizens as "not quite British" then they will continue to have difficulties in recognising the rights claims of their minority ethnic neighbours. Perhaps one of the reasons for governmental tentativeness in positively asserting the nature and purpose of their multi-ethnic policies is that they are all too aware of the ambivalent ideological basis of the majority ethnic community's acceptance of their legitimacy.

At the same time, in the past and currently, we have seen that restrictive border policies have also been legitimated in the name of tolerance and a commitment to harmonious community relations. However, it is apparent that such tolerance is regarded as having natural limits. Nation states appear to be very comfortable with the idea that there is a natural limit to their tolerance; that they should not be pushed too far in the name of equality and decency. BLOMMAERT/ VERSCHUEREN (1998), in their analysis of the Belgium response to ethnic diversity, identified the construction of an idea of "the threshold of tolerance". This is an idea which in its essentials asserts that there is a threshold (a limit) beyond which it is not reasonable to expect majority populations to continue with their "normal" level of tolerance. As, for example, when immigration rates or minority ethnic numbers become too high. In their words:

> The threshold of tolerance is an objectifying socio-mathematical concept that defines the conditions under which the all-European tolerance and openness may be cancelled without affecting the basic self-image. The European does not become intolerant, until this threshold is crossed. Just let him or her step back over the same threshold, i.e. just reduce the number of foreigners again, and the good old tolerance will return. In other words, even in moments of intolerance the European is still tolerant at heart, and the observed behaviour is completely due to the factual circumstances which render it impossible to exercise this essential openness. Needless to say, the threshold of tolerance is not an exclusively Belgian notion. It is commonly used in other European countries (p. 78).

The "magic" in this use of the notion of a threshold of tolerance lies precisely in its ability to define tolerance as an on-going property of the majority, which may regrettably be curtailed due to external conditions. From this perspective the proper politics of managing ethnic diversity lies in creating the environment in which tolerance can reign free. This, of course, may mean Draconian border policies excluding asylum seekers and/or restrictive citizenship criteria. Concretely, policies that fly in the face of humanitarian engagement with the lives of others are rendered meaningful as expressions of concern with internal "harmonious community relations". The whole, of course, permeated by an implicit nationalist xenophobia. It is hardly surprising that governments are so aggressively pursuing anti-asylum seeker policies.

In a period where Western capitalism has revealed awesome levels of corruption and fallibility; where the economically comfortable are financially neurotic about share values; where home owners have no reason to believe that their endowment policies are likely to fulfil their stated targets; and where pension schemes emerge as a new variant on the South Sea Bubble Corporation, large sections of the population feel deeply insecure. And, in a world where active participation in politics through the electoral system has almost become a minority activity, large swathes of the electorate are de facto politically irrelevant. In what J.K. GALBRAITH (1992) pointedly called "the culture of contentment", governments are likely to shape their policies to service the anxieties and priorities of this politically salient cohort. So perhaps again we can see why the robust claims of secure borders have greater political play than progressive policies aimed at securing equality of rights, and potentially difference of treatment, for minority ethnic citizens.

As short term pragmatic politics, this perverse differential pursuit of parallel politics may be "politically" understandable. But, as a collusive reinforcement of misguided majority population values and a denial of the political realities of multi-ethnic Britain this is an irresponsible nurturing of future troubles.

References

AHMED, W.I.U. (1993): (ed.) *"Race" and health in contemporary Britain.* Buckingham: Open University Press.

BANTON, M.; HARWOOD, J. (1975): *The race concept.* London: David & Charles.

BARZUN, J. (1965): *Race: a study in superstition.* New York: Harper & Row.

BLOMMAERT, J.; VERSCHUEREN, J. (1998): *Debating diversity: analysing the discourse of tolerance.* Routledge: London.

COLLEY, L. (1992): *Britons: forging the nation.* New Haven, CT: Yale University Press.

COMMISSION FOR RACIAL EQUALITY (1999): *The Stephen Lawrence enquiry: implications for racial equality.* London: CRE http://www.cre.gov.uk.

ELLIOT, J.; WALKER, R.; BALSON, G.; CHOUDHERI, S.; HUSBAND, C. (2002): *Getting on against the odds: how black and ethnic minority nurses can progress into leadership.* London: NHS Leadership Centre, Department of Health.

ERIKSEN, T.H. (1995): *Small places, large issues.* London: Pluto Press.

GALBRAITH, J.K. (1992): *The culture of contentment.* London: Sinclair-Stevenson.

GEDDES, A. (2003): *The politics of migration and immigration in Europe.* London: Sage.

GERRISH, K.; HUSBAND, C.; MACKENZIE, J. (1996): *Nursing for a multi-ethnic society.* Buckingham: Open University Press.

HARGREAVES, A.G. (1995): *Immigration, "race", and ethnicity in contemporary France.* London: Routledge.

HARTMANN, P.; HUSBAND, C. (1974): *Racism and the mass media.* London: Davis-Poynter.

HECHTER, M. (1975): *Internal colonialism.* London: Routledge and Kegan Paul.

HOBSBAWN, E.J.; RANGER, T. (1983): *The invention of iradition.* Cambridge: Cambridge University Press.
JORDAN, W.D. (1969): *White over black.* Harmondsworth: Penguin.
HUSBAND, C. (1974): (ed.): *White media black Britain*. London: Arrow Books.
HUSBAND, C. (1987): (ed): *Race in Britain: continuity and change.* London: Hutchinson Education.
HUSBAND, C. (2000): "Recognising diversity and development skills : the paper role of transcultural communication", in *European Journal of Social Work*, 3(3), pp. 225-234.
MASON, D. (1986): "Controversies and continuities in race and ethnic relations theory", in J. Rex and D. Mason (eds): *Theories of race and ethnic relations.* pp. 1-19, Cambridge: Cambridge University Press.
NAZROO, J.Y. (1997): *The health of Britain's ethnic minorities.* London: Policy Studies Institute.
OMNI, M.; WINANT, H. (1986): *Racial formation in the United States.* New York: Routledge.
SHARF, A. (1964): *The British press and Jews under Nazi rule.* London: Institute of Race Relations/Oxford University Press.
SOLOMOS, J. (1993): *Race and racism in Britain.* Basingstoke: The Macmillan Press.
TAYLOR, C. (1992): *Multiculturalism and "the politics of recognition".* Princeton NJ: Princeton University Press.

Mutual acceptance or rejection? Exploring social distance among German, Turkish and Resettler adolescents

Joachim Brüß

Introduction[1]

Since German reunification immigration into Germany, and the reactions to immigration, have become more important.[2] The current political debate on immigration legislation (see BADE/MÜNZ eds. 2002), indicates that the explosive nature of this subject might continue for quite some time. Moreover, research on the integration of immigrants has repeatedly pointed out that conflicts emerge during the process of integrating immigrants into a host society and that prejudice plays a considerable role in this respect (see for example BROWN, 1995; DUCKITT, 1992; TREIBEL, 1999; HECKMANN,1992).

The social relevance of this subject leads to the question of whether, and to what extent, ethnic prejudice or social distance among adolescents of various descent can be detected. Can we assume that mainly youths of German descent will reject immigrant youths or do these adolescents reject German youths as well? What are the dominant patterns of social relations between the immigrant groups? Can acceptance or rejection be found across all areas of social life, or are some attitudes particularly higlighted? Is it possible that acceptance and tolerance are prevalent in the cognitive area but when it comes to emotional

---

[1] This paper is based on research funded by the German Science Foundation (grant no. HE1385/5). Project directors are Prof. Dr. W. Heitmeyer and Dr. R. Möller.

[2] For the most violent expressions compare the development of rightwing extremist attacks against foreigners since 1990 (For details see the annual reports, *Verfassungsschutzberichte*, published by the German Ministry of the Interior or http://www.verfassungsschutz.de).

aspects, coldness and distance are the norm? This empirical field study attempts to assess the relationships between autochthonous, German, and allochthonous, Turkish (settled) and Resettler (recent) adolescents.[3] The main question is whether and to what extent social distance among three ethnic adolescent groups can be revealed and whether acceptance or rejection determines the interethnic relations.

Considerations for the measurement of mutual acceptance and rejection

The mutual perceptions among German, Turkish and Resettler adolescents are based on a survey that includes aspects of prejudice and social distance against distinct out-groups. In order to accomplish this, suggestions made by DUCKITT (1992), BROWN (1995), and BOBO/HUTCHINGS (1996) have been consulted. The construct *acceptance* versus *rejection* factors in emotional and behavioural components, cognitive attitudes and anxieties regarding declining resources. This instrument should be sensitive enough to tap into the difference separating "subtle prejudice" from "blatant prejudice", as has been widely used in American scholarship and research on race relations and prejudice.[4] Finally, the survey must incorporate questions appropriate to the level of adolescents, and they must be applicable for each group included in the research. These are central requirements for the measurement of mutual perceptions, particularly when considering that systematic scientific research in Germany involving two or more migrant groups is rarely found. Measurement instruments that have been primarily worked out for evaluating the attitudes of the majority population as for instance in ALLBUS or Eurobarometer surveys, offered suggestions, but could not be adopted completely.

---

[3] In order to keep the writing concise and to avoid overly complex analyses, adolescents without a migration background are defined as German adolescents. Adolescents with a migration background from Turkey, whose families started to arrive in the late 1950s, are described as Turkish adolescents. Finally, youths who came with their families from the ex-USSR, Romania or Poland since the mid 1980s are labelled Resettler (*Aussiedler*) adolescents. In addition, the group of Turkish immigrants can be described as settled, whereas the *Aussiedler* are seen as recent immigrants.

[4] See for instance McCONAHAY (1986), SEARS (1988) or PETTIGREW/MEERTENS (1995). In our case, we do not assume that blatant versus subtle prejudice constitute two distinct dimensions but rather presume that the different responses indicate an assessment continuum ranging from acceptance to refusal. Nevertheless, research on blatant versus subtle prejudice has worked out pertinent insights into the procedures of how to measure prejudice.

The attitudes regarding the mutual social relations of the three groups can be depicted by using an overarching perception continuum ranging from acceptance to rejection. The more often respondents express warm and favourable feelings, the more they consider mutual activities with members of the out-group, the more they accept the sociality of the out-group and the less they are afraid of resource anxieties, we will classify these attitudes as acceptance of out-group members. In the opposite case we will speak of rejection against the out-group and that overlaps with aspects of prejudice.

Social scientists define *prejudice* as comparatively rigid attitudes and rejection of other individuals and groups. According to BROWN (1995) prejudice is regarded as a) the holding of derogatory social attitudes or cognitive beliefs, b) the expression of negative affect, and c) the display of hostile and discriminatory behaviour toward members of a group on account of their membership of that group.

In addition to this, BOBO/HUTCHINGS (1996) note with reference to BLUMER (1958) that prejudice or hostilities between social groups are not only based on individually learned emotions and convictions but are also historically grown and carry a collective assessment of group position with them. Ethnic prejudice is then to be understood as a challenge for *group position*, and prejudice is used as a means of maintaining and securing the integrity and position of a dominant social group.

From the individual perspective, prejudices are social attitudes, acquired and maintained through an interaction of external influences (e.g. socialisation, culture), usual psychological functions (e.g. perception and categorisation), and through the personality structure of the individual. From a social perspective, prejudice is conveyed via the role "that prejudice played in supporting the society's racial caste system" (KATZ, 1991: p. 127). In this regard establishing and supporting group positions is of paramount importance and intergroup comparisons play a central role.

Favouring the ingroup and/or the out-group?

Since this study will include categories for ethnic identity, the analysis will also use theoretical assumptions of Social Identity Theory. In this theory, according to TAJFEL/TURNER (1986), individuals strive for a positive social identity which they gain from favourable intergroup comparisons. Experiments based on minimal group research designs have consistently shown that the effect of *categorisation* not only results in distinguishing in-group and out-group, but also that preferences for the in-group are expressed (TAJFEL, 1982). For this reason, a favouring of the in-group seems inevitable. Although this does not mean that in-group favouring automatically goes with rejection of the out-group, it is assumed that individuals are prone to such behaviour.

Based on results of several scientific studies on intergroup comparisons, HINKLE/BROWN (1990) robustly find that the same group shows a preference for the in-group and for the out-group as well as showing no preference for a particular group. This is a clear indication of a dependence on context and of the possibility of crossed categorisations for the comparisons in question. Results of their analysis indicate that the acceptance or rejection of out-groups is based on status. That is, lower status groups do not necessarily refuse out-groups with higher status.

An explanation for this is offered by Social Dominance Theory. SIDANIUS/PRATTO (1999) stress different potentials for and realisations of *social dominance* in a society that itself is structured as systems of group-based social hierarchies. According to them, the psyche of subordinates reflects not only the desire for positive regard and belonging but also their group's inferior position, just as the psyche of dominants mirrors their privileged position in society. The *asymmetry hypothesis* then posits, because in-group favouritism may be easier for and more valuable to dominants, that in-group favouritism will be stronger among dominants than among subordinates. Taking status into account, this implies that in-group favouritism is most prevalent among groups that have equal or greater status than the out-group. In contrast, out-group favouritism occurs more often when the out-group has higher status and when the social status hierarchy is perceived to be both legitimate and stable. Thus, Sidanius and Pratto help to explain the differences in favouritism by stating that, "both in-group favoritism on the part of dominants and out-group favoritism on the part of subordinates would seem to help maintain the system of group-based inequality" (1999, p. 230). Thus, in order to understand the group status for this study it is necessary to evaluate the social participation of our target groups.

Evaluating the status of the groups

The socio-economic background of the adolescents indicates a relative deprivation for the Turkish adolescents regarding education and parents' occupational status. In comparison with Resettler and German parents, Turkish parents do not often have a profession, though in some cases they have completed vocational training. Less frequently they have a technical diploma or even a university degree. For the mothers of Resettler adolescents it is important to note that they have less often completed vocational training in industry or administration. On the other hand, they more often have a technical diploma or a university degree than mothers of Turkish or German adolescents.

Regarding current job status, Turkish parents work less often in full- or part-time jobs in comparison with Resettler and German parents. Fathers of Turkish youths work more frequently in part-time jobs, and are more often retired or unemployed than fathers of German and Resettler adolescents. Mothers of Turkish youths work less often in part-time jobs and are more often home-makers than mothers of German and Resettler adolescents.

The relative deprivation of families of Turkish descent does not mean that they are entirely excluded from social participation. But regarding their socio-economic background, the command of a comparatively lower amount of resources has to be taken into account, especially when social participation in the labour market is concerned. Considering social position, this means that Turkish adolescents have a lower amount of resources and thus have less chance of social participation. In comparison, the positions of German and Resettler adolescents are well advanced.

This difference is even more substantial when political participation is taken into consideration. Resettler families are given German citizenship as soon as they enter the country after having proved that they are Resettlers and not Russian or Polish immigrants. In contrast, Turkish adolescents have to apply for citizenship if they wish to participate directly in politics, for instance in elections or for certain political or administrative posts.

Hence, the ascribed social status will be based on considerations of realised social participation of the three groups. The group with higher status is able to realise a higher amount of social participation measured by the average school education of the adolescents and by qualification and job type of their parents. Migrants of Turkish descent are still the most disadvantaged group amongst the guest-worker population, accounting for a comparatively high unemployment rate. Compare for example the statistics for Spanish, Greek, Italian and Turkish adolescents (Beauftragte der Bundesregierung für Ausländerfragen, 2000). However, changes in school education in the German state of North Rhine-Westphalia (NRW) indicate that the gap between Resettler and Turkish adolescents is getting smaller. The majority of these youths still attend the *Hauptschule*, but a tendency for Turkish adolescents to switch from the *Hauptschule* to the *Gesamtschule*, and for the Resettlers from the *Hauptschule* to the *Realschule*, can be observed. But the proportion of those who attend the *Gymnasium* is still low in comparison with German adolescents. Some scholars argue that this is an indication of institutional racism in Germany (e.g. GOMOLLA/RADTKE, 2002).

Taking this together, it is reasonable to categorise the group of German adolescents as members of the dominant group with high status. The group of Resettler adolescents will cautiously be regarded as subordinates having a medium status. The group of Turkish adolescents are classified as subordinates with low status given the comparatively low amount of realised social participation.[5] Since status serves as an additional relevant category for the analysis of intergroup differences, it will be discussed later to what extent the basic assumption of Social Identity and of Social Dominance Theory can be corroborated across all three groups in this field study. But before that, the model specification for the analysis is introduced.

Specifying the analysis

The complexity of the instrument stems from two sources. In taking the criticism by Katz seriously, and in order to include the central dimensions for a measurement of acceptance versus rejection, the construct is based on direct and indirect evaluations of the out-groups. First, to investigate the more individually or directly based relations, cognitive, emotional and behavioural evaluations were sought. On the other hand, in assessing primarily social or indirect relations, questions directed toward the social life of the out-groups, as well as perceived threats of declining resources were asked. Taken together, Figure 1 shows the ideal type structure for the analysis (for the specific items, see Appendix).

For mutual perceptions between German, Turkish and Resettler (Aussiedler) adolescents the following *hypotheses* will be investigated:

Relating to Social Identity Theory, across the groups we expect to find a clear in-group preference and a rejection of the out-groups.

- For the German adolescents, we expect to find that they will keep Turkish and Resettler adolescents at a certain distance. This assumption corresponds with BLUMER'S (1958) and BOBO'S

[5] This is not to say that individuals of any of these groups are per se dominant or subordinate or of high versus low status or prestige. The classification is explicitly made for an intergroup comparison and not meant to be derogatory for individual members of the particular groups.

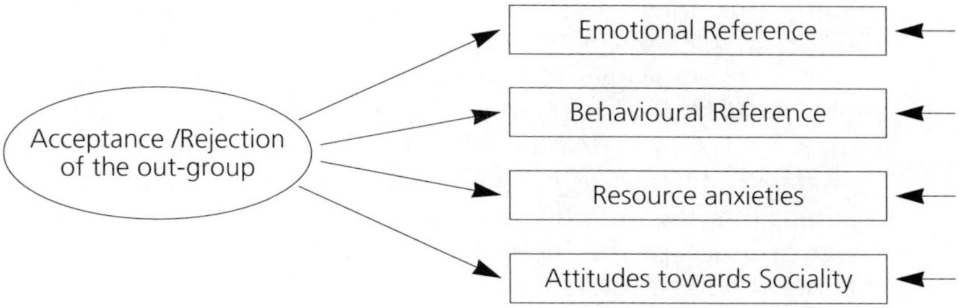

Figure 1
The attitude structure for the group comparison

(1999) approach of conceptualising prejudice as a threat to group position. According to this, prejudice and social distance aim at maintaining and securing group position in society. Further, from Social Identity Theory, there should be no incentives for a positive distinction for German adolescents if they accept members of migrant groups. Thus, this might lead to a rejection of the out-groups.

—For the adolescents with a migration background, the main assumption refers to a strong reason for migration in general: the expectation, or the wish, to improve one's living conditions. Thus, the answers from Turkish and Resettler adolescents are expected to be more friendly and accepting of German youths rather than expressing an attitude of rejection. In this case, out-group approval can indicate membership within the receiving society and this should support a positive social identity. Thus, for the two groups with lower social status we do not expect a refusal of the out-group with higher status.

—For social relations among immigrants, we expect a slight but substantial rejection of the "settled" group (in this case the Turkish youth) by the "recent" migrant group (here the Aussiedler adolescents) because of the particular conditions under which the Resettlers came to Germany. According to classical research on migration (BOGARDUS, 1930), the opposite would be a standard assumption. Under equal conditions, the newcomers would try to climb up the social ladder and the established groups might use prejudice and social distance to prevent or retard their social mobility. In our case, we cannot speak of equal conditions. Because of the political and governmental support for the Resettlers, we assume that they express prejudice and social distance against the Turkish adolescents in order to maintain their privileges. Moreover, it is to be expected that Resettler adolescents may identify more closely with the German youth, providing an additional reason to distance themselves from Turkish adolescents.[6] Finally, considering differences in group status Social Dominance Theory assumes that the Resettler adolescents in particular will reject the lower and accept the higher status group in order to maintain the intergroup structure.

Before we report on the results, a brief description of methods and sample structure will provide a better understanding of the scale of the study.

Methods

Sample selection

The *population* for this study consists of all pupils in the 10th grade (aged 16 to 17) who went to one of the four main state school types (*Hauptschulen*, *Realschulen*, *Gesamtschulen* and *Gymnasien*)[7] in NRW during 2001. This means that all pupils who come from a German, Turkish or Resettler family background in 54 urban and rural areas in NRW belong to the target population. The *selected sample* encompasses adolescents from these three ethnic groups from 24 urban and rural areas, with a comparatively high proportion of youths coming from a Turkish and Resettler background. The fieldwork was conducted in these areas, with roughly 69,200 German, 5,200 Turkish and 8,400 Resettler adolescents being potential respondents.

Fieldwork

In preparing the actual fieldwork we asked all state schools in the 24 urban and rural areas to participate. Those schools that agreed to participate received information for all the pupils in the 10th grade, as

---

[6] This seems particularly valid for the *Aussiedler* from the former Soviet Union, who were separated as so called *Volksdeutsche* (ethnic Germans) from the former ruling regime. This will have led to a stronger identification with the adolescents of German descent since their ethnic identity was not fully recognised in their former country and now they are able and possibly willing to develop the notion of a matching member- and citizenship.

[7] *Hauptschulen* are regarded as the least challenging schools in comparison with the *Gymnasien*, where attendance normally leads to further studies at universities.

well as material informing their parents about the study. The information was distributed in class and those pupils who wished to participate returned a letter of agreement. For the actual data collection, pupils received a questionnaire plus a small reward. In other cases, more often in the *Hauptschulen*, head teachers told us early on that the fieldwork should take place in the schools, otherwise there was a high probability that questionnaires would not be returned. In these schools the surveys were conducted in the classrooms. Of those 15,400 pupils who agreed to participate in the study (18.6 % of potential respondents), 60 % completed the survey at home and 40 % were surveyed at school. The subsequent surveys in this longitudinal study —last year and over the coming years— are self-report surveys.

The sample and its distribution

The *resulting sample* (72.7 % of those who declared participation), the IKG-Youth-Panel 2001, is composed of 6,055 German, 1,652 Turkish and 3,539 Resettler adolescents. This large number of participants is necessary as some respondents will not participate throughout the complete survey period of six years, panel mortality must be taken into account. The subgroups of immigrant youths must be large enough for comparative analyses, hence the over-sampling for them.

The distribution of pupils according to school attendance shows that the sample includes fewer adolescents from *Gesamtschulen* across all groups and fewer migrant youths from the *Gymnasium* compared with the population distribution. Regarding German adolescents, while there are too many pupils from the *Hauptschule* there are too few from the *Gymnasium* in our sample. In addition, the gender distribution is unbalanced.[8]

In order to match the sampling distribution with the population, the analysis was weighted to adjust for gender and school attendance in relation to the distribution in the population. Turkish and Resettler adolescents are classified according to their migration background, not only their citizenship. The classification is based on responses to questions about the pupils' descent (e.g. place of birth, passport) as well as including

---

[8] Particularly for the Turkish and the Resettler adolescents, the proportion of women is too high considering the normal demographic situation. For the German youths the gender distribution is appropriate. The combination of this distribution shows specifically that female migrants in the *Gymnasium* are over-represented while male migrant pupils from the *Gesamtschule* are under-represented. Concerning the German adolescents there are too many male pupils from the *Hauptschule* in the sample.

information on the parents' background and on the languages spoken in the household. The weights calculated range from 0.41 for female Resettler adolescents from the *Gymnasium* (n = 457) to 1.89 for male Turkish adolescents from the *Gesamtschule* (n = 119).

Results

This section describes and compares the interethnic attitudes for the three groups. Because of the very large sample size, all significance tests for differences in means and variances are carried out for an error probability of $p < 0.01$.

Looking for the general sentiment

To begin with, the overall emotional relations toward the particular groups are analysed with the help of a feeling barometer. Respondents were asked how they felt toward the out-groups and answers were marked on a 5 point scale, from "very negative" (–2) to "very positive" (+2). A first glance, comparing the values in the diagonal with those in the off-diagonal, clearly shows that the in-group assessments are frequently linked with more positive feelings than out-group assessments (see Table 1). This finding corroborates Tajfel's (1981) basic hypothesis of Social Identity Theory, that in a group comparison the preference is given to one's own group. Despite this, the findings indicate that we cannot completely corroborate a general out-group rejection based on responses to the feeling barometer.

Table 1

Average Responses to the Feeling Barometer[a]

General feelings	German adolescents	Turkish adolescents	Resettler adolescents
Toward German youth	m = 1.26 [a]	m = 0.90	m = 1.00
Toward Turkish youth	m = –0.24	m = 1.36	m = –0.26
Toward Resettler youth	m = 0.18	m = 0.41	m = 1.19

[a] The means are based on a 5-point scale with indicators at the extremes, labelled (–2) for a "very negative" and (+2) for a "very positive" feeling.
German adolescents n = 6,055
Turkish adolescents n = 1,652
Resettler adolescents n = 3,539

Source: IKG Youth Panel 2001

On average, feelings toward the German adolescents are quite positive and warm. In contrast, German adolescents do not express such warm feelings toward migrant youth, rather they remain indifferent. This corresponds closely with assumptions of Social Dominance Theory since the dominant group expresses closeness with the in-group but keeps the subordinate or the lower status groups at a certain distance.

Turkish adolescents receive the worst evaluations from German and Resettler adolescents. At the same time, they have the highest in-group values, though this is not related to a general out-group rejection. Turkish adolescents just express positive and warm feelings more often toward the in-group than toward the out-groups. In other words, the group with the lowest status expresses strong in-group feelings but also shows distinct inclinations to be on good terms with the higher status group.

In comparison with this, the Resettler adolescents show the largest differences in their feelings toward the out-groups. General feelings toward the German adolescents are nearly as warm and positive as feelings toward their own group. In contrast, emotional expressions of Resettlers toward the Turkish adolescents are much colder and more distant, thus we detect a tendency for emotional rejection. Corroborating the asymmetry hypothesis of Social Dominance Theory, the medium status group maintains the social hierarchy by expressing closeness with the dominant group but distance from the low status group.

Focusing on the group-specific attitude structures

For a more detailed analysis, 9 items provided the necessary complexity for measuring acceptance versus rejection across groups. Four major dimensions of mutual evaluations are used for the intergroup comparisons. These are:

—The *emotional factor* combines two evaluations that a) they like to be together with youths of the out-group with b) the general feelings toward the out-group.

—The *behavioural factor* consists of three assessments that a) they would lend something to members of the out-group, b) they would share personal problems with members of the out-group, and c) they would invite out-group members to a party.

—*Resource anxieties* are based on two propositions, a) that living conditions in the neighbourhood will be more difficult and b) there will be fewer options for vocational training if more out-group members live in the area.

—An *evaluation of the social life* of the out-group (its sociality) encompasses two items, a) that they like the way that out-group members deal with each other, and b) that members of the out-group are open-minded and friendly toward others.

Analysing the attitude structures

On the whole, answers from German adolescents (GA) indicate a more friendly and welcoming attitude toward the Resettler (RA) than toward the Turkish adolescents (TA). This is particularly highlighted by an emotional acceptance instead of an emotional rejection (26 % vs. 14 %; m = 0.11 w/RA, m = –0.30 w/TA; t = –23,1)[9], a less frequent rejection of the sociality of the Resettler than the Turkish adolescents (34 % vs. 47 %; m = –0.38 w/RA, m = –0.65 w/TA; t = –16,6), and a significantly stronger disapproval regarding resource anxieties favouring the Resettler and not the Turkish adolescents (47 % vs. 39 %; m = –0.53 w/RA, m = –0.32 w/TA; t = 10,2).

Table 2

Average approval and disapproval in the attitude structure[a]

Disapproval and approval of: [b]	German adolescents		Turkish adolescents		Resettler adolescents	
Regarding:	w/ TA	w/ RA	w/ GA	w/ RA	w/ GA	w/ TA
—Emotional acceptance	–0.30	0.11	0.91	0.28	1.00	–0.37
—Behavioural acceptance	–0.01	0.22	0.68	0.05	0.85	–0.27
—Resource anxieties	–0.32	–0.53	–1.12	–0.83	–1.15	–0.45
—Evaluations toward out-group sociality	–0.65	–0.38	*–0.14*	*–0.13*	–0.03	–0.52

[a] Means are based on a scale ranging from –2 for "strong disapproval" to +2 for "strong approval".
[b] Non-significant mean differences (p > 0.01) are printed in italics
GA: German adolescents n = 6,055
TA: Turkish adolescents n = 1,652
RA: Resettler adolescents n = 3,539

Source: IKG Youth Panel 2001

[9] See also Table 4, Appendix for more information on responses in per cent. For the mean differences, two-tailed t-tests were carried out. Degrees of freedom for German respondents are df = 12,108, for the Turkish group df = 3,302 and for the Resettler group df = 7,076.

The comparison for the views of Turkish adolescents corroborates that they tend to have better relations with the German than with the Resettler adolescents. In particular, Turkish youths significantly more often express emotional closeness toward German than toward Resettler adolescents (62 % vs. 33 %; m = 0.91 w/GA, m = 0.28 w/RA; t = 18.9). Moreover, Turkish youths more often approve activities with German than with Resettler adolescents (61 % vs. 37 %; m = 0.68 w/GA, m = 0.05 w/RA; t = 16.9). And finally, Turkish youths disagree with resource anxieties, and this more strongly regarding German than Resettler adolescents (71 % vs. 56 %; m = –1.12 w/GA, m = –0.83 w/RA; t = –8.8).

The most pronounced differences are revealed for the Resettler adolescents. Their answers clearly favour the German adolescents and keep the Turkish adolescents at a distinct distance. This is highlighted by their responses to the emotional factor (66 % vs. 14 %; m = 1.00 w/GA, m = –0.37 w/TA; t = 62.4) as well as the reply to the behavioural aspects in their relationship (67 % vs. 28 %; m = 0.85 w/GA, m = –0.27 w/TA; t = 43.2). Moreover, resource anxieties are far more rejected in relation to German than to Turkish adolescents (71 % vs. 42 %; m = –1.15 w/GA, m = –0.45 w/TA; t = –31.1). In order to complete the findings, Resettler adolescents tend to reject the sociality of Turkish youths whereas they express indifference toward the German youths (41 % vs. 19 %; m = –0.53 w/TA, m = –0.02 w/GA; t = 24.1).

Who is in and who is out? Comparing the attitude structures

Summarising the results for the group-specific attitude structures it is justified to argue that migrant adolescents express approval toward German youths very often regarding the emotional and behavioural acceptance of the relationships. In comparison to this, German adolescents remain more distant toward the out-groups. But they also reject evaluations stressing resource anxieties. Concerning German youth, migrant adolescents on average clearly reject resource anxieties.

The intergroup relations of the migrant youths are characterised by less interethnic proximity than with German adolescents. Particularly for the emotional and behavioural aspects Turkish and Resettler adolescents are more in favour of relations with German adolescents, than they are with those to each other. Turkish youths tend to remain indifferent toward Resettler adolescents, whereas for them a tendency for rejection of Turkish youths can be observed.

For acceptance and rejection on the whole it appears to be the case that German adolescents are widely accepted by the migrant youths. In contrast, Turkish migrants seem to be rejected or at least kept at a certain distance by German as well as by Resettler adolescents. The Resettler adolescents obtain slightly better evaluations from the German youths and they tend to reject Turkish adolescents. Hence Resettler adolescents do not seem threatened by social marginalisation, whereas Turkish adolescents might run the risk of becoming marginalised.

Summary and conclusion

At the beginning we asked whether and to what extent acceptance or rejection among adolescents of different descent could be detected and analysed. Can we assume that predominantly German adolescents exert social distance against the two migrant groups or can rejection also be found for the migrants against the German youths or between themselves? Additionally, we also sought to find out what attitude dimensions in particular are characterised by acceptance or rejection. The mutual evaluations of social proximity/distance can be summarised:

—The evaluations of adolescents with a migration background are friendly and accepting toward the German youths regarding the emotional and behavioural aspects in the relations. But in contrast, this is not fully the case for the notions of the German adolescents regarding the two migrant out-groups. Hence the relations between allochthonous and autochthonous adolescents are characterised by social proximity whereas for the reverse case a relation of social distance is observed.

—The comparison between the attitude structures of the two migrant groups reveals that German adolescents show a tendency toward social proximity regarding the Resettler youths. The relation with Turkish adolescents seems to be determined by social distance.

—Turkish adolescents experience social distance from German *and* from Resettler youths. This is particularly expressed by less approval with notions of emotional and behavioural attitudes.

—The aspect of social life (sociality) of the German adolescents is assessed ambiguously by the migrant adolescents. In contrast, the German adolescents specifically reject the sociality of Turkish youth, and to a certain degree also disapprove of sociality of the Resettler adolescents.

—On the whole, resource anxieties are most frequently dismissed, in particular by Turkish adolescents. However, German as well as

Resettler adolescents, though slightly less, do not reject resource anxieties against Turkish youths very strongly.

Linking empirical findings with theoretical considerations, it is now possible to agree that Blumer's approach to explaining prejudice using group positions within a society offers good guidance. The two groups who face possible threats in their group position, in our case German and Resettler adolescents, have expressed their views that match our theoretical assumptions. On average, they show a certain amount of social distance toward the group with lower status, represented in this case by the Turkish adolescents. This group, possessing a weak group position, reveals only limited reservations against the out-groups. It is more appropriate to say that Turkish adolescents combine a distinct in-group favouritism with friendly and warm evaluations toward the two out-groups.

Considering the main hypothesis of Social Identity Theory, an extension regarding social context seems necessary. This was already suggested in the paper by HINKLE/BROWN (1990). It is not true in all cases, that in-group favouritism is accompanied by a general out-group rejection. Specifically, the group with the strongest in-group bias, Turkish adolescents, do not express themselves according to the basic theoretical assumption. They may express some reservation but that cannot be seen as an out-group rejection per se.

Against the background of status considerations our results show that the group with lowest intergroup status, with on average less well-realised social participation, in this case Turkish adolescents, express more often than the other groups friendliness and acceptance toward the out-groups. In contrast to this, the answers of the group with medium status and comparatively well realised social participation, here Resettler adolescents, are split for the out-groups. Regarding the German adolescents, in our study the high status group, Resettler youths express distinct acceptance and approval whereas the group with lesser amount of realised social participation is rejected and kept at a certain distance. Although the rejection is not overwhelmingly strong, it is distinct. Finally, the high status group, in this case the German adolescents, expresses a certain amount of social distance toward the two out-groups and to a somewhat larger extent against the Turkish than against the Resettler youths. These findings corroborate a general assumption of Social Dominance Theory that groups with lower social status tend not to discriminate against groups with higher status. Moreover, SIDANIUS/PRATTO (1999) claim for groups in between, that they tend to discriminate against those with lower but accept those with higher status. In both cases groups are apparently prone to accept the given social hierarchy and order and are engaged in maintaining this. As we could see with findings for the German, Turkish and Resettler adolescents, this pattern could be examined regarding interethnic evaluations. Plus, recalling the fact the Turkish adolescents have been living in Germany much longer than Resettler adolescents, it is the ascribed social status backed by means of social participation that defines the intergroup setting. Given the current legislation in Germany and the low proportion of naturalised migrants from Turkey, the status distribution is likely to continue. But it remains to be seen whether the interethnic relations, the revealed structure of mutual acceptance or rejection, will be stable over time as well.

References

ALLPORT G. W. (1979): *The Nature of Prejudice.* Addison-Wesley, Reading, MA.

BADE K. J.; MÜNZ R. eds (2002): *Migrationsreport 2002.* Campus, Frankfurt am Main.

BEAUFTRAGTE DER BUNDESREGIERUNG FÜR AUSLÄNDERFRAGEN (2002): *Daten und Fakten zur Ausländersituation*. Selbstverlag, Berlin.

BLUMER H. (1958): "Race prejudice as a sense of group position." In *The Pacific Sociological Review,* 1, p. 3-7.

BOBO L. D. (1999): "Prejudice as group position: Microfoundations of a sociological approach to racism and race relations." In *Journal of Social Issues,* 55, p. 445-472.

BOBO L. D.; HUTCHINGS V. L. (1996): "Perceptions of racial group competition: Extending Blumer's theory of group position to a multiracial social context." In *American Sociological Review,* 61, p. 951-972.

BOGARDUS E. S. (1925): "Measuring social distance." In *Journal of Applied Sociology*, 9, p. 299-308.

BOGARDUS E. S. (1930): "A race-relation cycle." In *American Journal of Sociology,* 35, p. 612-617.

BREWER M. B.; HO H. K.; LEE J. Y.; MILLER N. (1987) "Social identity and social distance among Hong Kong schoolchildren." In *Personality and Social Psychology Bulletin,* 13, p. 156-165.

BROWN R. (1995) *Prejudice. Its Social Psychology.* Blackwell, Oxford UK, Cambridge MA.

DUCKITT J. (1992) *The Social Psychology of Prejudice*. Praeger, New York, London.

GOMOLLA M.; RADTKE F. O. (2002) *Institutionelle Diskriminierung: Die Herstellung ethnischer Differenz in der Schule*. Leske & Budrich, Opladen.

HECKMANN F. (1992) *Ethnische Minderheiten, Volk und Nation: Soziologie interethnischer Beziehungen.* Enke, Stuttgart.

HEWSTONE M.; ISLAM M. R.; JUDD C. M. (1993) "Models of crossed categorization and intergroup relations." In *Journal of Personality and Social Psychology,* 64, p. 779-793.

HINKLE S.; BROWN R. (1990) "Intergroup comparisons and social identity: Some links and lacunae." In *Social Identity Theory. Constructive and Critical Advances,* ed. M. A. Hogg and D. Abrams. Harvester Wheatsheaf: New York, p. 49-70.

KATZ I. (1991) "Gordon Allport's *The Nature of Prejudice.*" In *Political Psychology,* 12, p. 125-157.

MCCONAHAY J. B. (1986) "Modern Racism, ambivalence, and the modern racism scale." In *Prejudice, Discrimination, and Racism*, ed. S. L. Gaertner and J. F. Dovidio. Academic Press; Orlando, FL, p. 91-125.

PARK, R. E. (1924) "The concept of social distance." In *Journal of Applied Sociology*, 8, p. 339-344.

PETTIGREW T. F.; MEERTENS R. W. (1995) "Subtle and blatant prejudice in Western Europe." *European Journal of Social Psychology,* 25, p. 57-75.

SEARS D. O. (1988) "Symbolic Racism." In *Eliminating Racism: Profiles in Controversy*, ed. P. A. Katz and D. A. Taylor. Plenum, New York, p. 53-84.

SIDANIUS J.; PRATTO F. (1999) *Social Dominance: An intergroup theory of social hierarchy and oppression.* Cambridge Univ. Press, Cambridge, MA.

TAJFEL H. (1981) *Human groups and social categories*. Cambridge Univ. Press, Cambridge, UK.

TAJFEL H. (1982) "Social psychology of intergroup relations." In *Annual Review of Psychology,* 33, p. 1-39.

TAJFEL H.; TURNER J. C. (1986) "The social identity theory of intergroup behaviour." In *Psychology of Intergroup Relations*, ed. W. G. Austin and G. A. Worchel. Nelson-Hall, Chicago, p. 7-24.

TREIBEL A. (1999) *Migration in modernen Gesellschaften: Soziale Folgen von Einwanderung und Gastarbeit.* Juventa, Weinheim.

Appendix

Table 3

Items and indices measuring interethnic attitudes

Indices	Items [a]
Emotional Factor	1. I enjoy being with () youths. [b] 2. What is your general feeling toward () youths. [c]
Behavioural Factor	1. I would share my problems with a () youth. 2. I could imagine lending something to a () youth (e.g. my bike, clothes, roller skates). 3. I would invite them to a party.
Resource Anxieties	1. In our neighbourhood, the more () youths living there the more difficult it becomes. 2. There will be fewer opportunities for vocational training if more of them live here.
Evaluations toward out-group sociality	1. I like how () youths get along with one another. 2. () youths are open-minded toward others.

[a] Ordinal 5 point scales were used to tap the answers, ranging from "strongly agree" to "strongly disagree".
[b] Brackets are replaced in the questionnaire by the particular group name.
[c] The extremes for this question were labelled "very negative" to "very positive".

Source: Questionnaire for the IKG-Youth-Panel 2001.

Table 4

Approval and disapproval within the attitude structure[10]

Approval with the attitudes	German adolescents		Turkish adolescents		Resettler adolescents	
	w/ TA	w/ RA	w/ GA	w/ RA	w/ GA	w/ TA
—Emotional factor	14%	26%	62%	33%	66%	14%
—Behavioural factor	37%	44%	61%	37%	67%	28%
—Resource anxieties	18%	13%	4%	7%	2%	14%
—Evaluations toward out-group sociality	7%	9%	17%	14%	17%	8%
Disapproval with the attitudes	German adolescents		Turkish adolescents		Resettler adolescents	
	w/ TA	w/ RA	w/ GA	w/ RA	w/ GA	w/ TA
—Emotional factor	32%	18%	5%	17%	3%	38%
—Behavioural factor	36%	28%	14%	32%	10%	45%
—Resource anxieties	39%	47%	71%	56%	71%	42%
—Evaluations toward out-group sociality	47%	34%	25%	22%	19%	41%

GA: German adolescents n = 6,055
TA: Turkish adolescents n = 1,652
RA: Resettler adolescents n = 3,539

Source: IKG Youth Panel 2001.

[10] Indices are recoded by dividing the scale into three equal parts. Thus, answers are separated into approval (+2 to +0,67), indifference (+0,66 to –0,66), and disapproval (–0,67 to –2).

Voting rights for third country nationals in Vienna: a new step towards democratic participation in Austria?

Catrin Pekari

Introduction

Austrian migration policies have been of public interest since 2000, when the coalition between the ÖVP (*Österreichische Volkspartei, People's Party*) and the FPÖ (*Freiheitliche Partei Österreich, Freedom Party*) came to power. A lot has been said since then about racist and xenophobic tendencies,[1] and indeed the developments at the national level, especially the implementation of the "treaty for integration" (*Integrationsvertrag*),[2] have raised some new concerns.

Notwithstanding these facts, it seems that recently some progress has been made at the local level when in December 2002 the provincial parliament of Vienna decided to grant voting rights to third country nationals.[3] However, these voting rights are strictly local, allowing third

---

[1] The European Union assigned t independent experts to evaluate the "commitment of the Austrian government to the common European values, in particular concerning the rights of refugees, minorities and immigrants" and the "evolution of the political nature of the FPÖ"; see *Ahtisaari, Martti/Frowein, Jochen/Oreja, Marcelino:* Report, adopted in Paris on 8 September 2000. Their conclusion was that common European values were not violated, although concerns remained in some respects.

[2] The so called treaty for integration is part of the amending law No 126/2002 which changes certain provisions of the Alien Act (*Fremdengesetz*) 1997, the Asylum Act (*Asylgesetz*) 1997 and the Alien Labour Act (*Ausländerbeschäftigungsgesetz*). It introduces compulsory language courses for most third country nationals; if such a language course is not successfully completed within a certain time period, prolongation of the residence permit can be refused. The provision entered into force on 1 January 2003.

[3] See Resolution of the Viennese Provincial Parliament concerning the amendment of the Constitution of the City of Vienna and the Viennese Electoral Regulation, December 2002.

country nationals to participate in the election for the representatives of their municipal district, whereas they are still excluded from the elections to the city council. Furthermore, their right to stand as a candidate is restricted insofar as they can neither be elected to the office of the chief representative (*Bezirksvorsteher*) nor to that of the head of the Works Committee (*Bauausschuss*). These restrictions are necessary due to some provisions in constitutional law. In this paper I will explain the legal situation and legal obstacles to third country nationals' voting rights and discuss the arguments for and against political participation of non-citizens.

Local, provincial, national: voting rights within the Austrian federal system

Austria is a democratic republic established as a federal state, but the legislative and executive power of the nine provinces is rather limited compared to that of the federal institutions. Elections take place at three levels: national, provincial and local, whereas in some of the bigger cities the local level can be subdivided into elections to the city council and to the representation of the municipal districts. Additionally, referenda, petitions and plebiscites exist as instruments of direct democracy.

Voting rights for all these levels are determined by the Federal Constitution. It clearly states that the participation in political decision-making processes is restricted to Austrian citizens.[4] The only exceptions are the elections for the representatives of a municipal district; as they are not explicitly mentioned in the constitution, it seems possible to allow the participation of third country nationals in this case.

It was argued, however, that this is not true because the interpretation of the constitution has to be homogeneous in order to preclude the formation of different groups of voters for different elections. This implies that an individual excluded from the elections to the city council by the Constitution for nationality reasons cannot vote in municipal district elections either, even though this case is not mentioned in the Constitution. Now that Austria has became a member state of the European Union, this argument is no longer tenable. The implementation of Council Directive 94/80/EC, laying down the participation of citizens of EU member states in local elections in the state where they are

---

4 For the national level, the relevant provision is Art. 25 of the Federal Constitution, for the provincial level it is Art. 95 and for the local Art. 117.

resident, has already changed the group of eligible voters considerably. Although it could be said that with regard to the elections to the European parliament the homogeneity of the constitution has not been violated insofar as no Austrian elections are concerned, the fact remains that they form a different group of voters since they are included in local, but excluded from provincial and national elections.

There seems to be no obvious reason why the idea of homogeneity should be applied for third country nationals any longer, reserving voting rights at the local level to citizens of EU member states. This argument has a specific relevance in Austria, where the resident population of third country nationals is much higher than that of residents from other EU member states.

For all other forms of political participation of third country nationals, at the national and provincial level as well as with regard to city council elections, amending laws to the relevant constitutional provisions (Art. 25, 95 and 117 of the Federal Constitution) would be necessary. Such laws could be passed in Parliament only with a two-thirds majority, and since it is not entirely clear if that would mean a change to the Constitution *in toto*, the question might be subject to an obligatory plebiscite[5] too. After the last elections to the National Council in November 2002, negotiations for the new governments are still under way, but since there is a lack of political will in almost all political parties at the national level to overcome the constitutional obstacles for a voting right adapted to the concept of denizenship rather than to that of citizenship, a revaluation of the situation can probably not be expected within the near future.

So, with little expectation of changes at the federal level, alternatives are left only at the provincial level. The municipalities themselves, notwithstanding their important role within the federal system, have mere executive and no legislative power. It is therefore up to the Provincial Parliaments to decide upon the legislation concerning voting rights not only at the provincial, but also at the municipal level. Since they are bound by federal constitutional law, for the reasons discussed above they have no way of enacting regulations granting voting rights to third country nationals for elections to the Provincial Parliaments or to the city councils.

What remains within their competence is to guarantee the inclusion of third country nationals at the most local level, the elections for the

---

[5] The Constitution requires an obligatory plebiscite whenever an amending law means a change *in toto*. Such a plebiscite was held on 12 June 1994 for the approval of Austria's entry into the EU.

representatives of the decentralised administrative offices of the municipal districts. Due to historical reasons, this form of local governance is of relevance primarily in Vienna, while equivalents in other major Austrian cities do not show the same distinctive features. In rural areas, similar institutions with elected representatives do not exist; the political decisions are entirely left to the city council, and appointed, not elected officials are in charge of most executive agendas.[6]

The new legislation in Vienna concerning voting rights for third country nationals

The city of Vienna, capital of Austria, has a unique position within the Austrian federal system, because it is not only a municipality, but also one of the nine provinces with its own Provincial Parliament and Government. The Provincial Parliament is at the same time the city council, the Provincial Government has a dual function as town senate, and the Governor of the Province of Vienna is also the Mayor of the City. In December 2002, the provincial parliament decided to grant voting rights to third country nationals for the elections to the representatives of the municipal districts.

Such a representation is established in every one of the 23 Viennese districts, whereas the number of members depends on the population of the district, varying between 40 and 60. The elected representatives elect among them the chief representative and his/her deputies and the members of the edificial, the environmental and the financial board. The field of activities of the municipal offices is rather limited. They can co-decide or propose issues related to infrastructure, traffic, social measures and other initiatives which are of direct relevance for their district. However, they have a long tradition and an important role to play in the interaction between the city administration and the inhabitants.

The original proposal for this legislation, which has not entered into force yet, was made by the SPÖ (*Sozialdemokratische Partei Österreich, Social Democratic Party*), which is the current governmental party in Vienna, representing the mayor as well as the majority in the provincial parliament. The Green Party (*Die Grünen*) supported the proposal, while the Freedom Party and the People's Party voted against it.

---

6 These administrative units are the *Bezirkshauptmannschaften*, led by a district commisioner. In chartered towns (*Statutarstädte*) the mayor is in charge of a district commissioner's functions.

In order to enable third country nationals to vote in local election for the representatives of a municipal district, changes to two provincial laws were necessary: firstly to the Constitution of the City of Vienna (*Wiener Stadtverfassung*), secondly to the Viennese Municipal Electoral Regulation (*Wiener Gemeindewahlordnung*).

The most important amendment is that of § 16 (2) 2 of the Electoral Regulation, stating that non-Austrian and non-EU citizens who have been legally resident in Vienna for at least five years, are over 16 years of age and are not excluded from the right to vote due to other reasons can participate in the elections for the representatives of a municipal district. Regarding the right to stand as a candidate, § 42 refers to § 16, meaning that everybody who has the right to vote can be elected, too, with the restriction that the minimum age here is not 16, but 18. The other amendments to the Electoral Regulation mainly refer to necessary organisational changes such as the introduction of a specific statistical evidence of voters (§§ 19a, 19b).

The second law which was amended, the Constitution of the city of Vienna, makes an important restriction to the rights granted in the Electoral Regulation in § 61b (3), since it restricts the right to stand as a candidate for third country nationals insofar as it excludes them from certain positions. They cannot be elected as the chief representative of a municipal district nor as his/her deputy. Furthermore, according to § 66b (5), they are not allowed to become a member of the Works Committee. The reason for these restrictions is the constitutional regulation of Art. 2 of the Fundamental Laws (*Staatsgrundgesetz*) which limits the access to public service to citizens. The positions of the chief representative of a municipal district and his/her deputies as well as the membership (or even substitutive membership) in the Works Committee fall into this category of restricted public service because they involve specific tasks which belong to the core area of public administration.

For citizens of the EU, however, this constitutional obstacle has been derogated by the implementation of Council Directive 94/80/EC: they have the same right to stand as a candidate in all municipal elections as Austrian citizens. As already mentioned with regard to the participation in elections to the city councils, which take place with the participation of EU citizens, but without a right to vote for third country nationals, again it can be questioned if this discrimination is justified. The decision on who should be in charge of the representation of a district is up to the people living there, and, given the fact that for EU citizens the prerequisite of the Austrian citizenship does not exist, it is not clear why there should be no free choice among all candidates.

Even if seen from a historical perspective, the provision seems to be discriminating in a rather unfair way: The original purpose of Art. 2 of the Fundamental Laws was to ensure loyalty of public servants when deciding issues of direct political relevance, but since the loyalty of a district's chief representative should be to the district, it is not sure if the Austrian or EU citizenship is indeed a necessary requirement. The decisions to be made at this very most local level have little to do with concerns at the national level.

Taking into account the political situation in Austria, however, it seems unlikely that the necessary steps for a constitutional amendment at the federal level will be taken by the Parliament within the near future; still, discussion on this point is urgently needed.

Arguments for third country nationals' voting rights at the local level

The main argument for the participation of third country nationals in elections is the necessity to give all those who are affected by political decision-making processes the chance to decide who should represent them. This definition excludes *per se* tourists and other non-citizens without any intention of remaining in the host country, but argues for the inclusion of long-term residents. In a time of mass migration, not all long-term residents are citizens. Therefore, citizenship as a prerequisite for voting rights can open a rather huge gap between those who are able to participate and those who are not —while both groups are equally affected by political decisions. This is true especially in Vienna where the percentage of the foreign resident population reaches 33 % in at least one municipal district and more than 25 % in 4 districts, whereas the lowest number of third country nationals in a district is still above 7 %.[7] This leads to the conclusion that, even though restricted voting rights at the national level may be justified because of the need to show a certain intention to fully belong to a country's society as a citizen, this argument makes little sense at the local level.

The number of elected representatives in a municipal district depends on the whole population of a district —and not, as for the city council, on the number of citizens. This can lead to a further democratic deficit, because in districts with a high percentage of resident third country nationals who are excluded from the right to vote, a representative needs relatively few votes to be elected. At the same time, this

---

7 See *Wiener Integrationsfond:* MigranntInnen in Wien'99, at http://www.wif.wien.at/wif_site/wif_pages/se_ta_03.html. The data refers to the registered resident foreign population according to the statistical evidence of the City of Vienna as in 1999.

representative should cover the interests both of the citizens —who had the opportunity to vote for him or her— and the third country nationals, who did not have this chance.

Furthermore, municipal districts are more important than the rather abstract notion of a state for the identification of third country nationals with the host society. Studies show that third country nationals are not necessarily immigrating to a certain country, but rather to a certain town or even municipal district of a town where they find ethnic communities and social networks.[8] The daily routine of the integration process —such as finding accommodation and work or learning to understand a new language and culture— is of course dominated by the legal framework of the host country, but from an individual perspective, it may well be that the influence of the local community seems more important. Presumably, involvement in the political process at that level could further facilitate identification and integration also in a broader context.

Last but not least, it has to be mentioned that the relative restrictiveness of the provisions for obtaining Austrian citizenship is a strong argument for participation without citizenship. A regular application for citizenship can be filed only after 10 years of legal residence, still leaving some discretionary power to public authorities, whereas a legal claim comes into being only after 30 years. Additionally, dual citizenship is not permitted. This means that third country nationals are *de facto* excluded from voting rights for a long period, even if their integration process and their identification with the host country is already very advanced. Participation at the local level might provide some adjustment insofar as third country nationals can at least influence their direct environment at an earlier stage.

Concluding remarks

The very specific situation of Vienna as a province and a municipality as well as the historically important role of the decentralised municipal administrative offices and their elected representatives are rather unique phenomena in Austria. In Graz, the second largest city, with nearly 10 % foreign residents, some discussion on the possibility of granting voting rights to third country nationals at the local level has been going on in recent years, but no real conclusions have been reached so far.

---

[8] See *Bauböck, Rainer:* Wessen Stimme zählt? Thesen über demokratische Beteiligung in der Einwanderungsgesellschaft, Oktober 2002.

The Viennese regulation is therefore a particularity in the political landscape rather than a real breakthrough for Austrian migration policies and its implications for the country as a whole should not be overestimated. Still, it shows a very positive attitude towards integration in a town where the percentage of the non-Austrian resident population has reached a significant level. Even if the progress made is not more than a very small step —voting rights only in the municipal districts, with restricted rights to stand as a candidate— it definitely is a step.

The only way to reach a positive effect for integration in a broader context would probably be an amendment to Art. 117 of the Constitution in order to involve third country nationals in all local elections. This initiative would not necessarily conflict with higher level voting rights, where arguments for exclusive, citizenship based voting rights are much stronger. The more directly an individual is affected by a political decision, the more right one has to participate in the process leading to that decision. Experiences in other member states of the EU —namely Denmark, Ireland, the Netherlands, Finland and Sweden— have clearly shown that local and partly even provincial voting rights for third country nationals rather enhance than endanger the democratic stability of a country.

In any case the new law in Vienna could be of great importance insofar as it stimulates a discussion in Austria on this topic, and it might be that some political parties will implement this idea not only at the local, but also at the federal level.

Women migrants: invisible or creative actors?

Trinidad L. Vicente

Population movements are clearly one of today's most striking social phenomena. This is not due to their newness, given that such movements have always been part of human history. Rather, population movements in recent decades stand out for their specific features. Following CASTLES/MILLER (1998), we can highlight their growing globalisation (ever more countries are affected by these expanding population flows —whether as countries of origin, receiving countries, or both at once), their acceleration (migrations are increasing in volume in all the main affected areas), their diversification (reasons for emigrating are ever more varied —economic, political, studies, retirement, etc.— meaning that each receiving country tends to have distinct immigrant profiles) and their growing feminisation (woman currently comprise almost one half of the world migrant population (United Nations, 2002), with 85 million woman versus 90 million men migrants). The presence of women in migratory flows, however, is quite different depending on the area under consideration. By 2000, female migrants constituted nearly 51 % of all migrants in the developed world but about 46 % of all international migrants in developing countries.

In most countries in Asia, Africa and Oceania more men are emigrants that women, while in half the countries on the American continent women make up at least half of the emigrant population, a situation repeated in many European countries. According to the International Organisation for Migration, in one third of the receiving countries there are more migrant women than men. Women predominate in migratory flows to countries favouring permanent settlement, while men are the majority in flows to countries favouring labour-based immigration (ZLOTNIK, 1995, p. 231).

Table 1

Percentage of female migrants among the total number of international migrants, by major area, 1960-2000

Major area	1960	1970	1980	1990	2000
World	46.6	47.2	47.4	47.9	48.8
More developed regions	47.9	48.2	49.4	50.8	50.9
Less developed regions	45.7	46.3	45.5	44.7	45.7
Europe	48.5	48.0	48.5	51.7	52.4
Northern America	49.8	51.1	52.6	51.0	51.0
Caribbean	45.3	46.1	46.5	47.7	48.9
Latin America	44.7	46.9	48.4	50.2	50.5
Northern Africa	49.5	47.7	45.8	44.9	42.8
Sub-Saharan Africa	40.6	42.1	43.8	46.0	47.2
Southern Asia	46.3	46.9	45.9	44.4	44.4
Eastern and South-eastern Asia	46.1	47.6	47.0	48.5	50.1
Western Asia	45.2	46.6	47.2	47.9	48.3
Oceania	44.4	46.5	47.9	49.1	50.5

Source: United Nations, 2002.

Women as protagonists in migratory phenomena

The participation of women has generally been a constant in population movements throughout history. Interestingly, one of the earliest researchers into international migration, RAVENSTEIN (1885), identified the presence of women in international migration flows and the differences in the migratory behaviour of men and women, underlining the fact that women were not merely dependent beings and they also migrated on their own account for a variety of reasons.[1] Various later studies highlighted the greater proportion of women in the immigrant population of certain countries such as the US, where the feminine part of the immigrant population was greater than the masculine from 1930 to 1980 (HOUSTON *et al.*, 1984), at which point the number of male immigrants slightly surpassed that of females.

---

[1] In RAVENSTEIN's words (1885, p. 196): "Woman is a greater migrant than man. This may surprise those who associate women with domestic life, but the figures of the census clearly prove it. Nor do women migrate merely from rural districts into the town in search of domestic service, for they migrate quite as frequently into certain manufacturing districts, and the workshop is a formidable rival of the kitchen and scullery". In his well-known migratory laws, Ravenstein also pointed out that women migrants prefer to move shorter distances than men, although this is not born out by current evidence.

Yet, in spite of the fact that women have made up almost half of the migrant population for over forty years (1960-2000), most research focused on international migration has tended to ignore gender as a relevant variable in analysis. Gender continues to be relegated to the sidelines of social science research. As a result, much more is known about factors related to masculine[2] immigration than feminine.

According to the UN (1994), the reasons why the migration of women has been neglected are many, but some stand out:

—Migration theory. Because of the important role played by the human capital model in migration theory, the migration literature has focused heavily on autonomous or so-called "economic" migration, or migration motivated ostensibly for reasons of employment or economic opportunity (or to escape economic deprivation). Men have been generally more likely than women to report their moves as motivated primarily for economic reasons.

—Underestimation of women's economic activity and labour force participation, which is directly related to the above point. Since much of the economic activity of women is not classified as such in standard labour force and other surveys, it is implicitly viewed as irrelevant for migration analysis.

—The neglect of women in scholarly social science research in general (as well as in literature, art, politics, etc.). This is due to their generally lower status and presumably passive, dependent roles in society, which, however, are beginning to change in much of the developing countries.

—Most research on migration has been carried out by men. This is a fact, though it need not by itself have led to the neglect of female migrants since men as well as women are certainly capable of studying women's migration.

—Inadequacies in existing data on women's migration, at both the macro and micro levels, for reasons not unrelated to the above.

---

[2] The gender standpoint also calls for more thorough research into the impact that masculine immigration, or immigration of a female member of the family, has on the women left behind in the country of origin. Along these lines, some studies have shown the large negative effects that men's immigration has had on the women who stay in the country of origin, who in some cases are forced to take on still more responsibilities for the material survival of the community. At times, they must also abandon their home in order to join their husband's family, thereby losing part of their already scarce autonomy. In other cases, meanwhile, immigration by the head of the family has brought with it more positive than negative effects. This was the case in India, where a study concluded that immigration had led to a more favourable attitude towards the education of girls as well as boys (SUTCLIFFE, 1999).

> If data on overall international migration is scare, those relative to the migration of women are even less abundant. Consequently, the sex of migrants has to be inferred from the category in which they are admitted, assuming, for instance, that spouses are mostly women or that women constitute most of the migrants in certain occupations, such as nursing, domestic service or entertainment. Lack of information is hardly conductive to a more realistic assessment of women's participation in international migration or of their role as migrants (UN, 1995, p.1).

The presence of women in migratory phenomena began to attract notice in the seventies, especially after the oil crisis of 1973, with the growth of more restrictive immigration policies at a national and international level. These policies were also aimed at the so-called stabilisation of the foreign population already present in the country. The new migratory policies sought to slow down the arrival of new immigrants while encouraging the definitive return of those wanting to go back to their country of origin. They did not, however, similarly impede the entry of close family members of immigrants already established in the receiving countries, in a clear attempt to favour social integration and avoid social conflict. Many of those who until now have been regarded as "guest workers" (always represented by the image of an adult working man who moves to another country for a limited period, leaving his family behind, with the aim of improving his and his family's financial situation) have eventually decided to remain, regrouping their families in the host society. In part, this has been a response to the development of "Fortress Europe" policies. Woman immigrants thus became more visible in migratory movements, via family reunification.[3] However, they have usually continued to be regarded as passive subjects, dependent on the men in the process. For that reason, in most cases women's roles as economic and social agents, along with

---

[3] According to Zlotnik (1995), who studied the evolution of migratory flows in certain European countries such as Germany and Belgium between 1960 and 1990, these policies had a great effect on the gender distribution of the foreign population, although not as substantial as was claimed. Nor did these policies affect different national groups in each host country in the same way. Furthermore, Zlotnik points out that at no time during this period was feminine immigration in Germany and Belgium close to that of masculine. This fact refutes the generally accepted opinion that female immigration has been dominant from the time that family reunification became the main vehicle for legal immigration to those countries. However, a look at both countries shows a change in net immigration. Although negative for both men and women, the number of men leaving the country during the years under study is substantially higher than that of women.

their movement dynamics, their settlement guidelines, their own migratory projects and the consequences of these for the women themselves and for their family and social environment have all been downplayed.

The discourse on the feminisation of migration in Europe can thus be explained not only by a real increase in the feminine participation of population movements, but also by a conceptual opening to feminine immigration (OSO, 1998, p. 39-58), although this is obscured in the order of representations by specific reference to a homogeneous collective made up of the regrouped and dependent "woman immigrant".

There is still much research to be done, but various studies carried out in recent decades have clearly shown that there is no single model for the woman immigrant. Nor do these women share the same reasons for moving from one place to another. Such reasons can include the search for economic opportunity, family reunification, finding better opportunities for their children, the search for greater freedom as well as personal and social independence, the spirit of adventure, a desire for change, escape from situations of domestic or political violence, persecution for gender-related reasons, etc. The research already done has also brought to light the notable influence that a woman's specific situation in the country of origin has on her decision to emigrate, along with the significant influence of the particular dynamics in the destination country. These situations, which affect men and women differently, will be analysed in the following sections.

Women in the countries of origin

The majority presence of women in migratory flows into European countries hides important differences according to their place of origin and destination. In southern European countries (Portugal, Spain, Italy or Greece) which have only recently become magnets for immigration, the masculine proportion of the foreign population is substantially higher than in other European countries with a longer-running tradition of hosting international migration. Yet at the same time, there is a wide variety of composition by sex of each national group in these countries. In Spain, for example, the population of Latin American origin is mostly female (i.e. seven women for every three men among those coming from Colombia or the Dominican Republic). At the same time, men clearly predominate in the population with African origins (approximately three women for every seven men from North Africa, for example).

In light of the varying participation of men and women in migratory movements according to origin, we might want to look into the determining factors. Beginning with the situation in the societies of origin, we could consider two main points —women's family and social roles and the emigration regulatory policies that surely condition their mobility in different societies, while explaining why women seem more willing to emigrate from some places rather than others.

A woman's migratory experience will be heavily influenced by the personal and social conditions from which she comes, as well as by the goal of her migratory project. One must consider the socio-structural and cultural framework to which women migrate, as well as the family structure and sexual distribution of roles in the society of origin, in order to understand why some decide to emigrate and others not to in certain contexts. The decision to lead a migratory project is quite different in a society that controls and limits women's independence through rules, values and customs, restricting them to the private/reproductive sphere (such as in Moroccan society), from that of a society with looser control over women. Similarly, social and family structure can also help us to understand, because in many monogamous, patriarchal families (such as in the Philippines), especially with single-parent families (such as in Latin American countries), a woman's main role as child-bearer will lead her to emigrate as a strategy for maintaining and improving the family unit (GREGORIO, 1998; OSO, 1998).

Many contexts in the country of origin, with their mechanisms of control and the subordination of women, greatly condition the feminine presence in migratory flows. This does not mean, however, that women never assume a leading role in those flows. The social changes currently taking place even in the most traditional contexts —nourished by women's increasing access to education, urbanisation processes, the growing globalisation of communications and information and by value changes brought on by the emigration of other family members— are going to stimulate an ever greater number of women to set out on their own migratory project in order to find greater independence, to escape the social norms reigning in these family structures (arranged marriages, guardianship by the husband's family, etc.) and to flee from the negative opinions suffered in their societies arising from their status as divorcees, disowned, etc.

On the other hand, we must also look at the emigration policies of the countries of origin, which influence the ability of men and women to migrate through promotional, selective or prohibitive rules. Some Asian labour-exporting countries, such as the Philippines, India, Pakistan or Bangladesh, for instance, have attempted to prohibit the emigration of working women, largely owing to frequent abuse and attacks on their personal dignity in the receiving countries (mostly located in or around the Persian Gulf), which has had a major influence on the amount and selection of international migration. But the implicit views underlying many of these policies are —as UN (1995, p.3) remarks— that women are essentially vulnerable and that their respectability is likely to be compromised by the mere fact that they migrate on their own. News appearing in the media about cases of women who are exploited, trafficked and made to prostitute themselves have strengthened the idea that it would be better to stay at home, in the society of origin, where they will be protected by the males. There is no denying that the exploitation and the sexual abuse of women is a major problem that should be combated in all fronts, but it should not be treated as if it were a problem affecting primarily international female migrants. However, we must also recognise that women's greater level of vulnerability is the result of a social gender construction, which after relegating women to a secondary status, limits their access to resources and places them precisely in positions of lower status and social prestige. One way to fight against this would be to defend equal opportunity both at a national and international level —something that is still far off.

Female migrants in the receiving countries

We should also note the role played by receiving country immigration policies in the gender composition of international migration. European immigration laws and regulations developed in the seventies have left two main doors open to those from other countries. The first is through work, which is ever more restricted and requires a work permit. The second is through family reunification, a popular means used by women immigrants in recent decades for overcoming tightening border controls, although their migratory reasons are clearly work-related. Meanwhile, we must avoid mistaking a migratory project with the means of entry, something that can be clearly seen when the woman initiates the migratory process and the husband arrives later through family reunification.[4]

This "entry status" via family reunification is, however, helping to create an image of women as solely dependent immigrants, following a naturalised citizen or other immigrant (usually a man) who holds a

---

[4] In this case there is general agreement that the man's desire to work in the host country is what lies behind the decision to reunite the family. Here we are once again up against the stereotypes that view the man as an active subject with the responsibility for productive tasks carried out in the public sphere, while the women is relegated to the private sphere —her participation in economic activity thus undervalued.

residency permit and updated work permit. This latter person is economically active, with enough income to maintain the family members reunited in the host society. We can see this attitude in the European Charter on Migrant Worker Rights, which in article 17 maintains the right of immigrant workers to "bring their wife and children".

Since family reunification is one of the few legal avenues available for migration, many women will use this means of access to the host country, a process that will brand them with the status of legal immigrants who are economically dependent on their reuniting agent. They will thus not be regarded as residents in their own right, at least for a number of years —with far reaching consequences. The institutional dependency on the husband's permit will make the woman's life one that takes place in the private sphere, breaking the equality that exists between the married couple before the law. This, in turn, will establish and formalise hierarchies and areas of power within the family structure (MESTRE, 2001). For example, this situation will not allow many women to break the family link through separation —even in situations of conflict or domestic violence— since that move would place them in a situation where the risk of being deported is high and left to the arbitrary decision of the administration (MOROKVASIC, 1991). Moreover, their dependence will even be reinforced by the fact that family reunification offers a residency permit without a work permit —at least for a certain period. They will thus be deprived of their own economic resources, given that their only entry into the workplace, the underground economy, is deemed illegal. This brings with it the greater risk of suffering situations of economic exploitation. For all these reasons, recent studies on immigrant women in Europe still argue that women more often than men are denied full citizenship.

Another of the determining factors in the immigration of women to European countries is the economic status of their family members who have already emigrated and settled in the host country. Those earning lower salaries will have a more difficult time sponsoring the immigration of their closest relatives, especially when economic solvency is a necessary requirement for family reunification.

On the other hand, the arrival of some groups of women to certain European societies will be favoured by the migratory networks that have been established in those countries. Such networks include the family contacts, friendship and neighbourhood relations that act as channels for information, resources and all kinds of material and non-material goods and services that help the immigrant (GREGORIO, 1998, p. 34-37). As such, any explanation of the migratory flows into

Europe and their composition by sex must take into consideration such things as the volume, distribution, location and level of settlement of each migrant group. All of these features, along with the migratory policies, will be key aspects in explaining the evolution of foreign population flows.

The distribution of the sexes within each migrant group in each host society represents another important aspect from the gender perspective. Different studies have shown that many immigrant women have experienced a certain emancipation from their traditional roles, achieving independence or at least a relaxation in the levels of social control applied to them, in spite of the migratory policies of both the host and country of origin. This is especially true if the women are part of a group in which they are clearly the majority. Other women, however, will live within a reproduction of the family relations and social roles from their country of origin, especially if they belong to a group within the host country characterised by sexual equality. A third group, meanwhile, will live through still greater social control than that which exists in their country of origin. These are the women that enter by means of family reunification, and who represent a clear minority of their national group. However, a woman's situation within her family and community environment can change over time, depending on her level of success in terms of social and work integration in the new European context.

Female migration and gendered work

Mainstream migration theory has traditionally seen labour migration as predominantly male, with women viewed primarily as dependents (MOROKVASIC, 1984). Yearly data supplied by the OECD show, however, a substantial level of participation by women immigrants in the labour market in the different European Union countries. This is all the more impressive if we keep in mind that this section of the population often finds its workplace in the underground economy.

To date, European women have yet to enter the labour market under the same conditions as their male counterparts. However, this situation is much worse still for women immigrants in the EU. They reside on the bottom of the labour scale, behind the position held by the two national groups (men and women), and the group comprising their male immigrant companions.

Women immigrants in Europe are still mostly limited to the kind of work opportunities falling under the concept of "women's work": domestic work (internal and external), all kinds of cleaning work (offices,

Table 2

Participation rate and unemployment rate of nationals and foreigners by sex in EU countries 2000-2001 average

	Participation rate				Unemployment rate			
	Men		Women		Men		Women	
	Nationals	Foreigners	Nationals	Foreigners	Nationals	Foreigners	Nationals	Foreigners
Belgium	73.3	72.4	57.0	41.0	4.6	14.2	7.0	16.5
Denmark	84.1	71.2	76.2	53.0	3.6	12.2	4.9	7.2
Finland	79.4	83.1	74.6	60.2	10.0	24.2	11.2	29.9
France	75.1	76.6	63.3	48.6	7.1	17.1	10.7	23.9
Germany	78.9	77.6	64.7	50.7	7.2	13.4	7.8	11.7
Greece	76.2	89.2	49.0	56.0	7.2	7.6	16.2	17.6
Ireland	79.2	77.0	55.9	56.2	4.1	5.1	3.8	6.2
Italy	74.0	79.7	47.7	57.7	1.2	2.5	1.7	3.8
Luxembourg	84.9	69.5	67.2	49.0	1.9	4.7	2.9	7.0
Netherlands	84.6	82.1	76.8	67.2	3.7	5.3	3.4	4.5
Norway	79.0	81.5	64.0	65.3	3.1	8.4	5.1	9.6
Portugal	77.3	85.4	50.9	59.1	9.3	12.9	19.8	17.2
Spain	78.0	63.1	74.2	60.3	5.5	16.1	4.6	13.0
Sweden	83.1	75.6	68.4	55.8	5.5	9.8	4.4	7.9
U. K.	73.6	87.7	46.6	50.7	8.0	7.4	13.9	21.3

Source: Sopemi, 2003.

Note: Data cover the labour force aged 15 to 64. The data refer to the native and foreign-born populations.

hotels, etc.), health care, childcare, care of the ill and the elderly, restaurant and bar work (as waitresses, cooks, etc.) sales (street corner sales, etc.), sex shows, prostitution, etc. All of these employment areas offer an increasing amount of jobs, given that local workers tend to avoid them since they are so representative of gender discrimination. These jobs represent an entrance into the labour market for many immigrant women, although they are quite unstable (long workdays, low pay, high safety and health risks, low prestige and social protection, more relaxed control over compliance with contract conditions, part-time jobs, etc.). They are often performed without any contract at all, i.e., in the underground economy. Moreover, they rarely help in changing a woman's legal[5] status, due to the difficulty in obtaining the relevant

[5] A work contract or firm job offer is required for obtaining a work permit or renewal in European countries. Moreover, a work permit is often the requirement for a residency permit, which would allow the holder to emerge from hiding and obtain the yearned-for documents.

work permits or renewals. All of this leaves many of these women in an obvious situation of exploitation and social exclusion.

In addition, limitation to these "typically feminine" jobs leads to the professional disqualification of many of a women's degrees, resulting in the wasting of the training and capacities of many women who arrive with high academic and professional credentials (VICENTE, 2003). At the same time, this process reinforces the stereotypes applied to this group of women (supposedly made up of illiterates incapable of other kinds of work, with no professional future). In short, these women will quite often suffer a kind of double discrimination —immigrants and women workers in a society that confines them to badly regarded, badly regulated and badly paid jobs.

Domestic work and care of the elderly and children, for example, are common employment sectors for foreign women which have greatly expanded in recent years, especially in southern European countries which have only recently seen the incorporation of native born women into the workplace. These countries still have a low level of male or government participation in these tasks, creating a situation in which this work is quite often carried out in the underground economy. Yet even when the job is legal, applicable law does not always demand a written contract, making it tremendously difficult to legalise the immigration status of the foreigners (mostly women) working in those jobs. This situation also hinders the recognisance and protection of labour rights, since most work conditions in such jobs (hours, time present, salary and percentage of salary discounted for food, board and maintenance, etc.) are left to individual parties (MESTRE, 2001).

It would seem that immigrant labour is also becoming more and more prevalent in the sex industry, particularly prostitution. This is especially true among certain nationalities which are often identified with such activity. Prostitution work is usually identified with situations of exploitation, presenting women as victims of human trafficking rather than those who have freely immigrated. As such, they need protection, at least to the extent that they denounce their employers. Many studies, however, are showing that a large number of the women working in the European sex industry are active agents in migratory processes, people aware that their job would in some way be related to sex, if not prostitution itself, and who chose this path given the resources and job possibilities within reach (COLECTIVO IOÉ, 2001; BONELLI, 2001). In addition, many studies and reports have shown that trafficking or exploitation is suffered by many women working in many different sectors apart from the sex industry. As such, the fight against trafficking in human beings, and woman in particular, must be applied to many fronts —areas in which these people are left at the mercy of human trafficking networks. This phenomenon must be confronted with all means at our disposal.

In most cases, working conditions for woman immigrants are far from optimal. Yet as long as host countries offer woman migrants a more accessible means of entry (even if this is through family reunification), and better job prospects and salaries than their country of origin (although these are clearly stereotyped), women will continue to view the migratory process as an attractive option. Consequently, we should remain aware of the economic and social marginalisation caused by these precarious jobs, supporting these women with improved and more varied employment opportunities that will in turn allow them to improve their personal, family and social life.

Female migration and ethnic boundaries

When host countries describe a person as an "immigrant", we are externally applying a negative attribute, a stigma that will remain with that person forever (even after attaining citizenship). In fact, this stigma will continue with that person's descendants, who will be labelled (against all semantic logic) "second or third generation immigrants" (DELGADO, 2003, p.14). Immigrants, who are frequently referred to as "*the others*", have a series of defining characteristics. The most noteworthy of these is that of being regarded as from another land, of residing in the host country without having been invited, of being poor from the economic perspective and backwards from the cultural, of having come from less modernised societies, of representing a threat to the integrity of our society, etc.

All national collectivities are constructed around borders (legal/territorial lines) and boundaries (limit lines of collectivities), that delineate identities and separate the world into "us" and "them". The increasing foreign population entering Europe from non-EU countries is, in the opinion of many European citizens, bringing with it a questioning of our western culture by those from other civilisations, who reject integration into our society while adhering to and propagating the values, customs and cultures of their societies of origin (HUNTINGTON, 1997). With this in mind, woman immigrants come to represent "the others" par excellence.

Often stereotyped as unemployed immigrants who are economically and socially dependent on the male immigrant, these woman must often live between paternalism, and rejection by host societies that perceive and represent them as victims of subordination to backward cultural and social practices (such as being sold into marriage, the use of veils, genital mutilation, imprisonment in private quarters, sexual abuse/ violence, etc.) that they, in turn, transmit to succeeding generations. Similarly, these woman are associated with other social problems such as trafficking in human beings, prostitution, employment in inhuman conditions, etc. Meanwhile, the majority of Europeans believe that the settlement of foreigners should depend on the job market. Many still believe that it is better for immigrants to give up their native tongue, customs and traditions, while adopting those of their European host country. This is an especially relevant point if we keep in mind that, as different studies have shown, rejection of cultural diversity and the demand for assimilation serve as an excuse for exclusion. To the extent that a person does not perfectly assimilate to the new host society (an almost impossible task), he or she can blame no one else for their marginalisation apart from themselves —precisely for not "integrating".

Yet most of these foreign women will remain among us for a long period of time, and more will probably continue to arrive. This is an inescapable reality that we must accept as a starting point, one that compels us to ponder just how they will incorporate, or are already incorporating into the host societies (to which they already belong).

Final remarks

Feminine participation in migratory flows into the European Union cannot remain invisible. In spite of our relative lack of knowledge about feminine migratory processes, we can recognise their heterogeneity and complex causes. They may include situations in which the woman plays no role in the decision making process, as well as others in which the migration planning is done together with other family members (usually the husband). In many cases the women are the main actors, if not the sole, independent protagonists of these migratory processes. Women emigrating to European countries have a wide variety of origins, identities, migratory trajectories, leaving and arrival situations, connections with the original and receiving societies, etc. Moreover, these women's experiences differ in many ways from those of their male companions, due to their different social situation both in the original as well as destination society, to varying divisions of roles as well as to the ethic and sexual division of work. For all of these reasons, we must pay greater attention to the gender variable in the study of international migration if we want to truly extend our knowledge of this complex, current social phenomenon.

References

ANDALL, J. (2000): *Gender, migration and democratic service,* Aldershot: Ashgate.

ANTHIAS, F. (2001): "Gendering migration: the case of Southern Europe", in S. Ghatak and A.S. Sasoon (ed.): *Migrations and mobility: the European context,* Basingstoke: Palgrave, 146-167.

ANTHIAS, F.; LAZARIDIS, G. (eds.) (2000): *Gender and migration in southern Europe: women on the move,* Oxford: Berg.

APARICIO, R. (ed.) (1998): *Identidad y Género: Mujeres Magrebíes en Madrid,* Madrid: Dirección General de la Mujer.

BONELLI, E.; ULLOA, M. (Coord.) (2001): *Tráfico e Inmigración de Mujeres en España: Colombianas y Ecuatorianas en los Servicios Domésticos y Sexuales,* Madrid: ACSUR-Las Segovias.

BOYD, M.; GRIECO, E. (2003): "Women and migration: incorporating gender into international migration theory", Washington, D.C.: Migration Policy Institute (http://www.migrationinformation.org).

CASTLES, S.; MILLER (1998): *The age of migration*. New York: Macmillan.

COLECTIVO IOÉ (2001): *Mujer, Inmigración y Trabajo,* Madrid: Instituto de Migraciones y Servicios Sociales.

DELGADO, M. (2003): «¿Quién puede ser Inmigrante en la Ciudad?», Delgado, M (et.al.): *Exclusión Social y Diversidad Cultural*, Donostia: Gakoa.

GREGORIO, C. (1998): *Migración Femenina: Su Impacto en las Relaciones de Género*, Madrid: Narcea.

HOUSTON, M.F.; KRAMER, R.G.; BARREN, J.M. (1984): "Female predominance of immigration to the United States since 1930: a first look", *International Migration Review,* 18 (4): 908-963.

HUNTINGTON, S.P. (1997): *El Choque de Civilizaciones y la Reconfiguración del Orden Mundial,* Barcelona: Paidós.

MESTRE, R. (2001): «Inmigración, Exclusión y Género», in N. Fernández & M. Calvo García (coord.) *Inmigración y Derechos*, Huesca: Mira Editores, 97-109.

MOROKVASIC, M. (1991): "Fortress Europe and migrant women", *Feminist Review,* 39 (4): 69-84.

MOROKVASIC, M. (1984): "Birds of passage are also women...", *International Migration Review*, 18 (68): 886-907.

OSO, L. (1998): *La Inmigración hacia España de Mujeres Jefas de Hogar*, Ministerio de Trabajo y Asuntos Sociales, Madrid: Instituto de la Mujer.

RAVENSTEIN, E.G. (1885): "The laws of migration", *Journal of the Royal Statistical Society,* Vol. 48 (2): 167-235.

SUTCLIFFE, B. (1999): *Nacido en Otra Parte*, Bilbao: Hegoa.

UN (2002): *International migration report: 2002.* New York: Department for Economic and Social Information and Policy Analysis Population Division.

UN (1995): *International migration policies and the status of female migrants. Proceedings of the United Nations expert group meeting on international policies and the status of female migrants*, New York: Department for Economic and Social Information and Policy Analysis Population Division.

UN (1994): *The migration of women. Methodological issues in the measurement and analysis of internal and international migration*. Santo Domingo: INSTRAW.

VICENTE, T.L. (2003): «España: País de Inmigración Femenina», *Letras de Deusto,* 33, (99): 137-172.

ZLOTNIK, H. (1995): "The south-to-north migration of women", *International Migration Review*, 29: 229-254.